WRITING FUNDAMENTALS

Joseph T. Lyons, Ph.D.

Copyright © 2016 Joseph Lyons

All rights reserved.

ISBN:0692698353

ISBN-13:9780692698358

DEDICATION

FOR DIANE

Contents

Preface / xiii

CHAPTER ONE   **Beginning with the Foundation: Parts of Speech / 1**

A. Nouns / 1
B. Pronouns / 1
C. Verbs / 3
D. Adjectives / 3
E. Adverbs / 3
F. Prepositions / 4
G. Conjunctions / 4
    1. *Coordinate / 4*
    2. *Correlative / 5*
    3. *Subordinate / 5*
    4. *Conjunctive Adverbs / 5*
Exercise 1.1—Distinguishing Parts of Speech / 7

CHAPTER TWO   **Organizing Your Sentences / 9**

A. What Is a Sentence? / 9
B. The Complete Verb / 10
C. The Simple Subject and Verb / 10
Exercise 2.1—Locating the Subject and Verb / 11
D. Enlarging through Phrases / 13
    1. *Phrases Introduced by Prepositions / 13*
    2. *Phrases Beginning with -ing and -ed Verbs / 13*
    3. *Phrases Beginning with -ing Words as Nouns / 14*
    4. *Phrases with Infinitives / 14*
Exercise 2.2—Recognizing Phrases / 14
E. Expanding with Clauses / 16
    1. *Clauses as Adjectives / 17*
    2. *Clauses as Adverbs / 17*
    3. *Clauses as Nouns / 17*

Exercise 2.3—Identifying Clauses / 18
Exercise 2.4—Developing the Subject-Verb Structure / 19
F. Finding Sentence Errors / 21
    1. *Mending Fragments* / 21
    2. *Mending Run-on Sentences* / 21
Exercise 2.5—Detecting Sentence Fragments / 23
Exercise 2.6—Correcting Run-on Sentences / 24
Exercise 2.7—Revising Sentences in the Paragraph / 26
G. Variety in Sentence Patterns / 26
    1. *Simple Sentence* / 26
    2. *Compound Sentence* / 27
    3. *Complex Sentence* / 27
    4. *Compound-Complex Sentence* / 28
Exercise 2.8—Recognizing Sentence Patterns / 28
H. Combining into Patterns / 30
    1. *Joining through Coordination* / 30
    2. *Joining through Subordination* / 31
Exercise 2.9—Coordination / 32
Exercise 2.10—Subordination / 34

CHAPTER THREE   Checking for Agreement / 36

A. Ensuring Subject-Verb Agreement / 36
Exercise 3.1—Making Subject and Verb Agree / 38
B. Pronouns Agreeing with Nouns / 40
    1. *Person: Watch* You / 40
    2. *Gender: Guidelines for* He *and* She / 41
    3. *Number: Some Rules about Singulars and Plurals* / 41
Exercise 3.2—Making Pronouns Agree with Nouns / 42
Exercise 3.3—Review of Agreement / 44
Exercise 3.4—Revising the Paragraph for Agreement / 47

CHAPTER FOUR   Solving Special Problems with Verbs, Pronouns, Adjectives, and Adverbs / 48

A. Avoiding Verb Problems / 48
Exercise 4.1—Choosing Verb Forms / 52
Exercise 4.2—Correcting Verb Errors / 54
B. Detecting Pronoun Case Problems / 55
Exercise 4.3—Using the Proper Pronoun Case / 58
C. Confusing Adjectives and Adverbs / 60
D. Using Forms of Comparison / 61
Exercise 4.4—Confusing Adjectives and Adverbs / 62
Exercise 4.5—Revising the Paragraph to Solve Special Problems / 64

CHAPTER FIVE Making Sentences Clear / 66

A. Pronouns Must Refer Clearly to Nouns / 66
    1. *The Hazards of Ambiguity* / 66
    2. *Antecedents That Are Only Implied* / 67
    3. *Imprecise References Cause Confusion* / 67
Exercise 5.1—Improving Pronoun Reference / 67
Exercise 5.2—Revising the Paragraph for Clear Pronoun Reference / 69
B. Putting Modifiers in the Right Place / 70
Exercise 5.3—Misplaced Modifiers / 72
Exercise 5.4—Revising the Paragraph to Correct Misplaced Modifiers / 74
C. Detecting Dangling Modifiers / 74
Exercise 5.5—Dangling Modifiers / 75
Exercise 5.6—Revising the Paragraph to Remove Dangling Modifiers / 77
D. Employing Parallel Forms / 78
    1. *Correcting Faulty Coordination* / 78
    2. *Making Series Parallel* / 79
    3. *Watching for Incorrect Omissions* / 80
    4. *Making Comparisons Using* Than *or* As / 80
Exercise 5.7—Correcting Faulty Parallelism / 81
Exercise 5.8—Revising the Paragraph to Improve Parallelism / 83
Exercise 5.9—Review Exercise: Sentence Clarity / 83

CHAPTER SIX Keys to Better Spelling / 87

A. The Rules / 88
    1. *The* ie *and* ei *Words* / 88
    2. *Words Ending in* y / 88
    3. *Dropping the Final* e / 88
    4. *Doubling the Final Consonant* / 89
    5. *Plurals: Adding* s *or* es / 89
B. Words That Sound or Look Alike / 89
Exercise 6.1—Spelling / 93

CHAPTER SEVEN Punctuating Effectively / 97

A. Mastering the Comma / 97
    1. *Commas That Separate* / 97
Exercise 7.1—Commas That Separate Independent Clauses and Elements in a Series / 99
Exercise 7.2—Commas That Separate Coordinate Adjectives and Confusing Sentence Elements / 101
    2. *Commas That Set Off* / 103
Exercise 7.3—Commas That Set Off Non-restrictive Modifiers, Appositives, and Introductory Phrases and Clauses / 108

Exercise 7.4—Commas That Set Off Sentence Modifiers, Absolute Constructions, and Contrasting Elements / 110
Exercise 7.5—Commas That Set Off Names, Speakers, Echo Questions, and Mild Interjections / 112
Exercise 7.6—Comma Review Exercise / 114
B. Employing the Semicolon / 116
Exercise 7.7—The Semicolon / 118
C. Using the Colon and the Dash Properly / 120
   1. *The Colon* / 120
   2. *The Dash* / 121
Exercise 7.8—The Colon and the Dash / 122
D. When to Use Quotation Marks / 124
E. When to Use Italics / 125
Exercise 7.9—Quotation Marks and Italics / 126
F. What Should Be Capitalized? / 128
Exercise 7.10—Capitalizing Correctly / 131
G. The Functions of the Apostrophe / 133
   1. *To Show Possession* / 133
   2. *To Indicate Omission* / 134
   3. *To Form Plurals* / 134
Exercise 7.11—The Apostrophe / 134
H. The Distinct Uses of Parentheses and Brackets / 136
   1. *Parentheses* / 136
   2. *Brackets* / 137
Exercise 7.12—Parentheses and Brackets / 137
I. The Uses of the Hyphen / 139
Exercise 7.13—The Hyphen / 140
J. End Punctuation—The Period, Question Mark, and Exclamation Point / 141
   1. *The Period* / 141
   2. *The Question Mark* / 142
   3. *The Exclamation Point* / 143
Exercise 7.14—Periods, Question Marks, and Exclamation Points / 143
Exercise 7.15—Punctuation Review Exercise / 144

CHAPTER EIGHT   **Choosing the Right Words / 147**

A. Keeping Your Language Fresh: Clichés to Avoid / 147
Exercise 8.1—Detecting Clichés / 148
Exercise 8.2—Changing Clichés to Fresh Expressions / 149
B. Making Your Writing Precise: Watch Jargon / 150
Exercise 8.3—Replacing Jargon / 151
Exercise 8.4—Alternatives to Jargon / 153
C. Writing Concisely: Avoiding Wordiness / 153
Exercise 8.5—Making Sentences Concise / 154

D. Only What Is Necessary: Avoiding Redundancies / 155
Exercise 8.6—Removing Redundancies / 156
E. Proper Usage / 158
Exercise 8.7—Revising for Effective Diction / 171

CHAPTER NINE   Preparing an Outline / 173

A. What Is an Outline? / 173
B. The Benefits / 173
C. Types of Outlines / 174
   1. *Scratch Outline* / 174
   2. *Topic Outline* / 175
   3. *Sentence Outline* / 178
D. Ordering the Outline / 179
   1. *Grouping by Ideas or Analysis* / 179
   2. *Arranging Chronologically* / 181
   3. *Arranging by Location and Situation* / 181
E. The Elements of a Constructive Outline / 182
   1. *Balance* / 188
   2. *Unity* / 188
   3. *Completeness* / 188
Exercise 9.1—Preparing an Outline / 182

CHAPTER TEN   Constructing Effective Paragraphs / 195

A. What Is a Paragraph? / 195
B. Making Paragraphs Unified / 195
Exercise 10.1—Paragraph Unity / 196
C. The Topic Sentence: Point of View / 198
   1. *An Effective Topic Sentence* / 198
Exercise 10.2—Selecting the Topic Sentence / 199
   2. *Position of Topic Sentences* / 201
Exercise 10.3—Position of the Topic Sentence / 204
D. Three Paragraph Types / 205
   1. *The Introductory Paragraph* / 205
   2. *The Transitional Paragraph* / 205
   3. *The Concluding Paragraph* / 206
Exercise 10.4—Paragraph Types / 208
E. Creating Patterns of Development: The Expository Paragraph / 211
   1. *Classification* / 212
   2. *Comparison and Contrast* / 213
   3. *Narration and Description* / 214
   4. *Example* / 215
   5. *Enumeration by Details* / 216

6. *Cause and Effect* / 216
   7. *Process Description* / 217
   8. *Definition* / 218
Exercise 10.5—Topic Sentence and Patterns of Development / 219
Exercise 10.6—Selecting Topic Sentences and Constructing Patterns of
   Development / 220
Exercise 10.7—Selecting Topic Sentences and Constructing Patterns of
   Development / 221
Notes / 222

CHAPTER ELEVEN   Composing an Expository Essay / 224

A. What Is an Expository Essay? / 224
B. Preparing to Write / 224
C. The Parts of the Essay / 226
   1. *The Introduction* / 226
   2. *The Body* / 227
   3. *The Conclusion* / 227
D. The Well-Constructed Student Essay / 227
Exercise 11.1—Essay Assignment / 229
E. Examples of Effective Essays / 229
Exercise 11.2—Essay Assignment / 231
Exercise 11.3—Essay Assignment / 235
Exercise 11.4—Essay Assignment / 238
F. Citing Your Sources / 238
   1. *Examples of Citations within the Text* / 238
   2. *Works Cited* / 239
Notes / 241

Preface

The focus of this text is on the planning, organization, and structure of expository prose. Rhetorical or creative writing skills are not discussed. The writing style also continues to be precise and economical; the language does not patronize or talk down to readers, and the diction and vocabulary are appropriate for students on both the secondary and the post-secondary levels. Also, the text's North American orientation is natural, logical, and unintrusive, and the language is non-sexist.

   The flexibility of the text has also been maintained: it can be used for community college English courses, for developmental writing in first-year university courses, and for high-school students who must prepare for post-secondary composition and report writing. Furthermore, its organization and structure allow for use in self-paced and distance education programs that stress vocational writing skills.

   In sum, the text has the inclusiveness of a handbook and the utility of a workbook. Its organization permits the teacher to use it for in-class assignments, and its comprehensive discussion of grammar, syntax, and mechanics enables the student to use it as a self-study handbook. It provides an abundance of examples and exercises and prepares students for first-draft revision by obliging them to correct defective paragraphs and essays. Furthermore, the emphasis on skill development continues to be strong. From the presentation of grammar as a relationship among words, phrases, and clauses, to the use of outlining as the organizational foundation of paragraphs, essays, and reports, the text requires students to continually apply what they learn.

   By requiring students to balance sentences, correct inappropriate and redundant words and phrases, relate punctuation to speech inflection, and submit to the discipline of outlining, they become more sensitive to paragraph structure and more critical of first-draft composition.

   Finally, and most importantly, the text treats writing as a craft that requires thinking, planning, choosing, rearranging, and starting over.

Joseph Lyons

CHAPTER ONE

Beginning with the Foundation: Parts of Speech

All written and spoken communication depends on the sentence, since only the sentence contains a complete thought. And sentences themselves are composed of words with particular functions and assigned relationships; the term "parts of speech" simply describes how words function as sentence parts. With the exception of the interjection—a word whose abrupt emotional message is obvious (Help! Oh! Wow!)—each part of speech performs a particular role *within* the sentence. There are seven of them: nouns, pronouns, verbs, adjectives, adverbs, prepositions, and conjunctions.

A. NOUNS

A noun is a name; it names people, places, things, ideas, and general conditions. Some nouns, called *proper*, are capitalized because their names are particular.

> The *students* who graduated from *Glendale College* are invited to a reception hosted by *Professor Roberts*.

A noun's most important function, though, is as a subject (the doer) or an object (the receiver) in the sentence.

> **Subj.** **Obj.**
> *Marie* passed the *examination* with ease.
>
> **Subj.** **Obj.**
> Some *buildings* in Toronto have interesting *histories*.

B. PRONOUNS

Pronouns are noun substitutions, and they are used to avoid repetition. So instead of saying, "Peter and Peter's friend, Harold, took Peter and Harold's parents to the graduation party, where Peter and Harold and the parents of Peter and

Harold drank punch and ate tiny sandwiches...," you can say, "Peter and *his* friend Harold took *their* parents to the graduation party, where *they all* drank punch and ate tiny sandwiches."

There are three obvious kinds of pronouns: *personal, possessive,* and *indefinite.*

Personal	**Possessive**	**Indefinite** (*a partial list*)
I, me	my, mine	anybody
you	your, yours	anyone
he, him	his, hers	anything
she, her	its	everybody
it	our, ours	everyone
we, us	their, theirs	everything
they, them		somebody
		someone
		something
		all
		any
		each
		few
		many
		some

In the following sentences all three types are used:

> If *anybody* wishes to volunteer for *our* heart-fund drive, will *he* or *she* please step forward.

> Has *anyone* seen *my* textbook? *I* left it on *somebody's* desk.

Note that some indefinite pronouns are made possessive with an apostrophe and an *s*. See pp. 133-34.

Then there are *interrogative pronouns,* which ask questions: who, which, whom, whose, what.

> *What* was the colour of the book and to *whom* did it belong?

There are also *relative pronouns,* which link clauses to their antecedents: who, which, that, whom, whose.

> The *student (who* left the new textbook on the *desk) (that* is located in our school) is still looking for it.

And finally, there are *demonstrative pronouns*, which point out or demonstrate something: these, those, this, that.

> *Those* who leave their books on desks in unfamiliar classrooms will surely lose them—and *that* is the truth!

Note: Demonstrative pronouns also function as adjectives when they appear immediately before nouns: *these* cars, *that* house, *this* theory, *those* students.

C. VERBS

The verb is the heart of the sentence. It makes the sentence move and infuses it with vitality. In fact, you cannot write a sentence without a verb. Nor do you have to know what a word means to identify it as a verb, since it serves as the vital connecting link between the subject and the object.

> James *scrabbled* the test.
>
> The test *was scrabbled* by James.

Because the verb performs or receives an action or reflects a condition or an event, it provides the spark that lets a group of words project ideas.

> The flaming meteor *ploughed* into the field, *tore* through the treeline, and *crashed* against the mountain.
>
> The table lamp *was knocked* over by our cat while he *was playing* with the cord.

D. ADJECTIVES

An adjective is a word that modifies (describes, restricts, relates to) a noun or a pronoun and that answers the questions *which, how many,* and *what kind.* Other adjectives, called *articles*—a, an, the—answer the question *which one.* Adjectives usually, but not always, precede nouns and pronouns.

> The *morning* sun crept over the *blackened* rooftops and sent *cautious* probes of *pale* light into the *gutted* buildings.
>
> The *weary* traveller, *lonely* and *forlorn,* approached the outskirts of the *deserted* city.

E. ADVERBS

Adverbs are more flexible than adjectives. They can modify verbs, adjectives, and other adverbs, and can appear almost anywhere in the sentence. They normally answer the questions *where, when, how,* and *how much.* Adverbs not only determine the precise meaning of adjectives and other adverbs but also provide substance and glitter to verbs.

> *extremely* unhappy; *inconspicuously* clever; *fairly* mild; *quite* strong; *predictably* late
> (modifying adjectives and adverbs)

> While several sea birds wheeled *gracefully* over the undulating waves, others searched *casually* along the beach for discarded food.
> (modifying verbs)

F. PREPOSITIONS

Prepositions are important in sentences because they join with nouns and pronouns to form phrases that serve as modifiers of subjects, verbs, and objects. Here are some common prepositions: *at, by, for, from, in, of, on, to, with, between, over, under, through,* and *within.* They can start some very interesting things happening in sentences.

> (With simple dignity), (on the bed where he was born), he died (in silence).

Prepositional phrases are especially important in poetry, for they are often used to construct sensuous and powerful images.

> We sat grown quiet (at the name of love);
> We saw the last embers (of daylight) die,
> And (in the trembling blue-green of the sky)
> A moon, worn as if it had been a shell
> Washed (by time's waters) as they rose and fell
> (About the stars) and broke (in days and years).
>
> "Adam's Curse," William Butler Yeats

G. CONJUNCTIONS

Conjunctions are essential because they join similar sentence elements and thereby provide the sentence with balance and cohesion. There are four kinds of conjunctions: *coordinate, correlative, subordinate,* and the *conjunctive adverb.*

1. Coordinate

These conjunctions are the most frequently used and are therefore the most familiar. There are seven of them: *and, but, or, nor, for, yet,* and *so.* They connect grammatically equal sentence parts such as words, phrases, and clauses.

> WORDS: Bill *and* Frank; hit *and* run; tea *or* coffee

PHRASES:	(Around the corner) *and* (over the hill)
DEPENDENT CLAUSES:	No one knew (who he was) *or* (what he did).
INDEPENDENT CLAUSES:	(The director told me the actor's name), *but* (I have forgotten it).

2. Correlative

These conjunctions always come in pairs, and they are most often used for balance and emphasis. There are four important ones:

either...or; neither...nor; not only...but/but also; both...and.
(See the discussion of sentence coordination, pp. 30-31.)

> She is *not only* a portrait painter *but also* a concert pianist.
>
> Peter is *either* going to the University of Montreal *or* to an art college in Nova Scotia.
>
> *Neither* gambling *nor* drinking is permitted in this establishment.
>
> *Both* my father *and* my uncle are volunteer firefighters.

3. Subordinate

These conjunctions connect dependent and independent clauses, and their use is determined by the principles of subordination (see p. 31). Some of the most common subordinate conjunctions are *that, because, when, although, until, while, as,* and *if.*

> He discarded his life jacket *although* it was a dangerous thing to do.
>
> I always wear goggles *when* skiing downhill.
>
> *If* you volunteer, I shall support your efforts.

4. Conjunctive Adverbs

Conjunctive adverbs connect related independent clauses, and they are used in sentences to sequence, qualify, and conclude. They allow the writer added flexibility in conveying ideas and information. Some common conjunctive adverbs are *therefore, moreover, however, nevertheless,* and *consequently* (see p. 117 for a more complete list).

> He has not answered our summons; *therefore,* we shall proceed without him.
>
> Jane cannot babysit tonight; *however,* her brother has volunteered to take her place.
>
> Although the earthquake destroyed most of the town, people do, *nevertheless,* still manage to live there.

6 *Writing Fundamentals*

What is important to remember about parts of speech is how they combine to convey meaning. The correct positioning of verbs, pronouns, and adjectives will permit you to be not only coherent and precise but also original and emphatic.

Writing effective sentences is a constant challenge, but the rewards are worth the effort. When the proper words are used in the proper places, they can reveal the brilliance of the English language, as in sentences like these:

> Still falls the Rain—
> Dark as the word of man, black as our loss—
> Blind as the nineteen hundred and forty nails
> Upon the Cross.
>
> > "Still Falls the Rain," Edith Sitwell
>
> And we are here as on a darkling plain
> Swept with confused alarms of struggle and flight,
> Where ignorant armies clash by night.
>
> > "Dover Beach," Matthew Arnold
>
> Our birth is but a sleep and a forgetting...
>
> > "Intimations of Immortality,"
> > William Wordsworth
>
> Wit has truth in it; wisecracking is simply calisthenics with words.
>
> > *Paris Revue* [Summer 1956],
> > Dorothy Parker
>
> Let us go then, you and I,
> When the evening is spread out against the sky
> Like a patient etherized upon a table.
>
> > *The Love Song of J. Alfred Prufrock*,
> > T.S. Eliot
>
> Like flies to wanton boys are we to the Gods;
> They kill us for their sport.
>
> > *King Lear, Act IV, Scene I*,
> > William Shakespeare
>
> The beauty of the world has two edges, one of laughter, one of anguish, cutting the heart asunder.
>
> > *A Room of One's Own*, Virginia Woolf

Before we can hope to write sentences like these, however, we must first understand how they are made and patterned; these skills are examined in the following chapters.

Exercise 1.1 — Distinguishing Parts of Speech

In each of the following sentences identify the italicized words by writing the correct number in the blank at the right:

1. Noun   2. Pronoun   3. Adjective   4. Adverb   5. Preposition
6. Conjunction   7. Verb

EXAMPLE: Many *professional* football players do not enjoy playing *on* artificial turf.   _3_   _5_

1. Our old boat is docked *across* from the new *hotel*.
2. Please *take* your brother with you *when* you go to the store.
3. *She* swears that she was not in school when the *fire* started.
4. Milos *and* Catherine *prevented* the fire from spreading.
5. *You* should wash the fruit *before* eating it.
6. *Keep* your *head* down!
7. *Where* is *Carlos* going?
8. *Montreal* has many *excellent* restaurants.
9. Monty *wants* to go on a ski holiday, *but* Claude prefers to go to the beach.
10. *My* aunt *works* as a nurse in the general hospital.
11. The final rock concert this year was held in the *stadium where* our football team plays.
12. *Which* word-processing software package do *you* use?
13. Rojas and *he* are not coming with *us* tonight.
14. Your *pretentious* demeanour will make you *unpopular*.
15. *Talk* to your parents before you accept *their* invitation.
16. They *are* not to blame for your *poor* grades.
17. Is *it* her mother who *refuses* to join the exercise group?
18. Bill McLeod *and* Helen Freidlander *were chosen* for the leads in the school play.
19. It was *she*, not *he*, who travelled to India last summer.
20. *When* will she *visit* us again?

8 *Writing Fundamentals*

21. She broke the *blue* lampshade while trying to remove it *from* the packing crate. ____ ____
22. Franz Lorca is a *famous* opera singer from *Bolivia*. ____ ____
23. The Montreal Canadiens *and* the Detroit Red Wings *will play* an exhibition game tomorrow. ____ ____
24. *Their* privacy is *our* number one priority. ____ ____
25. They *travelled* throughout Europe *with* their dog, Ralph. ____ ____
26. *Where* will the plane land if the weather *is* unsuitable? ____ ____
27. Deirdre is a very *private* person; so is *her* sister. ____ ____
28. *How many* times has *Devon* struck out this year? ____ ____
29. Do *you* know *where* the Harrisons are moving? ____ ____
30. *Correct* the tests *with* the computer; the correction program is already loaded. ____ ____

CHAPTER TWO

Organizing Your Sentences

A. WHAT IS A SENTENCE?

A sentence is a group of related words containing a complete thought. It has both a subject and a verb, and can stand alone as an independent statement. The *subject* is the person, place, thing, or idea that the sentence is about, and the *verb* is the statement made about the subject. A sentence may consist of a simple verbal command without a stated subject—Follow me. Sit down. Turn to the right.—or it may have more than one subject and more than one verb, as in the following examples.

> **Mary and Lisa** are enrolled in the same course.
> (compound subject)
>
> The spectators *clapped and cheered* when the home team ran onto the field.
> (compound verb)
>
> **Students and faculty** *repaired and painted* the old classroom desks.
> (compound subject and verb)

The complete subject of a sentence includes the subject term and its modifiers—words and phrases that describe or limit—and the complete verb includes the verb statement and the modifiers that complete its meaning.

Complete Subject	Complete Verb
The **actor** who portrayed Count Dracula	*received* a standing ovation.
The **kind of music** I most enjoy	*is* dance music from the big-band era.
The small red and white **car**	*crashed* into a lamppost.

But always remember that, however numerous the subject and verb modifiers, the statement cannot stand alone without a simple subject and a simple verb.

(After being ignored time and time again,) **Mr. Roberts** *decided* (to remain silent during class discussions).

Without the words *Mr. Roberts* (simple subject) and *decided* (simple verb), the example above would not be a complete sentence.

B. THE COMPLETE VERB

1. The complete verb may have one or more helping words that reflect time or fix emphasis.

    It *must have been* he who wrote the letter.

    She *will have gone* by the time we arrive.

    I *should play* tomorrow.

2. It may have a direct object that completes the action and answers the questions *who* or *what*.

    Tom wrote his *term paper* yesterday. (Wrote what?)

    Squirrels eat *nuts*. (Eat what?)

    Jack drove *Carol* home last night. (Drove whom?)

3. It may have an indirect object that receives the action.

    He gave *me* (to me) his notebook to study.

    Steve told *me* (to me) a story about football.

    Her sister gave *her* (to her) new ski poles for Christmas.

C. THE SIMPLE SUBJECT AND VERB

If you remember that the subject is the focus of the sentence and the verb the statement made about the subject, the order in which they appear should pose no problem. First locate the simple verb, which is the word or group of words that states something: then ask who or what the statement is about. Consider the following examples:

1. Although the subject usually precedes the verb, the order may be reversed.

    s
    The *runner* is exhausted. (Who is exhausted?)

    s
    Is the *runner* exhausted? (Who is exhausted?)

>   s
> There is the exhausted *runner*. (Who is there?)
>
>   s
> From the runner came a *sigh* of exhaustion. (What came?)

2. In *There is (are)* and *Here is (are)* sentences, the verb always precedes the subject.

>   v   s
> There *is* only one *car* in the showroom.
>
>   v   s
> There *are* more *cars* in the parking lot.
>
>   v   s
> Here *is* the most expensive *car* on the market.
>
>   v   s
> Here *are* the most fuel-efficient *cars* that money can buy.

Note: *here* and *there* are never the subjects of sentences; they introduce the subject term but do not participate in its activity.

3. Sentences that issue orders, make strong requests, or give directions take *you* (meaning the reader or listener) as the implied subject.

>   (You) Go to sleep.
>
>   (You) Please find the correct file.
>
>   (You) Write your name and the date in your test booklet.

Exercise 2.1 — Locating the Subject and Verb

In the following sentences locate the simple subject and verb and then write them in the blanks at the right or on a separate sheet of paper.

		S	V
EXAMPLE:	Jack Reynolds, the star athlete, has won a scholarship for academic excellence.	Jack Reynolds	has won

1. Into the water dove the competing swimmers. ____ ____
2. Several of the puzzle pieces are missing. ____ ____
3. Please inform Sarah that she is wanted on the phone. ____ ____
4. When is our next anthropology class? ____ ____
5. Juan Martinez has a dental appointment today. ____ ____

6. Playing tennis is excellent exercise.
7. Some of the spectators are leaving early.
8. There were several choices that we had to make.
9. Our parents' anniversary is next Friday.
10. Many of our classes were cancelled yesterday.
11. Only one of us gave up smoking cigarettes.
12. Who took the chalk off the blackboard shelf?
13. Grapes and peaches were on sale last Friday at the local supermarket.
14. Several of our hockey players are still injured.
15. Here is my favourite talk-show host.
16. Douglas, after finally making the basketball team, had to cease all sports activities because of a heart murmur.
17. Some of the prizewinners were not eligible.
18. Beyond the next hill lies the farmers' market.
19. Please do not walk on the fresh cement.
20. Planting a flower garden is hard work.
21. Where did we meet last month?
22. Mr. Chang, after months of litigation, finally won his court case against his former employer.
23. How many hats does Greta own?
24. More than seven laws were broken by the convicted felons.
25. Outside the stadium there was a traffic jam.
26. All of our neighbours have paved driveways.
27. Swimming every day tones the leg muscles.
28. After the snowstorm we could not see our hedges.
29. While vacationing in the South of France, Jessica met her future husband.
30. Please try to be a little more patient with your baby brother.

D. ENLARGING THROUGH PHRASES

The subject-verb structure, the basic unit of thought that comprises a sentence, can be expanded by attaching to it related word groups called phrases and clauses. These word groups permit us to add variety and depth to statements.

A phrase may be defined as a group of related words without a subject and a verb and used as a single part of speech. The most common phrases are prepositional, participial, gerund, and infinitive.

1. Phrases Introduced by Prepositions

The prepositional phrase is introduced by a preposition—*across* the hall, *in* the house, *after* the game, *for* my sister—and is most often used as an adjective or an adverb.

> The manager *of our branch office* submitted her request *for a leave of absence.*

The italicized phrases above are used as adjectives because they modify the nouns *manager* and *request*.

> All final examinations are given *in the spring at the main campus.*

The italicized phrases above are used as adverbs because they modify the verb *are given* and answer the questions *when* and *where*. Other adverb phrases will answer the questions *why, how, to what extent,* and *under what conditions.*

2. Phrases Beginning with -ing and -ed Verbs

The participial phrase begins with a verb form ending in *ing* in the present and *ed* or *t* in the past. Participial phrases always function as adjectives.

> *Having treated the patient*, the doctor closed her bag and left the room.
> (participial phrase modifying *doctor*)
>
> *Penned in by his thoughtless owners*, the dog became extremely vicious.
> (participial phrase modifying *dog*)
>
> The threatening letter *sent by the accused* was used as evidence in the murder trial.
> (participial phrase modifying *letter*)

Sometimes the participial phrase begins with a verb form that has a vowel change.

> *Drunk with power*, the general issued an ultimatum.
> (participial phrase modifying *general*)

14 *Writing Fundamentals*

Note: When participles appear with *helping words* like *is, was, were,* and *have, has, had,* they function as *integral* parts of the verb:

> Father *is coming* home.
>
> The apartment *was rented* yesterday.
>
> I *have spent* my last dime on you.

3. Phrases Beginning with -ing Words as Nouns

The gerund phrase, like the present participle, begins with a verb form ending in *ing*; but, unlike the participle, it is *always* used as a noun. Therefore, the gerund phrase may serve as either the subject or the object of a sentence.

> *Skiing on ice* is very dangerous.
> (gerund phrase used as a subject, answering the question, "What is dangerous?")
>
> The teacher dislikes *listening to lame excuses.*
> (gerund phrase used as an object, answering the question "dislikes what?")

Remember, words ending in *ing* and answering the questions *who* or *what* are gerunds functioning as subjects or objects of sentences.

4. Phrases with Infinitives

The infinitive phrase begins with an infinitive—a verb preceded by the word *to*—and functions as a noun, an adjective, or an adverb.

> *To please everyone in the room* would be an impossible task.
> (infinitive phrase functioning as the subject)
>
> We were gathered together *to hear the election results.*
> (infinitive phrase used as an adverb answering the question *why*)
>
> He gave us permission *to begin our work.*
> (infinitive phrase used as an adjective modifying *permission*)
>
> We planned *to leave as early as possible.*
> (infinitive phrase used as a direct object)

Exercise 2.2 — Recognizing Phrases

In the following sentences identify the italicized phrase by writing the correct abbreviation in the blanks at the right (or on a separate sheet): *Prep.* for preposition, *Part.* for participial, *Ger.* for gerund, and *Inf.* for infinitive.

> EXAMPLES: I hate *standing in line*.   Ger.
>
> The house *on the left* has been sold.   Prep.

1. Monica does not want to go *with the rest of us.*
2. Kathy prefers *acting on stage,* not in films.
3. *During the basketball game* the assistant coach became ill.
4. The police officer *walking toward us* is my uncle.
5. *Swimming in salt water* is very refreshing.
6. *Discovering the origin of the universe* will be a major scientific undertaking.
7. Luke's favourite pastime is *playing chess.*
8. One of our highest-paid rock stars, *a multiple award winner,* has just been diagnosed with HIV.
9. *Competing in track and field* is my favourite sports activity.
10. I am flying out of Montreal *at precisely 1:00 p.m.*
11. *Shocked by the outcome of the trial,* the family members left the courtroom in embittered silence.
12. *Playing Scrabble with my sister and brother* is not my idea of a satisfying evening.
13. The new car, *parked near the courthouse,* belongs to the prosecuting attorney.
14. *Once purchased by the Queen of Belgium,* the famous blue, pear-shaped diamond is now being auctioned in London.
15. Abdullah Shaban certainly enjoyed *playing soccer in our new stadium.*
16. The old man *playing shuffleboard* was once a famous stage actor.
17. Our dog, Max, chased the squirrel *into the garage.*
18. Mary-Lisa hates *being the centre of attention.*
19. Farina and Talia decided to take computer programming courses on Tuesdays, *after their gym class.*
20. *To be an airline pilot* is my chief ambition in life.
21. *While acting in our school play,* Sheila slipped on a stage prop and broke her ankle.

22. *Famous for her role in <u>Anne of Green Gables</u>,* Catherine quickly became a member of a daytime soap opera cast. _____

23. *Working two jobs during the summer* enabled Kurt to pay his college tuition. _____

24. *To qualify for the accounting job,* we had to take a three-hour test. _____

25. *Enraged by her employer's lack of concern for the employees,* Danielle filed a grievance on their behalf. _____

26. The parking lot *next to the department store* is being repaved. _____

27. *Hiking in British Columbia* is one of the activities we are planning for next summer. _____

28. *To grow a perfect rose* is my wife's fondest dream. _____

29. They drove carelessly *on the unpaved road.* _____

30. The young outfielder *walking toward the bullpen* was my roommate in college. _____

E. EXPANDING WITH CLAUSES

Like phrases, clauses are groups of related words, and some function as a single part of speech; but unlike phrases, they have both a subject and a verb. There are two kinds of clauses: *independent* (or main) and *dependent* (or subordinate). An independent clause contains a complete thought and therefore stands alone. It may consist of simply a subject and a verb—*Students study*—or it may contain modifiers—Some *students study* very hard. An independent clause, then, is just another way of defining a simple sentence.

A dependent clause, on the other hand, does not stand alone. Although containing a subject and a verb, it begins with a relative pronoun (*whom, who, which, that*) or a subordinate conjunction (*if, as, since, because, while, when*) that makes it dependent upon the main clause.

> Jack fought a battle *that he couldn't win.*
>
> Adrienne, *who just celebrated her sixty-fifth birthday,* is now jogging around the block.
>
> *Since Hans is arriving late,* we shall start dinner without him.

Because dependent clauses function as single parts of speech, they can be divided into adjective, adverb, and noun clauses.

1. Clauses as Adjectives

An adjective clause, like an adjective, modifies a noun or pronoun and is usually introduced by a relative pronoun.

>Antonio is the student *who has been nominated for an academic award*.
>(adjective clause modifying student)

>Mr. Flynn, *who has just been appointed principal*, was one of my former teachers.
>(adjective clause modifying Mr. Flynn)

>The new car *that is parked in my driveway* belongs to my brother.
>(adjective clause modifying car)

2. Clauses as Adverbs

An adverb clause can modify a verb, an adjective, or another adverb, and it is usually introduced by a subordinate conjunction. An adverb clause will answer the questions *when, where, why, how, to what extent,* and *under what conditions.*

>He has not eaten anything *since his dog was killed by a car.*
>(adverb clause answering the question *when*)

>Marianne cannot take us to dinner *because she spent all her money.*
>(adverb clause answering the question *why*)

>The injured basketball player looked *as if she were going to faint.*
>(adverb clause answering the question *how did she look*)

3. Clauses as Nouns

A noun clause functions like a noun or pronoun, and can therefore be the subject, object, or subject complement of a sentence. The major difference between noun clauses and other dependent clauses is that, in most cases, you cannot remove the noun clause and still have an intelligible sentence.

>*That he could play any position on the field* was obvious.
>(noun clause functioning as the subject)

>We suggested *that he write his final essay.*
>(noun clause functioning as the object)

>The indisputable fact is *that we lost money last year.*
>(noun clause functioning as a subject complement)

Note: A subject complement always relates back to the subject and usually follows such linking verbs as *is, was, were, seem, become,* and *appear.*

>I will invest in *whatever company I think will make money.*
>(noun clause functioning as an object of a preposition)

Observe that in each case the noun clause is indispensable for the complete meaning of the sentence.

18 *Writing Fundamentals*

Exercise 2.3 — Identifying Clauses

Identify the italicized dependent clauses below by writing their functions in the blanks at the right (or on a separate sheet of paper): *N.* for noun clause, *Adj.* for adjective clause, and *Adv.* for adverb clause.

    EXAMPLES: I saw Romero enter the building *as I turned the corner.*   Adv.

    That she will win the final match is beyond question.   N.

1. *After you finish watering the lawn*, please sweep the driveway. _____

2. The English professor *who wrote the best-selling mystery novel* is now working on a screenplay for the CBC. _____

3. Maurice's new truck, *which he uses to haul produce*, has a broken axle. _____

4. *When I first saw Melissa*, she was a platinum blonde. _____

5. My new computer, *which has a Pentium chip*, is being repaired. _____

6. *When my birthday arrives*, I do not want a celebration party. _____

7. We believe *that everyone is entitled to a fair trial.* _____

8. The card game will begin *as soon as the other players arrive.* _____

9. *That Conrad Jellico will be elected the mayor of our city* is a foregone conclusion. _____

10. Who knows *when our bus will leave the station?* _____

11. Our city council is concerned about the allegations *that several construction firms overcharged the city for street repair.* _____

12. How can we know *what our school board's intentions are?* _____

13. *When Celeste arrived on campus*, the library committee had already concluded its business. _____

14. *If you think that your vote will make a difference*, we would be willing to reconvene the committee. _____

15. Garcia suggested *that we wait for final instructions.* _____

16. Do not overreact *when you hear your sister announce her candidacy for a city council position.* _____

17. The mid-term test *that was scheduled for next Friday* has been rescheduled for the following Monday. _____

18. Kim Chung is the woman *who won the applied science scholarship*.

19. My uncle, *who retired last month*, is now a consultant for a government agency.

20. We were told *that our airline fares were already paid*.

21. Our team responded to the fans' encouragement *as soon as our coach told us that our playoff chances were in jeopardy*.

22. The plane *that flew us to South America* is the same one that slid off the runway last week.

23. Who knows *how television network officials think*.

24. *When we heard about the brush fires near our property*, we rushed right home.

25. *What we know about past segregation practices* cannot be revealed.

26. Fred's old sawmill, *which he almost sold last week*, has just been declared a historical landmark.

27. Talk to *whoever is in charge of the investigation*.

28. Our team could not score a touchdown *because our star quarterback was out of action*.

29. Dr. Singh, *who was chief cardiac surgeon at University Hospital*, has just been awarded a lucrative research grant.

30. It was my family's cottage *that was severely damaged by the last hurricane*.

Exercise 2.4 — Developing the Subject-Verb Structure

In each of the following sentences, expand the subject-verb structure by adding appropriate phrases and clauses. Use as many kinds of phrases and clauses as you can, but be sure the meaning is clear and logical.

> EXAMPLES: George faced the jury.
> (*To hear the verdict*, George faced the jury.)
>
> Michelle left the room.
> (Michelle, *having finished her lunch*, left the room.)
>
> He is sure.
> (He is sure *that he knows who caused the accident*.)
>
> The boat has already been sold.
> (The boat *that Ian wanted to purchase* has already been sold.)

1. The stock market has been strong for months.
2. Calgary is a wonderful city.
3. He lacks ambition.
4. Don't deny your involvement with the criminal.
5. Pierre buys everything wholesale.
6. I can't eat broccoli.
7. Brian's new car was too expensive.
8. We toured Nova Scotia last July.
9. Paco studies English in the evening.
10. This pizza is too spicy.
11. Laptop computers are a convenience, not a necessity.
12. Please buy your own textbooks.
13. Cancel my two o'clock meeting.
14. Our cat received her rabies shots this morning.
15. My cottage is now winterized.
16. Stay where you are.
17. The house on the left has been sold.
18. Don't try to influence the election.
19. Franz telephoned about an hour ago.
20. Who wants an ice cream cone?
21. Ngu Peng has just become a Canadian citizen.
22. Send our condolences to the deceased's family.
23. Martin's retirement party is next Saturday.
24. Please watch the road.
25. The Canadian Rockies are ideal for a ski holiday.
26. My horse came in second.
27. Finish your homework before watching television.
28. Roland Garrett is a world-famous hairstylist.
29. My college does not allow smoking on the premises.
30. Lottery money helped us build our new hockey rink.

F. FINDING SENTENCE ERRORS

Fragmentary and run-on sentences are caused by the improper use of clauses and phrases. These sentences are written when we do not quite know what we want to say or how we want to say it. Thus, such sentences contain illogical and rambling statements. However, by thinking before we write, and by paying proper attention to the subject-verb structure that expresses action and thought, we can avoid these awkward constructions.

1. Mending Fragments

Fragments, as the name implies, are incomplete units of thought that cannot logically stand alone. Grammatically, they may be defined as dependent clauses and phrases (usually verbal phrases) that are expressed as if they were complete thoughts and written as if they were complete sentences. There are two common types of fragments:

(a) *Dependent-Clause Fragments*

> I stayed home from work yesterday. *Because I was sick.*
>
> Tom's new car was given to him by his uncle. *Who, I understand, is very rich.*
>
> Katrina learned to play the piano. *When she was very young.*

(b) *Verbal-Phrase Fragments*

> He was left without any money. *Having spent his last dime on a new guitar.*
>
> Karen was a potential heart-attack victim. *Being constantly frustrated and frequently overworked.*
>
> *Knowing how to win at cards.* He became a professional gambler.

Remember, a fragment cannot stand alone because it has no verb. Therefore, when proofreading, make sure you can identify the subject-verb construction that carries the meaning of each sentence.

Remember, too, that *ing* words, like *being, coming, having, doing, going,* cannot stand alone as verbs without being supported by a form of the verb *to be: is, are, am, was, were.*

2. Mending Run-on Sentences

Run-on sentences occur when two or more independent clauses are joined together without proper coordination or punctuation. The result is that two complete thoughts improperly overlap. The most obvious run-on mistake is the fused sentence containing two independent clauses without any punctuation.

> Brendan lost his textbook/that is why he failed the test.
>
> Our history teacher enjoys tennis/her husband enjoys golf.

The run-on sentence, however, is most often written as a comma splice, in which two independent clauses are incorrectly separated by a comma.

> Brendan lost his textbook, that is why he failed the test.
>
> Our history teacher enjoys tennis, her husband enjoys golf.

Run-on sentences are corrected in one of four ways, depending upon the relationship between the independent clauses:

(a) with a period when each clause is sufficiently independent from the other

> My father works for a tool company. The tools he makes are of the highest quality.

(b) with a semicolon when there is an implied connection between the independent statements

> Mike hits baseballs with power; Jacques hits them with ease.

(c) with a conjunctive adverb when you want to emphasize the specific nature of the relationship

> Jane has to work overtime; therefore, she will be late for dinner.

Note: The conjunctive adverb is still preceded by a semicolon to properly separate the independent statements.

(d) with a coordinate conjunction when the relationship between the two clauses is close, obvious, and logical

> My aunt is a doctor, and my nephew is a pharmacist.

Note: The coordinate conjunction must be preceded by a comma when it connects two independent clauses.

Remember, however, that when an independent clause can more logically be subordinated, you should write the sentence with one dependent clause.

> *Because my aunt was a doctor*, my nephew became a pharmacist.

Exercise 2.5 — Detecting Sentence Fragments

Identify the sentence fragments by writing *F* in the blank to the right or on a separate sheet of paper. If the sentence is complete, write *C*.

    EXAMPLES: Thinking in terms of racial minorities.   F

                         It is the correct position to take.   C

1. Forest fires can be prevented.
2. Without having to pretend.
3. Telling them again and again.
4. Stop driving so fast.
5. While we were waiting for our airplane to arrive.
6. Nothing is ever certain.
7. Although we were not the last ones to leave the party.
8. Your homework must be done now.
9. Whatever anyone says about our inability to win without a strong offensive line.
10. Let's keep it simple.
11. Appreciating someone else's point of view.
12. Try keeping your room clean.
13. Remember to exit your document file before turning off your computer.
14. Saving your document before exiting.
15. Where are you going?
16. How will you get there?
17. Staying home every Sunday evening.
18. To determine your next major goal.
19. Deciding what college to attend.
20. Will you commute or live away from home?
21. Organizing your time and scheduling different activities.
22. What are the possibilities?

23. Exercising every day.   _____
24. Stay out of trouble.   _____
25. Not caring what other people think about breaking the
    rules of the institution.   _____
26. Tell me your class schedule.   _____
27. To be excluded from all sporting activities is unfair.   _____
28. Can I be of any help?   _____
29. Smoking is not permitted.   _____
30. A troublesome period in the lives of the next door neighbours. _____

Exercise 2.6 — Correcting Run-on Sentences

Indicate which of the sentences below are run-on by writing *R*. Then correct the sentence by adding the proper punctuation or conjunction. If the sentence is correct, write *C*.

	EXAMPLES:	The men and women were working in the fields, and the children were picking strawberries.	R
		Every minute is important; every hour is crucial.	R
		She made the appointment, but she forgot to tell me.	C

1. I cannot think of the gentleman's name, maybe it was Frank.   _____
2. Nothing can be done for the victim his family, however,
   should be comforted.   _____
3. Please don't spread rumours get the facts before you speak.   _____
4. English is my most difficult course, I have to spend hours
   revising my essays.   _____
5. Our local library has a good children's section, but not a very
   large literature selection.   _____
6. Shopping for shoes is frustrating, I can never find a size
   small enough for my tiny feet.   _____
7. Even though our house is small, it is quite comfortable.   _____
8. However difficult the journey, we must complete it on time.   _____
9. We took the train to Toronto we were just too tired to drive.   _____
10. I'll order the food, you get us a table.   _____

11. Abdul Rahman was not born in Canada, however, he is now a Canadian citizen. _____

12. Trina hates the cold weather Janine loves to ski. _____

13. Did you bring your umbrella, I don't have mine. _____

14. We went to the game early, but we still could not find a parking place. _____

15. She can always be relied upon, however difficult the challenge. _____

16. Our school basketball team will be ready for the start of the season, in fact, we have already been picked to win our division. _____

17. The picnic table was set up, but the food had not yet arrived. _____

18. What will you do if your flight is delayed, will you cancel your speaking engagement? _____

19. The virus on my hard drive was transferred from one of my floppy disks, it has already corrupted one of my files. _____

20. Who drove home last night was it Malcolm? _____

21. The golf tournament will have to be cancelled and the money refunded. _____

22. Making hotel reservations on the Internet is easy, you should try it. _____

23. I cannot learn how to set up a spreadsheet, however hard I try. _____

24. Don't forget to pay the phone bill you can pay it at the bank. _____

25. Our city does not have a football team; however, it does have a highly regarded hockey team. _____

26. Wanting to please the efficient office staff, the general manager expanded their morning coffee break. _____

27. I'll collect our coats, you start the car. _____

28. Conchita has just bought a VCR, now she can tape her favourite TV programs. _____

29. Whatever the cost and however long it takes, we must arrive at our destination by Friday morning. _____

30. Having met its sales quota for the month, the marketing department decided to organize an office party, we were all invited. _____

Exercise 2.7 — Revising Sentences in the Paragraph

Rewrite the following paragraphs by correcting the sentence fragments and run-on errors. Be prepared to insert or delete punctuation and coordinating conjunctions.

> Food prices are increasing every year. Which places an extreme hardship on people who must budget their money carefully each month. That is why many people have changed their eating and shopping habits. For example, shoppers no longer buy as much red meat. Red meat is usually the most expensive item on the shopping list, its price has risen at least fifteen percent over the last few years. Instead, fish and chicken are often substituted, they are not only less expensive but more nutritious. Pasta is also increasingly replacing meat dishes. Indeed, meatless dinners and lunches are becoming quite common among people. Who are not only budget conscious but also want good nutrition.
>
> Also, consumers are not buying as much convenience food, frozen dinners and prepared delicatessen foods are now beyond many people's food budgets. Fresh fruit and vegetables in season are more in demand. In addition, store coupons and supermarket specials are also more common comparative shopping is now a necessity. For many low- and middle-income families.
>
> There are also fewer trips to fast-food restaurants; and more reliance on healthful and inexpensive snacks made at home. Yes, our eating habits are certainly changing. Not only because of rising costs. But also because of our desire for good nutrition.

G. VARIETY IN SENTENCE PATTERNS

Different combinations of dependent and independent clauses make up four basic sentence patterns: the simple, the compound, the complex, and the compound-complex. Learning when to use these different sentences will make your writing more flexible and emphatic. Depending upon what you want to say and how you want to say it, you will use each pattern for different reasons.

1. Simple Sentence

A simple sentence is the clearest, most direct self-supporting statement that one can make. It consists of only one independent clause, which may be long or short, and which may contain more than one subject and more than one verb. Despite its length, however, it must have only one subject-verb combination and make only one statement to be classified as a simple sentence.

> **Birds** *fly*.
> Many **birds** *fly* south in the winter.
>
> **Jack and Dan** study together.
> (compound subject)

Steve *washes and dries* the dishes.
(compound verb)

Yvette and Renée *live and work* together.
(compound subject and verb)

All of the above sentences are simple because they contain one idea. Do not be misled by a sentence with many modifiers; if it has a single subject-verb combination and says only one thing, it must be simple.

After our long and arduous journey, **we** finally *found* the ancient city, shining in all its glory.

2. Compound Sentence

A compound sentence consists of a grouping of two or more independent clauses usually joined by a coordinate conjunction (*and, or, nor, for, so, but*) or a conjunctive adverb (*however, therefore, moreover*; see p. 117 for a complete list of conjunctive adverbs). Each clause must bear equal weight for the sentence to be properly balanced.

(Bob won the bronze medal in the track meet), but (Spiro won the silver).

(Linda won the bronze medal); however, (Nicole won the silver).

Note: A comma precedes the coordinate conjunction, and a semicolon precedes the conjunctive adverb (see p. 97 and pp. 116-17).

When two independent clauses are closely related, a semicolon may be used to separate them.

(Hans took notes); (Yuri outlined the chapter).

(Mike made the beds); (his wife did the laundry).

Remember, compound sentences must contain at least two subject-verb combinations that can be broken into simple sentences when the connectives are removed.

(He wanted to be a salesman), but (he became an accountant).

(Students may drop one subject); however, (they must inform the registrar).

3. Complex Sentence

A complex sentence consists of one independent clause and one or more dependent clauses. Unlike compound sentences, complex sentences not only group statements but also indicate their order or importance. They inform the reader which statement carries more weight.

(When Deborah arrived), *Mario took the roast out of the oven.*
(The second statement contains the action; the first statement merely introduces it.)

The caretaker (who found the diamond ring) *was given a generous reward,* (which he immediately spent).
(The statements within the parentheses merely modify the words *caretaker* and *reward* in the independent clause.)

4. Compound-Complex Sentence

As its name implies, a compound-complex sentence has at least two independent clauses and one dependent clause. This type of sentence provides you with the greatest flexibility. It allows you not only to express ideas of equal significance but also to include other subordinate relationships within the structure of the sentence.

(Unless we improve the quality of our acting), *the director will hire new actors and actresses, or the producer will withdraw his money from the show.*

The pub opened on time, and the waiters were at their stations; however, the customers refused to enter (when they saw the pickets parading outside).

Exercise 2.8 — Recognizing Sentence Patterns

Identify each of the following sentences by writing one of the following abbreviations in the blank at the right or on a separate sheet: *S* for simple, *Cd* for compound, *Cx* for complex, and *Cd-Cx* for compound-complex.

EXAMPLES: During the music recital my sister became ill and had to leave.   **S**

The houses were built first, and then the apartment buildings were constructed.   **Cd**

Our company lost the building contract, which was unfortunate.   **Cx**

1. My brother lost the golf tournament, but he still won a prize. _____

2. Rudy Polanski and his brother, Stan, are my new teammates. _____

3. Neither the school board nor the teachers' association could suggest a compromise solution to end the stalemate. _____

4. The personal computer that I bought from a mail-order catalogue does not have enough memory. _____

5. Our garage is a new addition, but our patio came with the house. _____

6. My brother, who just graduated from a community college, already has a job out West, but my sister is still looking for employment. _____

7. The Thousand Islands International Bridge joins the state of New York and the province of Ontario. _____

8. Betty was flabbergasted when her number was drawn for the door prize. _____

9. I understand that your brother still smokes cigarettes but that your sister has just quit. _____

10. Don't go home yet; the party is just starting. _____

11. My printer, which is five years old, is working fine, but my home computer, which is new, has just crashed. _____

12. Retiring early is my main ambition, but I don't think that I will achieve it. _____

13. Johnny Chung rides a bike to school, but his sister walks. _____

14. After the movie, we all went to a fast-food restaurant. _____

15. Whenever our instructor gives us a test, she always tells us to manage our time properly. _____

16. Please reduce your intake of sugar and fried foods. _____

17. After planning our fishing trip for a month, we had to cancel it at the last minute. _____

18. Line up your putt; then stroke the ball gently. _____

19. Felix and Mai had to wait two hours for Kim and Michel. _____

20. What happens when our bus breaks down because the driver forgot to change the oil and check the tires? _____

21. Don't wait for us; we'll be late as usual. _____

22. We could not pay cash for our theatre tickets; instead, we used our credit cards. _____

23. For my parents' anniversary, which falls on the day after Christmas, we are sending them cruise tickets, but they may not use the tickets until the spring. _____

24. Bernhardt Saltzer, the tennis pro, will not play in the next tournament, but his brother will take his place. _____

25. Keeping secrets is difficult; telling them is easy. _____

26. My sister, who went to university on an athletic scholarship, is graduating next month. _____

27. Learning how to surf the Internet can be confusing. _____

28. Mary-Lisa drives too fast, and her brother, Steve, is worried about her. _____

29. Jackson Boulevard, which was recently repaved, is now closed because of median repairs, and the daily commuters are furious with the city works department. _____

30. However hard we try, we still cannot beat our high school rivals in football. _____

H. COMBINING INTO PATTERNS

In order to use sentence patterns correctly, you must understand the logic of co-ordination and subordination. When you coordinate ideas or statements, you place them in equal relationship, and when you subordinate them, you assign one idea more significance than the other.

1. Joining through Coordination

Coordination is the skill of joining together similar ideas with coordinating conjunctions (and, or, but) or with correlative conjunctions (either—or; neither—nor; not only—but also; both—and).

Proper coordination eliminates choppy sentence structure and reveals the precise relationship between similar ideas.

> CHOPPY: Bill Roberts is an athlete. He is a scholar. He is also a friend.
>
> COORDINATED: Bill Roberts is an athlete, a scholar, and a friend.
>
> CHOPPY: There are no classes held on Saturday. The school library is open until 5:00 p.m. Students may study there.
>
> COORDINATED: There are no classes held on Saturday, but the school library is open until 5:00 p.m. for students' convenience.

Each part of the sentence that is coordinated should have the same grammatical structure: phrases with phrases, clauses with clauses.

AWKWARD: A card-catalogue index file will not only help you find authors of books but also in finding subjects for term papers.

COORDINATED: A card-catalogue index will *not only* help you find authors of books *but also* subjects for term papers.

AWKWARD: He will either do as he is told or the boss will have to fire him.

COORDINATED: He will *either* do as he is told *or* be fired.

See Chapter 5 D, "Employing Parallel Forms," pp. 78-81 for more examples of proper coordination.

2. Joining through Subordination

A sentence with subordination contains one dominant idea that is modified by grammatically subordinate words, phrases, and clauses. Therefore, a subordinated sentence cannot have two equal parts, since it contains only one major idea.

Effective subordination eliminates wordiness and redundancy and reveals the logical relationship between unequal ideas.

FAULTY: Educational theory has changed in the last five years. Its change has been dramatic.

SUBORDINATED: Educational theory has changed *dramatically* in the last five years.

FAULTY: Our university is famous for its medical school. It has recently added a new school of international relations.

SUBORDINATED: Our university, *which is famous for its medical school*, has recently added a new school of international relations.

Effective subordination permits readers to focus on the main idea of the sentence; it ensures that the lesser ideas will be placed in dependent clauses or phrases.

FAULTY: When our new office building was completed, it was January 1978.

SUBORDINATED: Our new office building was completed in January 1978.

FAULTY: Threatening to call the police after the picketers locked the factory gates, the plant manager avoided a major crisis.

SUBORDINATED: The plant manager avoided a major crisis when he threatened to call the police after the picketers locked the factory gates.

32 Writing Fundamentals

The correct use of coordination or subordination is, finally, a matter of common sense. If we think through our sentences carefully, we should know when to use two equal thoughts or one major and one minor; we should know which statements can be developed by dependent clauses and which cannot. And we should know how to place emphasis by using a series of independent clauses or a combination of dependent and independent clauses. In short, we should know how to project significance by recognizing the implicit logic of English sentence structure.

Exercise 2.9 — Coordination

Correct the following sentences by eliminating unnecessary words or by using one of the following connectives: a coordinating conjunction, a correlative conjunction, or a conjunctive adverb.

>   EXAMPLE: We are going to the theatre, and then we are also going out to dinner.
>
>   CORRECTION: We are going to the theatre and then to dinner.

1. Santino might be quiet; he is certainly not shy.
2. Our small town has two theatres and four movie houses. It has only one hockey rink. However we are building another one.
3. Danielle is a hairstylist; she is not a manicurist.
4. Our local golf resort has two eighteen-hole courses. Each one accepts daily green fees. They both offer annual memberships.
5. Denzil is a travel agent or else he is an airline steward.
6. Our community college is not only the largest in the province, it is the most overcrowded as well.
7. Both of my brothers are basketball players; my sister is a basketball player, too.
8. Several students were caught cheating. The instructor confiscated their test papers. They were not suspended from school.
9. Her ice skates were misplaced or else they were stolen from the locker room.
10. I bought expensive skis, comfortable boots, and I even took a series of ski lessons from the local ski instructor. I still have trouble parallel skiing.
11. The football players were told to be on time for the bus departure, and they were also told not to forget their food vouchers. However, some of them still arrived late and some forgot their vouchers.

12. Song Wu and Tai Ming are neither swimmers and they are certainly not high-platform divers.
13. Her skin might be fair; it is unwrinkled.
14. Claudette was either in a car accident, or she may have been delayed by inclement weather.
15. My uncle is a college instructor, and he is a part-time musician, too.
16. Martina was warned not to jog without a warm scarf; she did, anyway, and she caught a bad cold.
17. Jason hates writing essays; he enjoys doing grammar exercises, though.
18. Our former beauty queen is now either an actress or else she is a physical-fitness instructor.
19. Deirdre wanted to join a ski club. She is bothered by cold weather. She decided to play indoor tennis instead.
20. His job is not only boring, it is physically difficult as well.
21. Skydiving is exciting and it is dangerous; it is not a sport for people who are physically unfit.
22. I am interested in politics and Canadian history, and I am also interested in environmental studies.
23. Pierre's new computer not only comes fully equipped with a monitor and a printer but it is also loaded with the latest business software.
24. Mohammed plays tennis and golf and basketball; he also plays racquetball as well.
25. Our physics professor is a basketball coach. He is also a volunteer with the Red Cross.
26. Jennifer's ideas have saved our company more than a million dollars during the last five years. She is our prime success story.
27. Our neighbourhood is located in a high-crime district; it is considered unsafe by our city police force and by our fire department as well.
28. My winter suit may look new. It is five years old.
29. The telephone company is not only raising its monthly rates, it is charging more for collect calls, too.
30. Seamus McCann thought he wanted to be an airline pilot; he suffers from claustrophobia. He is now a community-college professor.

Exercise 2.10 — Subordination

Rewrite the following sentences so that the main ideas are properly emphasized.

> EXAMPLE: After he fished for hours, Tom caught a five-kilo tuna.
>
> CORRECTION: Tom caught a five-kilo tuna after fishing for hours.

1. It injured more than ten people before the runaway Zamboni was finally brought under control.
2. Taylor's car was stolen yesterday; it is only two weeks old.
3. The first time I attended a professional football game it was 1959.
4. Our new car has a sunroof and anti-lock brakes. It was made in Germany.
5. When the stock market crashed in 1929, it occurred during the month of October.
6. Walking by the new fire station, we saw a spotted dog chasing a rabbit.
7. My father bought a new television; it has a twenty-seven-inch screen and stereophonic sound.
8. When he entered the locker room, our coach was carrying a canvas bag full of footballs.
9. He went to Pakistan last month where Nidal Mahti visited relatives and friends.
10. Skiing without heavy woollen mittens, some of Doris' fingers became frostbitten.
11. Roaring through our village, Hurricane Fran caused property damage in the millions of dollars.
12. Standing near the bus stop, Susan was almost run over by a swerving automobile that was trying to avoid a stray dog.
13. When our basketball team won its tenth game, it was in September.
14. Mowing the lawn last week with his riding mower, Pietro nearly ran over his Siamese cat.
15. While she was ice skating on our back pond, Bernice fell and nearly went through the ice.
16. After she drove in the pouring rain for nearly five hours, Tina developed severe muscle spasms in her lower back.
17. I am not sunburned. I put on sunblock before we went to the beach.
18. We were leaving the movie theatre when we saw the moving van back into the parked car.

19. Our small neighbourhood food market was once a thriving business; now it is losing customers to the large supermarket down the block.
20. While she was playing field hockey, Kristen tripped and tore the ligaments in her left knee.
21. It severely damaged more than two hundred homes before the Saginaw River floodwaters receded.
22. The morning newspaper did not arrive. The delivery boy is sick.
23. Carlotta's first novel was a best-seller; it is now being made into a movie.
24. When our young mayor was re-elected, it was 1996.
25. Riding on the Toronto subway, Maurice saw a man snatch an old woman's purse and run through the concourse.
26. My sister just moved from Halifax, Nova Scotia, to Ottawa, Ontario. She could not find a management job in Halifax.
27. The new movie has been rated "for adults only"; it has too much sex and violence for people under eighteen years of age.
28. I vacationed in Banff last summer, where I saw a black bear catching fish with its paws in a mountain stream.
29. When she finally arrived at the airport, Heidi's plane had already left the boarding gate.
30. Our examinations were the most difficult that I have ever taken. They are now finally over.

CHAPTER THREE

Checking for Agreement

A. ENSURING SUBJECT-VERB AGREEMENT

Subject-verb agreement indicates the proper relationship between the form of the verb and its subject. The verb always agrees with its subject in person (first, second, third) and number (singular, plural). Because of the various ways of organizing sentences, subjects are often camouflaged by intervening phrases and inverted word order. Therefore, to avoid using the wrong verb, we must become adept at finding the subject. The following suggestions may help.

1. Watch for modifying phrases beginning with prepositions like *on, of,* or *in* that come between the subject and the verb.

    A box (of nails) *was* on the workbench.

    One (of the football players) *is* not on the bus.

    Only **one person** (in five) *knows* the name of the British prime minister.

2. Watch for inverted sentences beginning with *there* and *here*.

    WRONG: There is a great many *people* at the game.

    CORRECTED: There are a great many people at the game.

    WRONG: Here is the most interesting *games* of chance.

    CORRECTED: Here are the most interesting games of chance.

    Remember, *there* and *here* never serve as subjects of sentences.

3. Do not confuse the subject with the subject complement.

    His **primary concern** *was* the sick employees.

    Helmut's **chief interest** *was* antique automobiles.

    My **favourite meal** *is* meat and potatoes.

4. Recognize singular subjects that appear to be plural.

> **Politics** *is* a popular sport in our community.
>
> **Economics** *is* not in our school calendar this semester.
>
> **Pediatrics** *is* a branch of medicine.

Remember, collective nouns take singular verbs when referring to a group as a single unit; however, when they refer to a group as a body of individual members, they take plural verbs.

> The **committee** *is submitting* its report.
> (used as a single unit)
>
> The **committee** *are working* in small groups.
> (used as a body of individual members)
>
> The **jury** *has* not *reached* a verdict.
> (used as a single unit)
>
> The **jury** *are* now *sealing* their votes in the jury room.
> (used as a body of individual members)

Logic should tell you when the collective noun is expressed as an indivisible whole; usually the word *members* is appended to the noun to indicate plurality: jury members; committee members; team members.

5. Singular subjects joined by *and* take plural verbs, but if they refer to the same thing, or function as a unit, they take singular verbs.

> A **pen** and a **pencil** *are* the tools of my trade.
>
> My best **friend and confidant** *has joined* the armed forces.
>
> **Law and order** *is* the issue.

6. Compound subjects with *each* or *every* take singular verbs.

> Each biology student, chemistry student, and physics student *is* responsible for his or her lab equipment.
>
> Every blonde, redhead, and brunette *was* judged according to her talents, not her hairstyle.

7. Compound subjects joined by *either...or, neither...nor* take singular verbs when both subjects are singular, and they take plural verbs when both subjects

are plural. When, however, one subject is singular and the other is plural, the verb agrees with the closer subject.

> Either **Charles** or **Hélène** *is* chairing the meeting.
>
> Neither her **pies** nor her **cakes** *were given* prizes at the country fair.
>
> Either the principal or the **students** *control* the student council's budget.
>
> Neither the actors nor the **director** *was* satisfied with the stage lighting.

8. Single subjects with intervening phrases like *together with, along with, in addition to,* and *as well as* take singular verbs.

   > **My sister**, along with her girlfriend, *is* going on the class picnic.
   >
   > **Tom's stereo**, as well as his car, *was* repossessed by the finance company.
   >
   > **Andre's notebook**, together with his history text, *was* stolen from his locker.

   Note: The commas around these phrases always separate them from the subjects of the sentences.

9. When the subject is a title, it always takes a singular verb.

   > Alfred Hitchcock's *The Birds* *is* coming to our local theatre next week.
   >
   > *The Russians* *was* an excellent television documentary.
   >
   > *Cats* *has been* one of the most successful Broadway musicals in the last five years.

Exercise 3.1 — Making Subject and Verb Agree

Select the correct verb in each of the following sentences and write it in the blank at the right or on a separate sheet.

1. Neither of Danielle's parents (is/are) going to our picnic lunch on Saturday. _____

2. The computer salesperson, as well as the technician, (was/were) correct in analyzing the problem with my laptop computer. _____

3. Neither the faculty members nor the college president (is/are) aware of the morale problems among our student body. _____

4. Each coach, team member, and sports fan (agree/agrees) that our city needs a new track-and-field facility. _____

5. There (was/were) a safety inspector and two members of the Ministry of Health investigating the fire that started in our restaurant's kitchen last week. _____

6. In the middle of the town square (stand/stands) the statues of our city's founders, Myers and McGillicudy. _____

7. There certainly (seem/seems) to be a solution for every problem. _____

8. The new rose bushes, as well as the bag of topsoil, (is/are) in the back of my pickup truck. _____

9. (Was/Were) American as well as Canadian literature courses scheduled last semester? _____

10. The hospital administrator, as well as the physicians on staff, (think/thinks) that our hospital needs a new chemistry lab. _____

11. The number of high-school dropouts (have/has) decreased during the last five years. _____

12. None of the salespersons (was/were) on the lot when the new Volvo was stolen. _____

13. Everyone who saw the Broadway cast perform in *Phantom of the Opera* (was/were) amazed at their versatility in adapting the play to our small stage. _____

14. Philippe and I are among the few who (practises/practise) the broad jump and the hammer throw on Fridays after school. _____

15. Anyone who thinks that he or she can function without the rest of the team members (is/are) very much mistaken. _____

16. Participating in the Red Cross blood drive (is/are) one of the members of our tennis team. _____

17. Neither the fresh peaches nor the skim milk (was/were) on sale this weekend. _____

18. *The Magnificent Ambersons* (was/were) included in the Orson Welles film festival at our local movie theatre. _____

19. Not one student in ten (knows/know) who wrote *The Ginger Man*. _____

20. Kimberly, together with her brother Alex, (has/have) decided to attend our local community college next year. _____

Writing Fundamentals

21. Neither Renko nor I (are/am) attending the music recital tomorrow evening. _____
22. Our crafts guild (was/were) discussing next week's quilt show when the earthquake tremor shook the house. _____
23. The selection of the jury (does/do) not mean that all ethnic groups will be represented. _____
24. Mako's physics project, together with her excellent mathematics test scores, (makes/make) her the student most likely to win this year's science scholarship. _____
25. Every electrician, toolmaker, and welder in our union (have/has) a right to vote in our next election. _____
26. We were informed that either Geoffrey or Liam (was/were) involved in the cheating scandal. _____
27. Our farm, along with our house and barn, (has/have) already been selected for sale at the auction next week. _____
28. Either the baseball players or the umpire (was/were) mistaken about the incorrect alignment of the left-field foul pole. _____
29. Sayed's favourite meal (is/are) chicken and rice. _____
30. One of the concert audience members (was/were) to blame for setting off the fire alarm. _____

B. PRONOUNS AGREEING WITH NOUNS

A pronoun must agree with the word it stands for (its antecedent) in person, gender, and number.

1. Person: Watch *You*

Agreement in person errors almost always occur with the incorrect use of the pronoun *you* or its possessive, *your*.

> INCORRECT: If anyone has to leave the room, *you* had better leave now.
>
> CORRECT: If *anyone* has to leave the room, *he* or *she* had better leave now.
>
> INCORRECT: When I first arrived on campus, I was told that *your* student fees helped to defray the cost of the school newspaper.
>
> CORRECT: When I first arrived on campus, I was told that *my* student fees helped to defray the cost of the school newspaper.

2. Gender: Guidelines for *He* and *She*

For the most part, establishing the correct gender for a pronoun does not present a problem to native English speakers. Since the use of masculine or feminine pronouns is properly reserved for people, you simply have to identify the person being referred to and your problems are solved.

However, a difficulty does arise when you wish to refer to any unspecified or hypothetical person. In the recent past it was considered correct to refer to such persons by the pronouns *he, him, his*. Used in this manner, these pronouns were considered to refer to both men and women.

This usage is still considered to be correct and is used by many writers. However, many other, equally careful, writers feel that the use of the masculine pronoun as a generic pronoun creates a sex bias in their writing. They avoid using the generic pronoun by using *he* or *she/his* or *her* constructions; by pluralizing the referent and using *they, their, theirs*; and by rewording sentences to avoid pronoun use altogether.

The following examples demonstrate these different responses to the problem of pronoun gender.

> Each member of the class must have all of his assignments turned in before he receives a final mark.
>
> Each member of the class must have all of his or her assignments turned in before he or she receives a final mark.
>
> All members of the class must have all of their assignments turned in before they receive their final mark.
>
> The student who left his books in the cafeteria must claim them before he leaves school.
>
> The student who left his or her books in the cafeteria must claim them before he or she leaves school.
>
> A child in nursery school may not be able to feed and dress himself.
>
> A child in nursery school may not be able to eat or get dressed without help.

3. Number: Some Rules about Singulars and Plurals

The rules for pronoun agreement in number are basically the same as those for subject-verb agreement:

(a) Single antecedents take singular pronouns; plural antecedents take plural pronouns.

> A few of the workers took *their* (not *his*) grievances to the supervisor.
>
> Any student who jogs near the construction site must watch *his or her* (not *their*) step.

(b) A collective noun expressed as a single unit takes a singular pronoun; collective nouns expressed as a group of individual members take a plural pronoun.

> The committee argued for hours, but could not decide how to make *their* (not *its*) recommendations public.
>
> The basketball team won *its* (not *their*) first game last Saturday.

(c) Singular antecedents connected by *or, nor,* or *but* take singular pronouns; however, when one is singular and the other plural, the pronoun agrees with the closer antecedent.

> Neither Claude nor Peter was asked to present *his* (not *their*) report to the class.
>
> Either the supervisor or the workers will win *their* (not *his*) grievance.

(d) In formal English, indefinite pronouns like *either, neither, anyone, everyone, someone, each, every*, and *somebody* take singular pronouns.

> Neither of the workers earned *his* (not *their*) salary last week.
>
> Everyone in class must buy *his or her* (not *their*) own lab manual.
>
> Somebody has left *his* (not *their*) jacket in the gym.

Remember, if you are not sure whether a pronoun should be singular or plural, locate the verb; it will usually reveal the number of the pronoun.

> The team *is ready* for its first game.
>
> Someone in the auditorium *has left* his or her car lights on.
>
> Neither the teacher nor the students *have agreed* on their debating topic.

Exercise 3.2 — Making Pronouns Agree with Nouns

Select the correct pronoun in the following sentences and write it in the blank at the right or on a separate sheet. Where possible, reword the sentence to avoid the pronoun problem.

1. The computer users committee is meeting this afternoon to discuss (its/their) financial report. _____

2. Anyone who wishes to participate in the hockey tournament should submit (your/his/their) name by next Tuesday. _____

3. Any person intending to vote in the city council election must first register (his or her/your/their) name at the voting office by tomorrow afternoon. _____

4. Everyone who intends to donate blood next week should give (their/his or her) name to the Red Cross representative on campus. _____

5. My neighbour was told that (you/he) had to make special arrangements for private trash collection. _____

6. Having considered all of the alternatives, the entertainment committee still could not decide on (its/their) next venue for the Halloween Ball. _____

7. Anybody who wants to babysit my little brother had better bring (his or her/their) Monopoly game; he loves playing board games. _____

8. Tanaka, together with her two brothers, was asked if (she/they) wanted to join the swimming team. _____

9. Everyone except Cleo passed (her/their) entrance exam. _____

10. Neither of the software writers could find (his/their) way to our new cafeteria. _____

11. Either the company president or the middle managers should have had (her/their) meeting last week with our union representatives. _____

12. The two new cars in the showroom window do not have (its/their) hood ornaments attached. _____

13. No team member will be permitted to arrange (their/his or her) own transportation to the tournament next Saturday. _____

14. Our investment club had (their/its) last meeting on Thursday. _____

15. Everyone in our Internet class should have (their/his or her) own home computer. _____

16. Both Francine and Hillary won (her/their) chess matches. _____

17. Neither the dancers nor the master of ceremonies wanted (his/their) performance to be videotaped. _____

18. Those of you who want to reserve orchestra seats had better send (their/your) money in by tomorrow. _____

19. Our Internet provider has increased (their/its) monthly fee by ten percent.

20. If anyone wants to have a thoroughly enjoyable time next weekend, (he or she/they) should attend our Riverfest celebration.

21. Every member of our union will have to turn in (his or her/their) strike vote ballot by tomorrow.

22. Both accident victims had (his/their) legs broken.

23. When Ricardo applied for a hockey scholarship, he was told that (you/he) first had to have a physical examination.

24. The local newspaper is printing all of (its/their) news photos in colour.

25. The student union committee argued for hours over the budget changes that (it/they) placed on the agenda last week.

26. Our board of education has informed us that (you/we) now have to build a childcare facility.

27. The coach, as well as the team members, thinks that (his/their) views are being ignored by the college officials.

28. No participant in the AIDS eradication drive will have to donate more than (his or her/their) time to Saturday's march.

29. Neither the lawyers nor the plaintiff could convince the jury that (her/their) arguments removed any reasonable doubt.

30. Each member of the curling association will be required to purchase (his or her/their) own team sweater.

Exercise 3.3 — Review of Agreement

Choose the correct verb and pronoun in each of the following sentences and write them in the blanks at the right or on a separate sheet.

EXAMPLE: The news of John's defection from the football team (were/was) known by the time the team played (their/its) first game.   P   V
   its   was

1. Somebody must be working late on the fourth floor; (he or she/they) (is/are) turning on all of the overhead lights in the front office.

2. Ranjit will enrol any student in his karate class, providing (they/he or she) (have/has) parental permission.

3. The college pep club (have/has) asked every student to lend (his or her/their) support in promoting next month's charity concert.

4. One of the young men in our class (believes/believe) that (his/their) grades were not properly recorded by the college registrar.

5. Neither Hector nor Pierre (want/wants) to have (his/their) name submitted for class president.

6. A pack of matches (was/were) left precariously near the fireplace; please remove (it/them) to a safer location.

7. Neither the police nor the firefighters (was/were) aware that (their/its) salary scales were under review.

8. Every member of our neighbourhood watch committee (is/are) requested to collect (his or her/their) window sticker as soon as possible.

9. Sufficient RAM, as well as a fast modem, (are/is) necessary for anyone who wants (his or her/their) computer to properly surf the Internet.

10. If either the dentist or the dental technician (answer/answers) the phone, please tell (her/them) that I must cancel my appointment for next Tuesday.

11. Among my favourite Canadian authors (is/are) Alice Munro and Margaret Atwood; I have read all of (her/their) novels and short stories.

12. Both my father and my uncle (feels/feel) that (he/they) should be the coach of our Little League baseball team.

13. Claudia, as well as Beryl, (think/thinks) that the new Boeing 777 is the most comfortable airplane that (they/she) has ever flown on.

14. Victor Gonzales is one of those small-business owners who (believe/believes) that (they/he) should put the customer first.

15. Every man and woman in this room (were/was) present when the conference-call message came from our home office; (he or she/you) should follow its instructions implicitly.

16. Chandra is one of the few travel agents who (provide/provides) the customer with (his or her/their) own computerized itinerary.

17. The bridge club (are/is) meeting this Friday to decide on the venue for (their/its) next tournament.

18. No one can understand dire poverty until (they/he or she) (travel/travels) to Calcutta, India.

19. Each of her sisters (are/is) working part-time to defray (their/her) tuition and travel expenses.

20. The building superintendent, along with the owners, (want/wants) each tenant to remove (his or her/their) clothesline from the balcony.

21. There (weren't/wasn't) anyone in the audience who did not have tears in (his or her/their) eyes after the performance.

22. Both our accountant and office assistant (has/have) already taken (his/their) summer vacations.

23. Neither the director of community relations nor the nursing-home volunteers (expect/expects) the city to reduce (their/her) monthly parking fees.

24. Veronica, in addition to Mona, (keeps/keep) (her/their) valuables in our bank's safety deposit box.

25. Each of our sales associates (meets/meet) (his or her/their) weekly sales quota by Thursday afternoon.

26. Every freshman, sophomore, and junior (are/is) required to collect (his or her/their) student identification card by Wednesday; seniors may collect theirs on Thursday.

27. Neither Fatima nor I (were/was) aware that the students, as well as the faculty, should pick up (his or her/their) graduation gowns on Saturday.

28. None of the grocery store clerks (were/was) allowed to remove (their/his or her) name tag during working hours.

29. Each of the two new employees (has/have) recently arrived from (his/their) respective country—Poland and South Korea.

30. The squash club (is/are) meeting tonight to announce (its/their) new bylaws and dues structure.

Exercise 3.4 — Revising the Paragraph for Agreement

Rewrite the following paragraphs by correcting the noun-pronoun/verb-subject agreement errors.

At some point in everyone's career we may be called upon to make a formal speech, and unfortunately you will probably not do a very good job. They will become nervous and hesitant, and forget what he or she want to say because they try to memorize lines as if you were actors on stage. You will also stumble over words that someone uses effortlessly in social or informal occasions, and they will speak either too briefly or too long; in either case his or her ideas will not be properly developed, which will cause their audience to become either bored or restless. If somebody has ever been in this situation, I have some tips that may help you take the pain out of speech making.

First, find out everything you can about the members of your audience. How much does it already know about your subject? For instance, does he or she know enough so that you can gloss over some of your points without going into detail? And does it have common interests? If your subject are aimed at a homogenous audience, such as community-college or university students, then we can use examples that appeals to his or her common experiences. Next, ask yourself why he or she is coming to hear you speak. What set of assumptions are they bringing that may cause your content to be either too narrow or too broad? If he or she assume, for instance, that you have knowledge to impart, then make sure that your thesis indicate the limited range of your subject.

Second, do not try to memorize your speech beforehand. Instead, jot down notes on index cards that covers your main points. You may glance at it while giving your speech to keep yourself from wandering off the subject, but the language used should be natural and delivered in our normal voice, with the proper inflections and hesitations. Speaking from memory can be very artificial and mechanistic, which may cause your audience to feel that someone is speaking down to it.

Third, use as many examples and visuals as you can to illustrate your ideas. Charts, graphs, and pictures on an overhead projector is extremely effective because it clarifies your information and raise your audience's interest level. Concrete examples and visual information also eliminates vagueness and the excessive use of descriptive words.

Therefore, if one strives to know as much as you can about your audience by putting oneself in its place; if he or she avoids an artificial delivery by eliminating their dependence on memorization; and if you clarify and tighten your content by using significant visuals and concrete examples, you will find that our next speech will not only be easier to deliver but also more interesting to your audience.

CHAPTER FOUR

Solving Special Problems with Verbs, Pronouns, Adjectives, and Adverbs

A. AVOIDING VERB PROBLEMS

Using the wrong verb is one of the most frequent and obvious errors of the ill-educated. Fortunately, our ears usually tell us when a verb is used incorrectly. For instance, we would probably never say:

> I *throwed* the ball thirty metres.

But if we were only vaguely familiar with verb tenses, we might well say:

> We *begun* the job yesterday.

Thus you should know that all verb tenses are formed from the principal parts of the verb: the present, the past, and the past participle. You should also know that most verbs add *d* or *ed* to the present infinitive to form the simple past and the past participle:

Present	**Past**	**Past Participle**
(to) move	moved	moved
(to) watch	watched	watched
(to) fill	filled	filled

> PRESENT: I *soak* my feet every afternoon.
> PAST: Yesterday I *soaked* my feet for two hours.
> PAST PARTICIPLE: I *have soaked* my feet every day for the past two years.

Other verbs, however, change forms completely. These verbs are called irregular, and they are the ones that give us the most trouble (a list of some irregular verbs is found on p. 51).

Present	Past	Past Participle
(to) see	saw	had seen
(to) do	did	had done
(to) go	went	had gone

If you remember the following rules you should be able to avoid the most common errors of verb usage.

1. Always add *d* or *ed* to the past and past participle of regular verbs.

    I *used* (not use) to play football in high school.

    He was *supposed* (not suppose) to report to the counsellor's office.

    We finally *passed* (not past) our chemistry examination.

2. Do not use past participle forms to express the simple past.

    I *saw* (not *seen*) the snow yesterday.

    She *drank* (not *drunk*) all of her milk.

    He was the one who *did* (not *done*) it.

3. The auxiliary form of the verbs *to be* and *to have* are used with only the past participle, not with the simple past.

    I have already *seen* (not *saw*) the television program.

    When the race was *run* (not *ran*) we were inside.

    If I had only *known* (not *knew*).

    You are too late; they have already *gone* (not *went*) to the rock concert.

4. Four irregular verbs deserve special attention because they are frequently misused.

(to) lay	laid	laid
(to) lie	lay	lain
(to) sit	sat	sat
(to) set	set	set

Whenever you have occasion to use these verbs, try following these rules:

(a) When you mean "placing" or "positioning" something, use the verb *lay*.

> I *lay* my books on top of my locker every morning.
>
> Yesterday I *laid* my books on the table.
>
> I *have* always *laid* my books on top of my locker.

(b) When you mean to recline or to remain in a fixed position, use *lie*.

> *Lie* down before your headache gets worse.
>
> The dishes *lay* in the sink all day.
>
> He *had lain* in bed for more than a week before he saw a doctor.

(c) When you mean to place something in position, use *set*.

> I always *set* my briefcase beside my desk.
>
> They *set* the coffee machine next to the water cooler.
>
> He *has set* himself the goal of becoming the vice-president of the company.

(d) When you mean to hold yourself in a sitting position, use *sit*.

> I *sit* in the same chair every day.
>
> Yesterday I *sat* in a different chair.
>
> I *have sat* in this chair ever since I can remember.

5. The third principal part of the verb (past participle) is used for the following reasons:

(a) To indicate an action completed at some indefinite time before the present. It uses the auxiliary words *have* or *has*, and is defined as the present-perfect tense.

> We *have completed* our tasks.
>
> She *has* already *finished* her homework.

(b) To indicate an action that was completed before another past action. It uses the auxiliary word *had* and is defined as the past-perfect tense.

> We *had completed* our tasks an hour before she arrived home.
>
> She *had completed* her homework by the time her brother returned.

SOME COMMON IRREGULAR VERBS

Present	Past	Past Participle
begin	began	begun
bite	bit	bitten
blow	blew	blown
break	broke	broken
bring	brought	brought (not *brung*)
burst	burst	burst
choose	chose	chosen
come	came	come
do	did (not *done*)	done
draw	drew	drawn
drink	drank (not *drunk*)	drunk
drive	drove	driven
eat	ate	eaten
fall	fell	fallen
fly	flew	flown
forget	forgot	forgotten
freeze	froze	frozen
give	gave	given
go	went	gone (not *went*)
grow	grew	grown
know	knew	known
lie	lay	lain (not *layed*)
ride	rode	ridden
ring	rang	rung
run	ran	run
see	saw (not *seen*)	seen
sing	sang	sung
sink	sank	sunk
speak	spoke	spoken
steal	stole	stolen
sting	stung	stung
swear	swore	sworn
swim	swam	swum
swing	swung (not *swang*)	swung
take	took	taken
tear	tore	torn
throw	threw	thrown
wear	wore	worn
write	wrote	written

(c) To indicate an action to be completed before a specific time in the future. It uses the helping words *shall have* or *will have*, and is defined as the future-perfect tense.

We *shall have completed* our tasks by the time she arrives home.

She *will have completed* her homework by the time her brother returns.

6. When the verb in the main clause is in the present tense, the verb in the subordinate clause should also be in the present tense. Remember to be consistent in your use of verb tenses, for a paragraph containing sentences that shift tenses abruptly can be extremely awkward and confusing:

   I believe that our school system *had been designed* (past perfect) by a computer programmer, one that *has* (present) no sense of humour. For instance, when I *asked* (past) the program coordinator if she *is able* (present) to judge a student's total performance merely on the basis of true or false questions, she *said* (past), "No, of course not; only our computer *had been able* (past perfect) to do that."

   Corrected
   I believe that our school system *was* designed by a computer programmer, one that *had* no sense of humour. For instance, when I *asked* the program coordinator if she *were* able to judge a student's total performance merely on the basis of true or false questions, she *said*, "No, of course not; only our computer *is* able to do that."

Exercise 4.1 — Choosing Verb Forms

Select the correct verb form in each of the following sentences and write it in the blank at the right or on a separate sheet.

1. (Set/Sit) the salad bowl on the drainboard next to the sink. _____

2. The rotted tree trunk has (lain/laid) in our backyard since last July. _____

3. There is the worker who is (suppose/supposed) to help us erect the scaffolding. _____

4. Jasmine is the woman who (swum/swam) for our college swimming team. _____

5. The Flannigans (use/used) to be our next door neighbours. _____

6. Caroline has already (began/begun) her quilting classes. _____

7. The party guests had already (ate/eaten) when the dinner-music ensemble arrived twenty minutes late. _____

8. The Salvation Army workers had almost (frozen/froze) on the street corner during the cold spell a week before Christmas. _____

9. Only a few children (rang/rung) our doorbell on Halloween night. _____

10. I do not believe that convicted murderers are (hung/hanged) anymore in North America. _____

11. My grandmother has (flew/flown) over 15,000 kilometres since my aunt moved to Vancouver. _____

12. If Rachel and Tanya had (chose/chosen) another airline, they would not have been delayed five hours in Chicago. _____

13. The chorus had already (sang/sung) its opening number before most of the audience was seated. _____

14. I did not know that Maurice already (seen/saw) our new play. _____

15. How many paintings were (hanged/hung) yesterday at the art gallery opening? _____

16. We tried to skate on the back pond, but the ice was (broke/broken) in several places. _____

17. When I was dieting, I (drunk/drank) at least eight glasses of water every day. _____

18. Toys were (laying/lying) all over the floor when I entered my son's bedroom. _____

19. My younger brother has (grew/grown) two inches since last February. _____

20. After Martina's term paper had been (wrote/written), her sister, who is a high-school English teacher, proofread it. _____

21. Our train had already (went/gone) by the time we arrived at the station. _____

22. The football fans were just (rising/raising) the banner above their heads when a gust of wind blew it over the railing. _____

23. How could the pitcher have (threw/thrown) the baseball over the catcher's head when the tying run was on third base? _____

24. Victor Chung may have (rode/ridden) on the snowmobile if he had worn warmer clothes. _____

25. Has anyone in the class (brung/brought) a copy of today's newspaper? _____

54 Writing Fundamentals

26. Who (sung/sang) "O Canada" at the hockey game last night? _____

27. Bernice's stamp collection was (stole/stolen) while she was visiting her uncle in Calgary. _____

28. The plate glass window was (broke/broken) when I arrived this morning to open the grocery store. _____

29. If we had known that the movie was showing for only one week, we would have (saw/seen) it. _____

30. The bedroom door slowly (swang/swung) open to reveal the bloodstained carpet. _____

Exercise 4.2 — Correcting Verb Errors

Write the number of any incorrect verb form in the first blank to the right; then write it correctly in the second blank. Write *C* if the verb is correctly used. Alternatively, write your answers on a separate sheet.

EXAMPLE: As we watch the football game, we *became*¹ excited.   <u>1</u>   <u>become</u>

Coins were first invented as a form of money by three separate civilizations: the Chinese, the Greeks, and the Indians. Even though these people *had*¹ no contact with each other, they all _____ _____

invented metal coins and *had chosen*² them as the best form _____ _____

of money. The first coins *had been*³ very simple and heavy, _____ _____

and did not have an exact value. Silver coins *become*⁴ very _____ _____

popular among the Greeks for several reasons. First, since silver is so strong, people *have used*⁵ the coins over and _____ _____ over without the money breaking. Second, the coins *were* 6 ____ ____

small, so they *are* easy to carry or to store at home. Third, 7 ____ ____

silver is a beautiful, soft metal, and coins that *have been* 8 ____ ____

made of silver *are* easy to imprint with designs, letters, and 9 ____ ____

numbers. Most importantly, however, the value or cost

of silver *will stay* the same longer than cheaper metals. 10 ____ ____

B. DETECTING PRONOUN CASE PROBLEMS

Case refers to the change in form (or inflection) of a noun or pronoun to indicate its function in a sentence. The three cases are *nominative* (used for subjects), *objective* (used for objects of verbs, prepositions, and infinitives), and *possessive* (used to indicate possession). Since nouns do not change form in the nominative and objective cases, and since their change in the possessive is indicated by an apostrophe (see p. 133), they present no problem. It is the pronoun that gives us trouble. Most personal pronouns and the relative pronoun *who* change forms in all three cases.

Nominative	Possessive	Objective
I	my, mine	me
we	our, ours	us
you	your, yours	you
he	his	him
she	her, hers	her
it	its	it
they	their, theirs	them
who	whose	whom

The usage rules for the pronoun case are fairly straightforward, but the application of these rules can be confusing.

1. When the pronoun functions as the subject of the verb or follows some form of the verb *to be* (is, am, was, were), it takes the nominative case.

    He broke the cup.
    (simple subject)

    It was *she* who acted on stage.
    (subject complement)

2. When the pronoun functions as the direct or indirect object, the object of a preposition, or the object of an infinitive, it takes the objective case.

    Ivan told *him* about the class trip.
    (direct object)

    She gave *me* an assignment.
    (indirect object)

    He is coming for *me* in an hour.
    (object of the preposition *for*)

    My employer told me to meet *her* at the airport.
    (object of the infinitive *to meet*)

Many usage problems occur when pronouns are used in certain compound constructions, or when they align themselves too closely with nouns:

1. When a pronoun functions as one part of a compound object containing a noun, read the sentence without the noun. Your ear will usually tell you which pronoun to use. You might write, "The coach had a meeting with he and the quarterback," but you would probably never write, "The coach had a meeting with he." Therefore, the correct use of the pronoun is evident without the noun: "The coach had a meeting with him and the quarterback."

2. For pronouns preceding nouns, you may apply the same test used for compound construction: read the sentence without the noun. Again, you might write, "Us workers on the assembly line deserve a pay raise." But you would not write, "Us deserve a pay rise." Therefore, common sense and the process of elimination will ensure that you write, "We workers on the assembly line deserve a pay raise."

3. When the words *like* and *but* are used as prepositions, their pronouns take the objective case.

    Everyone but *him* (not *he*) came to the party.

    Your daughter looks like *her* (not *she*).

4. In clauses that follow the words *as* or *than*, the pronoun may function as either the subject or the object of the implied verb.

> She is older than *I* (am).
>
> I like Bill better than (I like) *him*.
>
> My brother earns more money than *he* (earns).

Note: When the verb is supplied, the form of the pronoun becomes obvious.

5. In informal English, pronouns that follow forms of the verb *to be* are often placed in the objective case; in formal English, however, the nominative case is preferred:

> It was *he* (not *him*) who had been given the responsibility.
>
> The major vote-getters were *they* (not *them*).

6. The case of the relative pronouns *who/whoever* and *whom/whomever* is determined by their function in a clause. The easiest method of determining which case to use is by mentally rearranging the clause and then substituting *he* or *she* for *who* or *whoever*, and *him* or *her* for *whom* or *whomever*.

> It is he whom the police want for questioning.
> (The police want *him* for questioning.)
>
> It is she who, I am told, went to Europe last summer.
> (*She* went to Europe last summer.)
>
> Please send the message to whoever is on duty.
> (*He* is on duty.)
>
> We will save the work for whomever they send to replace the supervisor.
> (*They* send *him*.)

7. Compound personal pronouns—for example, himself, herself, itself, themselves—should be used only to emphasize information already given by a noun or pronoun, or to direct the action of a verb back to the subject. These two uses of the compound pronoun are called intensive and reflexive.

   (a) Intensive (emphasizing a noun or pronoun):

   > The minister *himself* arranged the social function.
   >
   > I *myself* served as the host.
   >
   > The administrators *themselves* are to blame.

(b) Reflexive (directing the action to the subject):

>I hurt *myself* on the exercise bicycle.
>
>We have insured *ourselves* against fire and theft.
>
>They found *themselves* without a leader.

Do not use a compound pronoun unless the noun or pronoun to which it refers is used in the same sentence. Never, for example, say:

>The players gave the game ball to Juan and *myself.*
>
>(to Juan and *me*)
>
>*Herself* and Jennifer Carson are tied for the lead.
>
>(*She* and Jennifer Carson are tied)

Note also that *hisself* and *theirselves* are severely ungrammatical and should never be used.

8. A pronoun used before a gerund (an *ing* verb form used as a noun) is always in the possessive case.

   >I was surprised at *his* (not him) not wanting to go on the camping trip.
   >
   >*Your* (not you) coming and going is driving me crazy.
   >
   >*His* (not him) wanting to study medicine came as a pleasant surprise.

   Do not confuse pronouns that function as direct objects with pronouns that precede gerunds.

   >My mother saw *him* (not his) working in a construction camp.
   >
   >I noticed *you* (not your) running around the track.

Exercise 4.3 — Using the Proper Pronoun Case

Select the correct pronoun in each of the following sentences and write it in the blank at the right or on a separate sheet.

1. Fuad Shamaz and (I/me) bought the members of the soccer team pizzas for winning their final game of the season. _____

2. No one on the team is faster than (she/her). _____

3. Just between you and (I/me), the anniversary dinner will not be held at Sal's Restaurant. _____

4. We were not prepared for (his/him) complaining about the lack of team spirit. _____
5. It was not (he/him) who won the new car in the raffle yesterday. _____
6. (Whomever/Whoever) is ready may tee off first. _____
7. Please inform Kerry and (I/me/myself) what time you will pick us up tomorrow evening. _____
8. My Web site was designed by (her/she) and Brian. _____
9. It must have been (they/them) who started the vicious rumour. _____
10. (Whom/Who) are the leading candidates for the job? _____
11. (We/Us) club members had better vote in the next election. _____
12. None of us thought that (their/them) booing their own team was appropriate behaviour. _____
13. Everyone but (she/her) wanted to participate in the student-council election. _____
14. Please return the locker room keys to either Jasmine or (me/I/myself). _____
15. Our committee will present the most valuable player award to (whoever/whomever) has scored the most points during the hockey season. _____
16. No one but (he/him) could swim the length of the lap pool underwater. _____
17. Even the coach (hisself/himself) thought that our split end was out of bounds when he caught the ball. _____
18. The second prize in the lottery was five hundred dollars, which was divided equally between Johnny Wu and (I/me/myself). _____
19. The church choir members (theirselves/themselves) thought that choir practice was rescheduled for Friday evening. _____
20. It was (they/them), I believe, who went white-water rafting on the Ottawa River. _____
21. Emma, the live-in house maid, and (he/him) are finally getting married. _____
22. I cannot understand (she/her) telling the cheerleaders that they are not sufficiently enthusiastic when leading the cheers. _____

23. My husband was not as excited as I about (my/me) taking
    flying lessons.   _____

24. No one was more disappointed than (I/me) when our debating
    team lost last week.   _____

25. Don't do anything rash until you hear from Rachel and (I/me).   _____

26. Please give the donation to (whoever/whomever) qualifies as
    a worthy recipient.   _____

27. Father did not know that both my sister and (I/me) are ski
    instructors in British Columbia.   _____

28. Will you provide Michelle and (I/me/myself) the information
    that we require to reserve discount airline tickets?   _____

29. I cannot understand (them/their) insisting that we report to
    work a half-hour early.   _____

30. Is it (them/they) who will host the bazaar next Saturday?   _____

C. CONFUSING ADJECTIVES AND ADVERBS

Adjectives and adverbs are distinguished only by the words they modify. Adjectives modify nouns and pronouns; adverbs modify verbs, other adverbs, and adjectives. Many adverbs are formed by adding *ly* to the adjective, but many others take the same form as adjectives: *fat, well, ill, much, far*. In fact, there are so many exceptions to the *ly* rule that it is just barely a rule.

Despite the inconsistency in spelling, surprisingly few adverbs and adjectives give us trouble. Here are some rules that may help you avoid confusing them.

1. Adjectives modify nouns and pronouns—and nothing else!

    > He is a *proper* gentleman at all times.
    > (adjective modifying the noun *gentleman*)
    >
    > > but
    >
    > My stereo does not work *properly*.
    > (adverb modifying the verb *work*)
    >
    > He wears *conservative* ties.
    > (adjective modifying the noun *ties*)
    >
    > > but
    >
    > He dresses very *conservatively*.
    > (adverb modifying the verb *dresses*)

This is a *real* sealskin coat.
(adjective modifying the noun *coat*)

but

Julio is a *really* fine swimmer.
(adverb modifying the adjective *fine*)

2. Verbs of the senses (*to smell, to hear, to feel, to taste, to look*), forms of the verb *to be* (*is, are, am, was, were*), and other linking words, like *appear, become, seem*, are followed by adjectives that modify the subject.

She feels *bad* (not *badly*).

The peaches tasted *sweet* (not *sweetly*).

His closet seemed *neat* (not *neatly*).

We were *late* (not *lately*) for dinner.

When these verbs denote action, however, they take adverbs, not adjectives.

He looked *suspiciously* (not *suspicious*) at the new employee.
(modifies *looked*)

The alarm rang *loudly* (not *loud*) but no one was in the building to hear it.
(modifies *rang*)

The burglar felt *carefully* (not *careful*) around the door jamb.
(modifies *felt*)

D. USING FORMS OF COMPARISON

Adjectives and adverbs change form to show degrees of quality or quantity: these degrees are positive, comparative, and superlative. The comparative form of short modifiers is made by adding *er* to the positive form. The superlative form is made by adding *est*. The comparative and superlative forms of adverbs ending in *ly* or having two or more syllables are created by adding *more* and *most* to the positive form.

Note: Some adjectives and adverbs change forms completely in all degrees of comparison—good, better, best; bad, worse, worst.

Positive	Comparative	Superlative
cold	colder	coldest
fat	fatter	fattest
careful	more careful	most careful
quickly	more quickly	most quickly

1. The comparative form of adverbs and adjectives is used to compare two persons, things, or ideas.

    My horse is *faster* than yours.

    Alice is *more joyful* than her sister.

    He is *more enthusiastic* than Ahmed.

2. The superlative form compares more than two persons, things, or ideas.

    My horse is the *fastest* on the track.

    Alice is the *most joyful* of the three sisters.

    Jay is the *most enthusiastic* member of the team.

3. Some adjectives are absolute in meaning, and therefore cannot logically be compared.

    My cup is empty. (not *the emptiest*)

    Her costume is unique. (not *the uniquest*)

    Lina is pregnant. (not *more pregnant than Angela*)

4. Avoid double comparisons.

    My friend is stingier (not *more stingier*) than your friend.

    He is the angriest (not *the most angriest*) man I ever met.

    She is my dearest (not *most dearest*) friend.

Exercise 4.4 — Confusing Adjectives and Adverbs

Select the correct adjective or adverb in each of the following sentences and write it in the blank at the right or on a separate sheet.

1. Our Thanksgiving meal was (really/real) sumptuous. _____

2. The captain of our basketball team felt (bitter/bitterly) about not being selected for the all-star team. _____

3. Martha is an (awfully/awful) fine dressmaker. _____

4. The whole class felt (bad/badly) when our teacher, Mrs. Reagan, was transferred to another school. _____

5. Our company's accounting office operates quite (efficient/efficiently) despite being understaffed. _____

6. We did not eat any (different/differently) than the other tourists, but we still became ill. _____

7. My husband always dresses (conservatively/conservative) when we have dinner with our friends. _____

8. Both Carmen and Felicia did (good/well) on their mid-term examinations. _____

9. Kurt eats (sensibly/sensible) when we go out for buffet dinners. _____

10. That small girl on the bench is (sure/surely) not a member of the school basketball team. _____

11. I felt (strange/strangely) when I entered the room alone. _____

12. All of us felt (good/well) about the size of our donation to the Children's Aid Society. _____

13. We advised Liam to drive (slowly/slow), but he ignored our admonition and received a speeding ticket on the highway. _____

14. Donata is the (most thinnest/thinnest) woman in our cooking class. _____

15. I felt (sick/sickly) after I ate the chocolate fudge sundae. _____

16. Clara told us that she played (poor/poorly) in our annual college golf tournament. _____

17. Timothy is much (more heavier/heavier) than his friend Sam. _____

18. My family is the (most/more) gregarious of any family in our neighbourhood. _____

19. Our hockey team is (most frequently/frequently) faster on the ice than our competitors. _____

20. Those lemons tasted very (sour/sourly) in our lemonade. _____

21. Charles Chang is the (more qualified/most qualified) employee in our marketing department. _____

22. Harold certainly looks (different/differently) since he had his hair coloured. _____

23. I believe that last month was the (most warmest/warmest) month on record. _____

24. Creative Solutions is the (more recent/most recent) software development company to move into our industrial park. _____

25. We cannot give you a (more accurate/more accurately) account of our department's monthly expenditures. _____

26. This year our basketball team is the (most strongest/strongest) it has been since the 1993–94 season. _____

27. My rowing coach is (most knowledgeable/knowledgeable) about high-protein diets. _____

28. Please don't play your saxophone too (loudly/loud). _____

29. I think that Ottawa is the (most coldest/coldest) city in which I have ever lived. _____

30. Odette's is the (most elegant/more elegant) dress shop of the two in our small town. _____

Exercise 4.5 — Revising the Paragraph to Solve Special Problems

Rewrite the following paragraphs by eliminating the pronoun case errors as well as all the problems related to adverbs and adjectives.

Last winter my wife and me decided to take a summer golf vacation with two other young couples who we have known for near ten years, before they were married. Since all of us were most avid golfers, we thought that a two-week holiday focussing on golf would be a lot of fun.

We decided on the Carolinas. We thought that a week spent at Myrtle Beach, South Carolina, and a week in the mountains of North Carolina would be more enjoyable and entertaining. We were right: my wife and myself both agreed that it was one of the best holidays that we have ever had.

We left Canada on June 15 in two cars, three people in each car. The trip to Myrtle Beach took us two full days, but we drove more slower than the speed limits and made small side trips along the way, including a stop in Gettysburg, Pennsylvania, where the famous Civil War battle was fought.

In Myrtle Beach we stayed in a charmingly small hotel right on the beach; our rooms were adjoining, and each had cooking facilities. The couple whom owned the hotel were the most friendliest and obliging people that my wife and me have ever met. They were also, theirselves, real fine golfers and gave us helpful tips on which courses to play. We decided, on their advice, to play four different courses, each with differently degrees of difficulty, including more extensive water hazards and large sand traps along the fairways. In the evening we ate in different ethnic restaurants, most of which served wonderful fresh seafood. And the prices, I and my wife discovered, were quite reasonable for the quality of the food and the sophistication of some of the restaurants in which us and our companions ate.

We also took a day off from golf and spent some time on the beach. The water was awful warm for that time of year, and the sand was white and clean, which we were not use to, since we live in the Ottawa Valley, where beaches are few and farther between. And, of course, what Canadian, including us, travels south and does not go shopping? So we shopped in factory outlet malls during the one rainy day we had that week. The women, for the most part, bought clothes and we all purchased golf accessories.

At the end of the week, on Sunday, we drove—more quicker this time—to the Blue Ridge Mountains of North Carolina, where we checked into a golf resort with lodging and restaurant facilities. The resort had twenty-seven holes of golf as well as fine manicured tennis courts and a large swimming pool. The mountain courses were quite interesting, and most challenging, with raised tees and greens, and fairways that followed the contours of rolling hills and wide valleys. The tall southern pine trees were real magnificent, and the view from several of the tee areas was most breathtaking. We spent a great deal of time taking pictures of the beautiful vistas. Again, the food was first rate, and there was dancing and entertainment in the evening for whoever was energetic enough to stay awake after playing twenty-seven holes of golf. The weather, as in Myrtle Beach, was absolute perfect: warm days and cool nights, especially in the mountains, where the air was fresh and dry.

At the end of our holiday, we all agreed that us choosing the Carolinas for a golfing holiday was a stroke of genius. We also agreed that we would recommend the holiday to anyone whom loves golf, good food, and most wonderful scenery.

CHAPTER FIVE

Making Sentences Clear

To write clear, concise, and balanced sentences, you must be able to structure your statements so that the proper relationship of your ideas comes through. You must pay close attention to the important transitional links that connect sentence parts and be aware of the logical pattern of parallel words and statements that give sentences balance and cohesion. Your ability to write such sentences will depend on your avoiding errors in pronoun reference, dangling and misplaced modifiers, and parallel construction.

A. PRONOUNS MUST REFER CLEARLY TO NOUNS

Pronouns are used in place of nouns to avoid repetition and to connect ideas. However, if you have not made clear what nouns the pronouns replace, your sentences will lack coherence and thus create confusion in the mind of the reader. The following pronoun reference errors are the most common.

1. The Hazards of Ambiguity

Ambiguity occurs when a pronoun can refer grammatically to more than one antecedent.

> The teacher informed the student that he needed another test booklet.
> (Who needed the test booklet?)
>
> Mother told Anna that her pickles were not canned properly.
> (Whose pickles?)

Even though the reader may logically deduce your meaning, your sentence may appear ridiculous if the pronoun lacks a clear reference.

> Paula heard her daughter speak her first word upon returning from her tennis match.
> (Whose tennis match?)
>
> The dean of the college told the student that his bicycle needed a taillight.
> (Whose bicycle?)

2. Antecedents That Are Only Implied

Do not use a pronoun whose antecedent is implied only by the wording of a sentence. Make sure that your pronoun refers clearly to one antecedent.

> FAULTY: In the armed services *they* can retire at an early age. (Who are "they"?)
>
> CORRECTED: The men and women in the armed services can retire at an early age.
>
> FAULTY: I am attending a western university where *they* teach petroleum engineering. (Who teaches?)
>
> CORRECTED: I am attending a western university where petroleum engineering is taught. (Eliminating the pronoun sometimes clarifies the meaning.)
>
> FAULTY: The English teacher tried hard, but *it* went right over our heads. (What went over our heads?)
>
> CORRECTED: The English teacher tried hard, but the lesson went right over our heads.

3. Imprecise References Cause Confusion

Do not use a pronoun that refers vaguely to an entire clause or to a complete sentence. When words like *this, which*, or *it* refer to general statements, confusion results.

> FAULTY: When it rained in the valley, *it* was because of a low pressure system.
>
> FAULTY: The relationship between Canada and the United States has always been close, *which* has benefited business in both countries.

Usually, sentences like these can be easily corrected by rewriting them without the pronoun.

> REVISED: It rained in the valley because of a low-pressure system.
>
> or
>
> The valley had rain because of a low-pressure system.
>
> REVISED: The close relationship between Canada and the United States has benefited business in both countries.

Exercise 5.1 — Improving Pronoun Reference

After each of the following sentences containing a faulty pronoun reference, write *F* in the blank at the right or on a separate sheet. Then rewrite the sentence correctly. If the sentence is correct, write *C* instead of *F*.

68   *Writing Fundamentals*

EXAMPLE: I am learning how to lay bricks because I want to
be one, like my father.   F

REVISED: I am learning how to lay bricks because I want to
be a bricklayer, like my father.

1. Carlotta spends a great deal of time collecting stamps because it is her favourite hobby.   _____
2. Eileen told Maureen that her hairdresser was seriously ill.   _____
3. My uncle from Toronto bought my brother a new computer, which took him completely by surprise.   _____
4. My sister has never played tennis, but she is quite interested in learning it.   _____
5. The music on the radio is too sombre; it is not the kind of sound that I enjoy.   _____
6. When I saw my first baseball game, I decided that I wanted to be one when I grew up.   _____
7. When I went to the unemployment office, they told me to return next Monday for an interview with an employment counsellor.   _____
8. When the star baseball player hit a home run, everyone gave him a standing ovation.   _____
9. Gregory asked Brian if he could meet him for lunch on Sunday.   _____
10. Our gym instructor told us that it had been a successful workout.   _____
11. I attended my first cricket match, but I couldn't understand it.   _____
12. On the menu outside the restaurant, they indicate that the soup of the day is cream of asparagus.   _____
13. Everything I do seems to annoy you, and this confuses me.   _____
14. I never went to a bullfight, but I am fascinated by them.   _____
15. Deirdre failed the final exam, which was the reason she had to attend summer school.   _____
16. Because we left the football game early, we failed to see them score the final touchdown.   _____
17. The captain of the cruise ship asked the passengers if it had been enjoyable.   _____
18. The dentist told the doctor that his tooth had to be extracted.   _____

Chapter 5 / Making Sentences Clear   69

19. Helen called the hospital and told them about being overbilled. _____
20. Their exam scores were low, which disappointed them. _____
21. When it hit the coast of North Carolina, it achieved hurricane-force winds of one hundred and sixty kilometres per hour. _____
22. After living in France for the last ten years, I have come to enjoy it. _____
23. Carl told Fred that his tie was made of silk. _____
24. I spend a lot of money on stamps because it is my favourite hobby. _____
25. In William Frazier's *Cold Mountain,* he writes about a soldier returning to his home in the North Carolina mountains during the civil war between the northern and southern states. _____
26. When the airline pilots went on strike, this surprised us very much. _____
27. The members of our hockey team bought the coach a gold watch at the end of the season, which was a very nice gesture of appreciation. _____
28. The jury members were surprised when the judge informed them that they had to stay in the hotel overnight. _____
29. When Beryl volunteered to work overtime on Friday, it was appreciated. _____
30. In the Middle East they speak mostly Arabic. _____

Exercise 5.2 — Revising the Paragraph for Clear Pronoun Reference

Rewrite the following paragraphs, eliminating the pronoun reference errors.

1. When a foreign-language credit was a requirement for high-school graduation, this greatly increased their sensitivity to the structure of language, including English. It was important for students because there was a skills transfer, especially knowledge of verb tenses and of common prefixes and suffixes.

    Also, they developed a disciplined approach to learning grammar rules, and this helped their knowledge of English syntax. It tended to make them more careful writers. It is too bad that students today do not have to study a foreign language, because it would certainly make them better users of their native tongue.

2. When I first travelled overseas I was worried that they would not understand me, for I could not speak a foreign language. But this was not the case at all, because I found that in every European country I visited they could understand what I said. This, of course, was because most of them had to study English in both grade school and high school.

   It made me feel inadequate because the people were at least bilingual—some even trilingual—and everyone I met was eager to talk to me in order to increase his or her knowledge of English, especially our slang expressions. It made me suspect that my lack of knowledge about other people and other cultures stemmed from my unwillingness to learn a foreign language.

   Therefore, since my first trip overseas five years ago, I have learned two foreign languages fluently and am conversant in two more. It also increased my appreciation of other cultures, because I soon realized that language is the key to understanding how they think and feel. This is a lesson that I will not soon forget.

B. PUTTING MODIFIERS IN THE RIGHT PLACE

The position of a modifier usually determines the precise meaning of your sentence. If it is placed incorrectly, your statement will be illogical and confusing. To avoid this error, place your modifiers as close as possible to the word or words they modify.

1. Almost any modifier can be misplaced if there are two or more words in the sentence to which it could possibly attach itself. Consider the following modifier errors:

    MISPLACED: The old man walked into the lamppost going to the optician. (Who has bad eyesight, the old man or the lamppost)?

    CORRECTED: While going to the optician, the old man walked into the lamppost.

    MISPLACED: The performers danced while we joined hands with gusto. (Who is gusto?)

    CORRECTED: The performers danced with gusto while we joined hands.

   Also watch out for dependent clauses beginning with *which* or *that*; if they do not immediately follow the word they modify, you may write sentences like these:

    MISPLACED: He crossed the stream in a canoe, which was recently stocked with fish.

    CORRECTED: He crossed the stream, which was recently stocked with fish, in a canoe.

MISPLACED: The football game was played in our stadium, that was full of penalties.

CORRECTED: The football game that was full of penalties was played in our stadium.

2. Make sure you place words like *only, nearly,* and *almost* immediately before the words or phrases they modify. If you do not, your sentence will be illogical, or it may even change in meaning:

ILLOGICAL: During the summer vacation she nearly earned a thousand dollars. (You cannot nearly earn.)

LOGICAL: During the summer vacation, she earned nearly a thousand dollars.

ILLOGICAL: He almost ran thirty kilometres in the marathon race. (He did not almost run.)

LOGICAL: He ran almost thirty kilometres in the marathon race.

Consider how the following sentences change their meaning when the word *only* is shifted:

He *only* drove a car until he bought a bicycle.
(He did nothing else except drive a car.)

He drove *only* a car until he bought a bicycle.
(He drove nothing else.)

Only he drove a car until he bought a bicycle.
(No one else drove.)

He drove a car *only* until he bought a bicycle.
(He stopped driving when he bought a bicycle.)

3. Do not make your modifier ambiguous by placing it in such a way that it could modify either of two parts of a sentence. This error is referred to as a "squinting modifier."

SQUINTING: Students who study often get good grades.
(Does *often* modify *study*, or does it refer to *good grades*?)

CORRECTED: Students who often study get good grades.

or

Students who study get good grades often.

4. Good writers may sometimes use a split infinitive to achieve clarity or to place emphasis; but unless you know precisely what you are doing, avoid splitting infinitives, especially with phrases and clauses.

> SPLIT: We intend *to*, if our money holds out, *travel* out west during our semester break.
>
> CORRECTED: If our money holds out, we intend *to travel* out west during our semester break.
>
> SPLIT: I promise *to* faithfully and diligently *do* my work.
>
> CORRECTED: I promise *to do* my work faithfully and diligently.

Exercise 5.3 — Misplaced Modifiers

After each of the sentences containing a misplaced modifier, write *M* in the blank at the right or on a separate sheet, then rewrite the sentence correctly. If the sentence is correct write *C* instead of *M*.

> EXAMPLE: We nearly took in three hundred dollars at the crafts show.   *M*
>
> REVISED: We took in nearly three hundred dollars at the crafts show.

1. No one can fix the bicycle without a tool kit. _____

2. Raymond asked Leslie on Monday for a date. _____

3. We started the automobile race on Sunday morning without qualified mechanics in the pits. _____

4. People who overeat frequently have high cholesterol. _____

5. By 7:00 p.m. most of the dinner guests had already arrived. _____

6. Singing frequently relieves tension. _____

7. They intend to, if the coach is agreeable, have a pizza party in the locker room on Saturday night. _____

8. Please inform us if you received your free box of chocolates on the enclosed postcard. _____

9. By the end of the meal I had almost consumed all of the lemon meringue pie. _____

10. We attended the annual fundraising party for AIDS research at our high-school gymnasium. _____

Chapter 5 / Making Sentences Clear   73

11. Do not buy a used car from a friend without a maintenance record. _____

12. My father did not intend to, please believe me, offend you by offering to pay for your wife's dinner. _____

13. Our volunteer recycling team almost collected three hundred discarded aluminum cans. _____

14. Everyone in my class completed his or her assignment before the due date. _____

15. I finally found my wristwatch under the car seat without the gold band. _____

16. My son's pen pal visited us on Saturday from New Orleans. _____

17. The mechanic told me on Friday to have my car's oil changed. _____

18. Greg and Sally only finished their homework ten minutes before class. _____

19. We will not agree to, under any circumstances, accompany you to the class reunion this Saturday. _____

20. We often go to the movies on Friday night. _____

21. Our hockey team played last year's championship team with trepidation. _____

22. She almost telephones her sister every night at 8:00 p.m. _____

23. Mai Ling's gold ring was lost in the airport with a two-carat diamond. _____

24. Denise did not intend to, I am certain, insult the cocktail waitress last night. _____

25. Drinking Gatorade often prevents dehydration. _____

26. Never drive at night on country roads without fog lights. _____

27. Gerta only ran in the five-kilometre race. _____

28. Frank nearly swam ten kilometres across Lake Tuckahoo. _____

29. Ranjit sold a necklace to Chandra with a broken clasp. _____

30. Our Little League team played last Saturday without proper uniforms. _____

Exercise 5.4 — Revising the Paragraph to Correct Misplaced Modifiers

Rewrite the following paragraphs, eliminating the misplaced modifiers.

> Last summer we held our annual company barbecue in Grove Park that only included chicken, hot dogs, and hamburgers. By eliminating steak, we nearly saved over two hundred dollars. Also, we wanted to, if the park authorities had agreed, have soccer games and Frisbee-throwing contests, but they refused us permission because of lack of space and potential danger to other picnickers.
>
> Despite this restriction, though, we still managed to have fun. We organized potato-sack races for the children and horseshoe-throwing contests for the adults with real horseshoes. There were also watermelon-eating contests in which everyone nearly participated. It was a perfect afternoon for the families of our employees without oppressive heat or humidity. And we had only one minor injury: our vice-president of marketing cut his finger while slicing a watermelon on a slippery plate with a knife.

C. DETECTING DANGLING MODIFIERS

Whenever you use a phrase or a clause that refers to a specific word, make sure you arrange the sentences so that the reader knows how the word and its modifier are attached. If you fail to relate clearly the modifier to the word modified, the reader will become confused and may lose interest in what you have to say.

A dangling modifier is a phrase or an elliptical clause (a clause without a subject or verb—or both) that is illogically separated from the word it modifies. Thus it appears awkwardly disconnected from the rest of the sentence. Here are a few examples of dangling constructions:

PARTICIPIAL PHRASE:	*Cited by the writer*, the student did not know the source of the quotation.
	(The quotation, not the student, was cited.)
GERUND PHRASE:	*Approaching the guard rail on Lookout Mountain*, a vast expanse of farmland could be seen.
	(Who—or what—approached the guard rail?)
INFINITIVE PHRASE:	*To appreciate the English language*, reading must be done.
	(Who must read?)
PREPOSITIONAL PHRASE:	*After four weeks at sea*, my wife was happy to see me.
	(Who was at sea?)
ELLIPTICAL CLAUSE:	*When on the top floor of the tall building*, the cars looked like tiny fish in a stream.
	(Where are the cars? Where is the speaker?)

To correct dangling modifiers, you must reword the entire sentence; unlike misplaced modifiers, the fractured syntax of dangling constructions cannot be cured by shifting one or two words around.

1. One method of correcting a dangling modifier is by locating its implied subject (by asking yourself who or what is responsible for the action), and then making it the stated subject of the main clause.

   DANGLING: After three hours of practice, a large mug of root beer was what the thirsty dancers wanted.
   (Who was practising?)

   REVISED: After practising for three hours, the thirsty *dancers* wanted a large mug of root beer.

   DANGLING: Before submitting any written work, careful proofreading must be done.
   (Who must submit the work?)

   REVISED: Before submitting any written work *you* must carefully proofread it.

2. Another method of correcting dangling construction is by expanding the dangling phrases or elliptical clause into a full dependent clause.

   DANGLING: Watching the parade, my wallet was stolen.

   REVISED: While I was watching the parade, my wallet was stolen.

   DANGLING: Although tired and hungry, the drill sergeant would not let us rest.

   REVISED: Although we were tired and hungry, the drill sergeant would not let us rest.

Exercise 5.5 — Dangling Modifiers

After each of the following sentences containing a dangling modifier, write *DM* in the blank at the right or on a separate sheet. Then rewrite the sentence correctly. If the sentence is correct write *C* instead of *DM*.

   EXAMPLE: When very young, my father took me to the circus.   DM

   REVISED: When I was very young, my father took me to the circus.

1. Concerned by the threat of lightning, the golf match was delayed by the head official. _____

2. During the drive between Edmonton and Calgary, many serious accidents could be seen on the icy roads. _____

3. While cross-country skiing without sunblock, my face became painfully sunburned. _____

4. To play golf in the low eighties, many hours of practise are required. _____

5. Before buying my new car, I did a lot of comparison shopping. _____

6. After waiting two hours for the plane to arrive, the airline announced that the flight had been diverted to another airport because of inclement weather. _____

7. Concerned by the spreading brush fires, the homes were ordered evacuated by the firefighters. _____

8. While waiting for the bus to arrive, Serena used her mobile phone to make a dinner reservation. _____

9. Once on the open road, my worries seemed to disappear. _____

10. As an expert in tax law, this business deduction is completely unwarranted. _____

11. After listening to him speak, my opinion of his management skills has not changed. _____

12. When sailing on the St. Lawrence River, the Thousand Islands International Bridge appeared suddenly through the morning mist. _____

13. When I first met Beverly, I thought that she was a fashion model. _____

14. Like many of today's TV programs, violence and sex is what makes this program so popular with today's youth. _____

15. When thoroughly plastered, the painter decided to let the wall dry overnight. _____

16. To become a successful actor, voice training is essential. _____

17. Seeing the snow fall in late afternoon was like being a child again in the province of Quebec. _____

18. During our lunch hour the fire alarm went off inadvertently, and the building had to be temporarily evacuated. _____

19. When jogging in the hot sun, a sweatband should be worn. _____

20. After a large dinner, a heavy dessert is not a good idea. _____

21. To remain thin, exercise and a low-fat diet are necessary. _____

22. As a long-time resident of Montreal, this city needs better, and more modern, public transportation. _____

23. When sunbathing on the beach, watch out for the Frisbee players. _____

24. While word-processing on my computer, I always save my work during—not after—the writing process. _____

25. After becoming pregnant, the doctor put Zelda on a strict diet. _____

26. Regretting her refusal to participate in the bake sale, Kathy decided to volunteer as a ticket seller for the charity bazaar. _____

27. To enjoy the winter months, cross-country skiing can be a great family sport. _____

28. After reading Stephen King novels in bed, the light must always be on. _____

29. Knowing when to stop drinking alcohol, Harvey is always elected the designated driver. _____

30. While attending the Calgary Stampede, Donna's purse was stolen from her hotel room. _____

Exercise 5.6 — Revising the Paragraph to Remove Dangling Modifiers

Rewrite the following paragraphs, eliminating the dangling modifiers.

    The motor trip that my wife and I took along the Rhine and Moselle river valleys was a once-in-a-lifetime experience, for it was both delightful and educational. Flying from Montreal to Frankfurt, rough weather was encountered, causing our flight to arrive late. But after spending a quiet and restful night in a Frankfurt hotel, the next morning we rented a small German car and drove to Mainz, where we began our Rhine River trip.

    Taking the two-lane road that ran alongside the river, small towns and villages could be seen. We visited vineyards and wineries where different grades of white wines were made and bottled. A cable-car ride was also taken to a lookout point above the river, where the small ships looked like toy boats in a bathtub. And in the old town of Boppard we saw the ruins of an old Roman fortress. One morning, taking a boat cruise along the Rhine, a guide pointed out the history of that waterway, especially as a daunting means of transportation during the time of the Robber Barons, who levied heavy tolls and exorbitant custom duties along the river's stretch from Mainz to Cologne. After sightseeing, shopping in the small villages, and visiting ancient churches and cathedrals, overnight stays in *gasthauses*, which can be compared to bed and breakfast inns throughout North America, were a welcome respite.

When we reached the town of Koblenz, we joined the Moselle river valley. The wine vineyards there were on the sides of steep hills that guarded the river, and the workers had to be tied around the waist with a rope in order to tend the grapes. While driving along the Moselle, several small towns were having wine festivals, in which we actively participated. We also ate our lunches—wursts, schnitzels, and red cabbage—in quaint *biergartens*, toured several castles, and visited Roman ruins in the old town of Trier.

During the trip many friendly German villagers were encountered who extended us their hospitality and good will. We even learned to say "bottoms up" in German. At the end of the trip, we realized that we had just travelled through one of the most beautiful parts of southern Germany, and that our knowledge and appreciation of the German people and their history had increased tenfold. We also learned an important lesson: One should never try to lose weight while touring through the German wine country.

D. EMPLOYING PARALLEL FORMS

We signal the reader that two or more ideas have equal value by placing them in the same grammatical form; this enables us to express these ideas clearly and emphatically. To position parallel ideas properly, however, we must pay close attention to the logic of grammatical relationships.

1. Correcting Faulty Coordination

When word groups are linked by a coordinating conjunction, they should each have the same grammatical construction. Consider the parallel structure of the following word groups:

> Our locker room is small, chilly, and dirty.
> (parallel adjectives)

> I enjoy playing basketball and hockey.
> (parallel nouns)

> Our dog ran across the lawn and under the hedge.
> (parallel phrases)

> We requested that he sing our favourite songs and that he allow us to record them.
> (parallel clauses)

> I want to learn English, and she wants to learn French.
> (parallel sentences)

Notice how awkward sentences look and sound when they contain unequal elements.

> She works diligently and at night.

> He spends a great deal of money and foolishly.

> I was told to report to the supervisor and that I should bring my tools.

Two very common types of error in coordination involve the use of *and who/and which* constructions and the use of correlative conjunctions, which must be used correctly before your sentences can be properly balanced. These errors are discussed in the following sections.

(a) *And Who/And Which Constructions*
The awkward *and who/and which* construction is one of the most common yet most serious errors made by students, resulting in an illogical link between dependent and independent clauses. To avoid this error, follow this rule: Never use *and who* or *and which* clauses unless they are preceded by *who* or *which* clauses.

> FAULTY: Tom Clark, wise and intelligent, *and who* is our union representative, has been promoted to foreman.
>
> CORRECTED: Tom Clark, *who* is wise and intelligent, *and who* is our union representative, has been promoted to foreman.
>
> FAULTY: James Joyce's *Ulysses*, a long and complicated novel *and which* is on our reading list, has been banned by the school board.
>
> CORRECTED: James Joyce's *Ulysses*, *which* is a long and complicated novel, *and which* is on our reading list, has been banned by the school board.

(b) *Correlative Conjunctions*
Correlative conjunctions are always used in pairs: *either...or; neither...nor; not only...but also; both...and*. Because they are used to compare and contrast similar statements, each part of the conjunction must be followed by the same grammatical construction. The proper use of correlative conjunctions will enable you to write clear, well-balanced sentences.

> UNBALANCED: I want either to study English literature or study world history.
>
> BALANCED: I want to study either English literature or world history.
>
> UNBALANCED: Our new car not only is more economical but also it is more comfortable than our old one.
>
> BALANCED: Our new car is not only more economical but also more comfortable than our old one.

2. Making Series Parallel
When words or groups of words are placed in a series, they must be parallel in both meaning and structure. Observe how the proper use of parallel series tightens your sentence structure and clarifies your meaning.

> FAULTY: When we arrived home we unpacked our suitcases, took showers, and then we went to sleep after eating our lunch.
>
> REVISED: When we arrived home we unpacked our suitcases, took our showers, ate our lunch, and went to sleep.
>
> FAULTY: Many people choose air transportation because it is fast, offers convenience, and it is not very expensive.
>
> REVISED: Many people choose air transportation because it is fast, convenient, and inexpensive.
>
> FAULTY: You should strive to cooperate with your colleagues to bring about change, for improving communication, and professional development.
>
> REVISED: You should strive to cooperate with your colleagues to bring about change, to improve communication, and to further professional development.

3. Watching for Incorrect Omissions

By omitting essential words in a parallel construction, you force one word to serve the grammatical requirements of two different statements.

One of the most common omissions in student writing occurs in the *has/have...will/shall* constructions.

> He always has and always will compete for the highest honours.
>
> I always have and always shall practise diligently.

To correct this type of omission error, test the verb with each of its auxiliary words; if it appears in the wrong tense, the construction is unparallel.

> CORRECTION: He always has competed (not *compete*) and always will compete (not *competed*) for the highest honours.
>
> CORRECTION: I always have practised (not *practise*) diligently and always shall. (Practise is understood.)

4. Making Comparisons Using *Than* or *As*

When *than* or *as* are used to join parallel constructions, make sure that the things or ideas they compare are logically and grammatically alike.

> ILLOGICAL: The students attending our school are more intelligent than your school.
> (compares people—students—to a thing—a building)
>
> LOGICAL: The students attending our school are more intelligent than the students attending your school.

ILLOGICAL: His learning is as extensive as Paul.
(compares an abstract quality—learning—to a proper noun—Paul)

LOGICAL: His learning is as extensive as Paul's learning.
(or simply Paul's)

Exercise 5.7 — Correcting Faulty Parallelism

After each of the following sentences containing errors in parallel construction, write *P* in the blank at the right or on a separate sheet. Then rewrite the sentence correctly. If the sentence contains no error, write *C* instead of *P*.

EXAMPLE: I cannot decide whether I should remain in school or to withdraw.   __P__

REVISED: I cannot decide whether to remain in school or to withdraw.   __C__

1. I moved to Vancouver because of its milder winters, for the close access to the University of British Columbia, and to be near my youngest daughter. _____

2. My uncle George was a bricklayer, a construction worker, and finally he became a professional wrestler. _____

3. Our high-school gym teacher, a strict disciplinarian, and who is the treasurer of the local teachers' union, has just been indicted for embezzlement and bribery. _____

4. Calvin not only wants to learn how to play tennis, he wants also to learn golf and curling, too. _____

5. My new car is comfortable, economical, and easy to drive. _____

6. The golf pro's putting is much more accurate than Paul. _____

7. She is either an actress or maybe she is a fashion model. _____

8. The Muslim faith, one of the world's fastest growing religions, and which is attracting new worshippers in Canada every year, requires strict fasting during the holy month of Ramadan. _____

9. Tam Sung's apartment is not only small, it is unfurnished as well. _____

10. I was asked to pick up the laundry, put gas in the car, buy headache pills at the pharmacy, and then I was supposed to rent a movie at our local video store. _____

11. He is either going to the local community college or he might attend the University of Western Ontario.

12. Fenimore always has and always will support the Calgary Stampeders football team.

13. My tennis game is not as well developed as Luke.

14. The airline that I am using offers neither frequent flyer miles nor non-stop service from Vancouver to Montreal.

15. I cannot decide which kind of fruit I want: a pear, orange, or an apple.

16. She jogs every day and for at least an hour.

17. Our city's pollution bylaws are not as strict as your city.

18. Françoise is participating as well as benefiting from the new community campaign to modernize garbage collection.

19. Donn is both an officer as well as a gentleman.

20. My parents always have voted in the national election and always will.

21. We were told that our evening flight would be delayed indefinitely and to be prepared to wait until the early morning flight.

22. My daughter babysits for our neighbour's little girl and quite willingly.

23. Cross-country skiing is good for the heart and lungs and which is highly recommended for muscle tone.

24. I can play poker, pinochle, gin rummy, and I also play canasta.

25. Manuel's credit-card debt is not as large as Paco.

26. He is not only a navigator but also a pilot.

27. Mandy and Mickie are both cousins and they are best friends as well.

28. My cat, Max, catches neither mice nor does he catch any other rodent that could possibly injure him.

29. The hockey game that we saw last night was rough, exciting, and it was also full of penalties.

30. If I had my choice of owning either a Mercedes or Oldsmobile car, I would choose the Mercedes.

Exercise 5.8 — Revising the Paragraph to Improve Parallelism

Rewrite the following paragraphs, eliminating errors in parallel structure.

> It is not easy to permanently and safely lose weight, for there is no magical diet pill that will guarantee substantial weight loss without risk. Furthermore, fad diets not only do not work, they may even be harmful to your health. The most important facts to remember are that permanent weight loss takes time, involves a change in lifestyle, and you require exercise as well. Through the correct combination of the right foods and exercise, you need to establish a daily deficit of approximately five hundred calories to lose that pound a week.
>
> You need to control your eating not only for the duration of the diet but as well for long after you have lost the desired pounds. Food rich in fat calories is more readily converted to body fat than food high in carbohydrates and proteins. A high-fat diet is a risk factor for heart disease, contracting diabetes, and to avoid some kinds of cancers. Diet experts advocate a fat intake of 25 percent of total calories, which is substantially lower than the 38 to 40 percent most North Americans consume and is ideal for maintaining a long-term weight loss.
>
> After a certain amount of time, your fat deficit, along with exercise, can slim your body to a point where it functions so efficiently and where you stop losing weight. At this point, having become used to both the dietary changes you have made as well as to your daily exercise regimen, you can then go ahead and cut your fat intake far enough to reach the target weight you have set for yourself. But you must remember that losing weight always has and always will require a combination of diet and exercise—one without the other will not, in the long term, be effective.

Exercise 5.9 — Review Exercise: Sentence Clarity

After each of the following sentences containing sentence clarity mistakes, write the following in the blank at the right or on a separate sheet: *PR* for faulty pronoun reference, *M* for misplaced modifier, *DM* for danging modifier, and *P* for faulty parallelism. Then on a separate sheet rewrite the sentences correctly.

EXAMPLES: I am learning computer programming because I want to be one when I graduate.	PR
We almost bought ten dollars worth of provincial lottery tickets.	M
When running in a marathon race, dehydration is always a problem.	DM
Connie's examination score was higher than Greg and Sonia.	P

1. I moved to North Carolina because I like the milder weather, for the golfing opportunities, and the lower cost of living. _____

2. Once out on the open sea, our worries seemed to disappear. _____

3. As the representative for the clean air committee, this proposal, as far as I'm concerned, will not help our cause. _____

4. Tanya informed Paula that her lost dog was finally found by her brother. _____

5. Always purchase a computer from a reputable store with a fast modem and sufficient memory. _____

6. Whenever I go to the post office, they find something wrong with the way I wrap my parcels. _____

7. She always has and always will vote for the political party that supports affirmative action. _____

8. When typing a letter, your word processor should have a spell-check capability. _____

9. To safely and efficiently lose weight, your exercise routine should include at least a half-hour of either walking or jogging. _____

10. Mendez almost ran fifteen kilometres in the marathon race. _____

11. The flight attendant forgot to tell us to buckle our seat belts during the turbulent weather, and this was noticed by all of the passengers in my section. _____

12. Sergio not only finished first in the marathon race, he broke the speed record as well. _____

13. After we arrived at our lakefront cottage, we carried in our belongings, stowed our fishing gear, slid our boat into the water, and then we decided to go swimming. _____

14. The football players who are late for practice often are placed on probation and suspended for one game. _____

15. All of us wanted to, if the rain had continued, cancel the volleyball game and have our picnic lunch inside the school cafeteria. _____

16. Caroline's English test score was much lower than Phil and Kurt. _____

17. I have never seen an African bee, but I am terrified of them. _____

Chapter 5 / Making Sentences Clear **85**

18. While attending the estate auction, the grand piano slid off the mobile stage and smashed into a dining-room table. _____

19. Kylie is interested and excited by the new Canadian rock star. _____

20. Emory is either a ballet dancer or else he is a soccer player. _____

21. The gym instructor told us on Friday to meet the school bus at 9:00 a.m. _____

22. The coach asked her players if it had been an easy game. _____

23. The hockey team played its last game with sadness and regret. _____

24. Please allow me to, if the rain stops, attend the outdoor rock concert. _____

25. Our college tennis team is far better than your college. _____

26. After a gruelling six weeks of spring training at football camp, my family was glad to have me back home in Canada. _____

27. When it rained in the mountains it melted the snow and caused some flooding. _____

28. Out of a field of fifty-four teams in the golf tournament, the team of Durer and Sullivan only broke par on the first day. _____

29. We finally decided to purchase the car from the used-car dealer that had a sliding moon roof and an ABS package. _____

30. When completely fried, Sally removed the flounder from the Teflon pan. _____

31. Garth plays tennis because he enjoys the competition, for the exercise, and because his girlfriend is a tennis pro. _____

32. Once on top of the CN Tower, the cars looked like small toys racing along the thin parkway. _____

33. Stacy always has and always will exercise strenuously at least three times a week. _____

34. Claude's new detective novel was favourably reviewed and which is now on the best-seller list. _____

35. To swim competitively, your legs and shoulders must be very strong. _____

36. My husband forgot our wedding anniversary, and this disturbed me very much. _____

37. He is either lazy or he must not be interested in success. _____

38. I have never seen a great white shark, but I am deathly afraid of them. _____

39. Johnny Chung only won ten dollars playing blackjack. _____

40. My father is irritated and disappointed in his employees' tardiness and lack of ambition. _____

CHAPTER SIX

Keys to Better Spelling

Poor spelling is not an incurable disease. True, some people have better visual memories than others, and some have great success in sounding out words phonetically. But most people, with a little concerted effort, can easily overcome their spelling handicap. Here are a few suggestions.

1. **Write with a Dictionary** If you are not sure of the spelling of a word, get into the habit of looking it up in a dictionary. If you look up the word often enough, your mere exposure to it will help you spell it correctly.

2. **Divide Words into Syllables** If you are not quite sure how to spell a word, pronounce it carefully by breaking it into syllables. Although many English words are not spelled the way they are pronounced, many more are; by pronouncing words first you will not write *atheletics* for *athletics*, or *grievious* for *grievous*, or *villian* for *villain*, or *envirment* for *environment*.

3. **Proofread Everything You Write** This simple device for picking out spelling errors is too often ignored by students. Many errors result from simple carelessness and are therefore easily revealed by a careful rereading. If you have left letters out, or transposed letters, or confused one word with another because of its sound, proofreading will enable you to find virtually all of these mistakes.

4. **Make a List** Compose a list of the words you most frequently misspell and write them correctly. As you learn to spell them more proficiently and encounter new words that give you trouble, you will continually add new words to, and subtract old words from, your list. In doing so, you will always have a running record of your rate of improvement.

5. **Read Something Every Day** Simply exposing yourself to words will aid your spelling when you write. Reading is the easiest and least onerous method of learning to spell. Memorizing the spelling of words that you rarely see in print (because you do not read) is next to useless. You might as well try to learn punctuation by watching television. So whatever else you do to improve your spelling, make sure you read—every day.

A. THE RULES

Although English spelling has almost as many exceptions as rules, there are several useful rules that will help you to spell hundreds of words correctly.

1. The *ie* and *ei* Words
The *ie* rhyme is still the most effective way to learn this rule:

> Write *i* before *e* except after *c*
> or when sounded as *a*
> as in *neighbour* and *weigh*.

Examples of *i* before *e*: achieve, grief, field, piece, relief

Examples of *e* before *i*: sleigh, receipt, foreign, ceiling

Common exceptions: either, neither, weird, seize, height

2. Words Ending in *y*
(a) Words ending in *y* preceded by a consonant change *y* to *i* before adding all suffixes except *ing*.

EXAMPLES:	mercy/merciful	study/studying
	try/tried	hurry/hurrying
	fry/fried	worry/worrying

(b) Words ending in *y* preceded by a vowel retain the *y* before all suffix endings.

> EXAMPLES: stay/stayed; portray/portrayed; enjoy/enjoyed
>
> COMMON EXCEPTIONS: lay/laid; say/said; slay/slain

3. Dropping the Final *e*
(a) The final *e* is dropped before a suffix beginning with a vowel; it is retained before a suffix beginning with a consonant.

> EXAMPLES OF FINAL *E* DROPPED: change/changing; force/forcing; desire/desirable
>
> EXAMPLES OF FINAL *E* RETAINED: hope/hopeless; use/useful; excite/excitement
>
> EXCEPTIONS: argument, truly, awful, ninth, wholly

(b) The final *e* is also retained after a soft *c* or *g* if the suffix begins with *a* or *o*.

> EXAMPLES: notice/noticeable; change/changeable; advantage/advantageous; courage/courageous

4. Doubling the Final Consonant

(a) Double the final consonant following a single vowel before you add a suffix beginning with a vowel when the following conditions occur:

> The word has only one syllable
> EXAMPLES: swim/swimming; trip/tripped; ship/shipped

> The word is accented on the last syllable
> EXAMPLES: begin/beginning; compel/compelled; occur/occurred

(b) If the accent shifts to the first syllable when a suffix beginning with a vowel is added, do not double the final consonant.

> EXAMPLES: prefer/preference; confer/conference; defer/deference

5. Plurals: Adding *s* or *es*

(a) Add *s* to nouns ending in *y* preceded by a vowel.

> EXAMPLES: valleys, keys, clays, guys

(b) Add *es* to form the plurals of words ending in *ch, x, sh,* or *s*.

> EXAMPLES: axes, marshes, taxes, churches, buses

(c) Add only *s* to nouns ending in *o* preceded by a vowel.

> EXAMPLES: cameos, folios, radios, rodeos

B. WORDS THAT SOUND OR LOOK ALIKE

1. **accede/exceed**
   accede means to comply with; *exceed* means to surpass

2. **accept/except**
   accept means to take or receive; *except* means to exclude

3. **adapt/adopt**
   adapt means to adjust; *adopt* means to choose or take possession of

4. **advice/advise**
   advice is a noun meaning information given or recommendations made; *advise* is a verb meaning to give counsel

5. **affect/effect**
   affect as a verb means to influence or to change; *effect* as a noun means result or outcome, and as a verb to fulfill or to bring about

6. **altar/alter**
   an *altar* is a part of a church; *alter* is a verb meaning to change

7. **beside/besides**
   beside means by the side of; *besides* means in addition to

8. **born/borne**
   born means brought into life; *borne* means carried or endured

9. **breath/breathe**
   breath is a noun meaning respiration; *breathe* is a verb meaning the act of inhaling and exhaling, respiring

10. **choose/chose**
    choose means to select; *chose* is the past tense of choose

11. **cite/site/sight**
    cite is a verb meaning to quote; *site* is a noun meaning a place; and *sight* is a noun meaning vision or a particular view

12. **clothes/cloths**
    clothes means wearing apparel; *cloths* are fabrics from which clothes are made, or simply pieces of fabric

13. **coarse/course**
    coarse means rough or common; *course* can mean the direction taken, a plan of action, a path of movement, or a fixed plan of study (as in a school subject)

14. **complement/compliment**
    complement is a noun meaning that which completes or fulfills; *compliment* as a verb means to praise, and as a noun means a flattering remark

15. **conscience/conscious**
    conscience is a noun meaning the sense of right and wrong; *conscious* is an adjective meaning aware, able to think and feel, in the normal waking state

16. **council/counsel**
    council is a noun meaning an assembly; *counsel* as a verb means to give advice, and as a noun means an attorney (or anyone whose advice is sought)

17. **decent/descent**
    decent means proper or commendable; *descent* means a decline, a way down, a downward slope, and also ancestry

18. **desert/dessert**
    desert as a noun means a barren land, and as a verb means to abandon; *dessert* is the last course of a meal

19. **device/devise**
    device is a noun meaning a mechanical contrivance, a design; *devise* is a verb meaning to plan or scheme

20. **dyeing/dying**
    dyeing means changing the colour of something; *dying* means approaching death

21. **emigrate/immigrate**
    emigrate means to leave a country in order to live in another country; *immigrate* means to enter a country for the purpose of taking up permanent residence

22. **farther/further**
    farther means at a greater distance, and it refers to space; *further* means in addition to, and it refers to time, quantity, or degree

23. **formally/formerly**
    formally means in a formal manner; *formerly* means before or preceding

24. **heal/heel**
    heal means to cure; *heel* as a noun means a part of the human foot, a part of a shoe or sock, and as a verb means to furnish with a heel, or to walk closely at someone's heels

25. **its/it's**
    its is the possessive form of it; *it's* is a contraction of it is

26. **later/latter**
    later means after a period of time or after a previous event; *latter* means the second in a series of two (the opposite of former)

27. **lead/led**
    lead as a verb means to guide and as a noun means a type of metal; *led* is the past tense of the verb to lead

28. **lesson/lessen**
    lesson is a noun meaning an exercise designed to teach something; *lessen* is a verb meaning to make small

29. **liable/libel**
    liable means responsible; *libel* as a verb means to defame and as a noun means a malicious misrepresentation of someone

30. **lightening/lightning**
    lightening means making lighter; *lightning* means an electrical discharge in the atmosphere

31. **lose/loose**
    lose means to suffer the loss of something; *loose* as an adjective means unbound and as a verb means to release

32. **passed/past**
    passed is a tense of the verb meaning to move along or move by; *past* is a noun meaning time gone by

33. **peace/piece**
    peace means calmness, serenity, the absence of conflict; *piece* means a portion of something

34. **perfect/prefect**
    perfect means without fault; *prefect* means a type of official

35. **personal/personnel**
    personal means private or belonging to a certain individual; *personnel* means the staff of a company or an organization

36. **precede/proceed**
    precede means to go before; *proceed* means to advance or go ahead

37. **prescribe/proscribe**
    prescribe means to order or advise; *proscribe* means to forbid

38. **principle/principal**
    principle means a general rule; *principal* as an adjective means the first, and as a noun means a sum of money that draws interest or a chief official of a school

39. **quiet/quite**
    quiet means calm, silent; *quite* means entirely, completely

40. **respectively/respectfully**
    respectively means in a given order; *respectfully* means in a courteous manner

41. **rite/right/write**
    rite means a ceremony or ritual; *right* means correct; and *write* means to inscribe

42. **stationary/stationery**
    stationary means fixed, unmovable; *stationery* means writing materials

43. **strait/straight**
    strait is a water passageway; *straight* means not crooked

44. **than/then**
    than is a conjunction that compares; *then* is an adverb meaning at a given time

45. their/there/they're
their is a possessive pronoun meaning belonging to them; *there* is an adverb meaning in that place; and *they're* is a contraction of they are

46. threw/through/thorough
threw is the past tense of throw; *through* can mean in one side and out the other, or from end to end, or it can mean by use of, or completed; and *thorough* means carried to completion, omitting nothing, painstaking

47. to/two/too
to is a preposition meaning toward; *two* is the number 2; and *too* is an adverb meaning more than enough, more than average, or also

48. vice/vise
vice means sin, wickedness, or an undesirable habit; *vise* means a type of clamp

49. weather/whether
weather refers to the state of the atmosphere; *whether* means if

50. were/where
were is the past tense of the verb to be; *where* is an adverb meaning a place in which

51. whose/who's
whose is the possessive of who; *who's* is a contraction of who is

52. your/you're
your is a possessive pronoun; *you're* is a contraction of you are

Exercise 6.1 — Spelling

Identify the misspelled words in the following sentences, and then spell them correctly in the blank at the right or on a separate sheet. If the sentence contains no spelling error, write *C* in the blank or beside the number of the sentence on your worksheet.

1. We cannot except any more donations at this time. _____

2. I think your in that new play we saw last night. _____

3. Would you please advice my daughter about the available opportunities for post-secondary education? _____

4. She does not know weather to major in dentistry or medicine. _____

5. We cannot alter our rules on attendance and lateness. _____

6. There are to many cooks in the kitchen.

7. Josef was borne on July 1, Canada's birthday.

8. They're peace proposal was unacceptable to the Security Council.

9. Whoever they chose as a candidate must be acceptable to the election committee.

10. I'd rather sail through the Straight of Gibraltar than through the Straight of Hormuz in the Arabian Gulf.

11. He is thinking of dyeing these plain cloths a bright orange.

12. The holy rights of the Anglican Church are similar to those of the Catholic Church.

13. The formal recognition of his past accomplishments was the best complement he could have received.

14. Darlene is quiet strong for her size and weight.

15. Our city council is liable to overturn the school board's decision on further funding for school construction.

16. Smoking on campus is prescribed by our school's clean-air policy.

17. These immigrants come from one of the dessert countries along the Arabian Gulf.

18. Who's in charge of our personal department?

19. I do not know whether its Thursday or Friday.

20. May I have a peace of pie for dessert?

21. He looks too young and inexperienced to have lead soldiers into battle.

22. Please do not loose your temper when addressing city council tonight.

23. When did your legal counsel file the liable suit?

24. Can you exceed to her wishes with good conscience?

25. Who's in charge of the stationery department?

26. I don't know how the personnel department will adopt to his aggressive management style. _____

27. Do you know were the principal is right now? _____

28. Do you think that this coarse of study will help you obtain a decent job? _____

29. He has too many vises to be a prefect of discipline at our school. _____

30. We just passed the building cite for our new gymnasium. _____

Some Frequently Misspelled Words

absence	apologizing	commitment	desirable
accept	apparent	committee	despair
acceptable	appearance	comparable	desperate
accessible	approximate	comparatively	despised
accidentally	approximately	compelled	develop
accommodate	argument	competition	disappeared
accomplish	aroused	completely	disappoint
accumulate	arrangement	conceivable	disastrous
accustomed	athlete	condemn	dissatisfied
achievement	attendance	conquer	effect
acquaintance	basically	conscience	efficiency
acquire	becoming	conscious	eighth
address	believe	consequently	elementary
adequate	benefited	consistent	eligible
adjustment	bicycle	conspicuous	embarrass
adolescent	boundaries	continually	eminent
advantageous	bulletin	counterfeit	emphasize
advisable	bureau	courteous	enforceable
affect	calendar	curiosity	entrance
aggravate	candidate	deceive	environment
aisle	careful	decent	equipped
allot	cemetery	deficiencies	equivalent
altogether	changeable	definitely	especially
amateur	chargeable	delinquency	exaggerated
analyze	colonel	dependent	except
answer	commission	descend	excitement
anxious	commit	describe	exhausted

existence	lieutenant	prejudiced	serviceable
explanation	loneliness	preparation	similar
extraordinary	maintenance	prevalent	solemn
familiar	marriage	primitive	sophomore
fascination	mathematics	privilege	staring
February	miniature	probably	strength
foreign	mischievous	procedure	studying
fortunately	morale	proceed	succeed
forty	mortgage	professional	successful
fulfilled	necessary	professor	sufficient
government	niece	profitable	supersede
grammar	ninety	prominent	superstitious
grateful	noticeable	pronunciation	supplement
grievance	obstacle	psychology	suppress
guarantee	occasion	pursue	surprise
height	occurred	pursuing	surround
heroes	occurrence	quantity	syllables
hindrance	omission	quitting	synonym
humorous	omitted	receipt	temperament
hypocrisy	opportunity	receive	temporary
immediately	optimistic	recipes	thorough
immigrants	parallel	recognize	through
imminent	paralyzed	recommend	tragedy
importance	parliament	recurrent	transferred
incidentally	particular	reference	truly
independent	peaceable	referred	twelfth
indispensable	perceive	relieve	typewriter
inevitable	permanent	repetition	unanimous
influential	permissible	resemblance	undoubtedly
intelligence	perseverance	resistance	unnecessary
interesting	persistent	restaurant	usually
interfere	personnel	rhythm	varieties
interpreted	phenomenon	ridiculous	vegetable
interrupt	planned	satisfactorily	vengeance
irrelevant	possess	scarcely	vigorous
irresistible	possession	schedule	villain
knowledge	possibility	scissors	weird
laboratory	potato	secretary	wholly
legitimate	practically	seized	withhold
leisurely	precede	sensible	
library	preference	separate	
licence	preferred	sergeant	

CHAPTER SEVEN

Punctuating Effectively

Punctuation marks may be understood as signposts that guide readers through our written statements, or they may be compared to the verbal inflections we employ in speech. When we pause between statements, raise or lower our voices, or adjust the pitch, we are controlling the meaning of what we say. The same thing happens in written expression. When we punctuate properly we permit readers to follow our ideas and to respond to the stress we place on those ideas.

Punctuation, then, is our directive to our readers, informing them how we want them to read our prose. They will accept our control so long as we are consistent— so long, that is, as our ideas and statements flow in a steady and logical pattern. The omission or misuse of punctuation marks short-circuits this flow of ideas and causes readers to lose confidence in our ability to convey meaning. Thus proper punctuation permits us to place emphasis, to convey mood, and to marshal ideas.

A. MASTERING THE COMMA

Because commas serve more functions inside the sentence than any other mark of punctuation, they are the most difficult marks to master. But, when used properly, they tighten and clarify sentence structure, pace our readers through our thoughts, and substitute for the many important inflections that we employ to convey meaning in speech.

The comma's function may be divided into two general areas: (1) to separate internal sentence elements that otherwise would destroy clarity and confuse the reader, and (2) to set off parenthetical sentence elements that interrupt the flow of thought between words, phrases, and clauses.

1. Commas That Separate
(a) *Separating Independent Clauses*

When two independent clauses are joined by a coordinating conjunction (and, but, or), they must be separated by a comma.

> We mowed the lawn, but we failed to water the garden.

> The workers went on strike, and the citizens supported their demands.

Conjunctions that do not join independent clauses do not require commas.

> Depending on the weather, Mr. Robinson will *fly* or *drive* to his business meeting.
> (two verbs; no comma)
>
> The ball sailed *over the goalpost* and *into the stands*.
> (two phrases; no comma)
>
> We think *that he is breaking the law* and *that he will soon be caught*.
> (two dependent clauses; no comma)

(b) *Separating Elements in a Series*

A series consists of three or more words or word groups that have the same grammatical function in the sentence. When a coordinating conjunction joins the last two elements, a comma is placed before it.

> *Faisal*, *Bruno*, and *Elizabeth* were all invited to the school dance.
> (a series of nouns)
>
> My parents *shopped* in London, *dined* in Paris, and *skied* in Switzerland.
> (a series of verbs)
>
> The stray dog ran *down the hall*, *through the laboratory*, and *into my office*.
> (a series of phrases)
>
> We were told *that the test would be long*, *that it would be difficult*, and *that it would count towards our final mark*.
> (a series of dependent clauses)
>
> "*I came, I saw, I conquered.*"
> (a series of short, independent clauses)

Note: The comma may be omitted in a series when a conjunction is used to connect each element.

> Enrique *and* Tom *and* Andre all made the starting team.
>
> Please take off your coats *and* sit down *and* listen.
>
> For his birthday, I shall buy my younger brother a toy fire engine *or* a wind-up racing car *or* a picture puzzle.

(c) *Separating Coordinate Adjectives*

Two or more adjectives are coordinate when they equally modify the same noun or pronoun. To test whether or not adjectives are coordinate, reverse their order and place *and* between them. If they read intelligibly, separate them with commas.

The alert, energetic students passed the test.

The energetic *and* alert students passed the test.

The clear, cold mountain stream flowed near our camp.

The cold *and* clear mountain stream flowed near our camp.

Observe how the adjectives below differ from the coordinate adjectives:

She was wearing a tattered fur coat.

Aldo became an accomplished modern dancer.

If we try to reverse their order and insert a conjunction, the sentences become nonsensical, for the last adjective is too closely related to the noun.

She was wearing a fur *and* tattered coat.

(the word *tattered* modifies *fur* as well as *coat*)

Aldo became a modern *and* accomplished dancer.

(the word *accomplished* modifies *modern* as well as *dancer*)

(d) *Separating to Prevent Misunderstanding*

Some words and phrases must be separated from the rest of the sentence by a comma to avoid confusing—and sometimes amusing—the reader.

CONFUSING: Outside the crowd pressed against the police barriers.

REVISED: Outside, the crowd pressed against the police barriers.

CONFUSING: When basting Mother often covers the turkey with a cheesecloth.

REVISED: When basting, Mother often covers the turkey with a cheesecloth.

CONFUSING: At nine thirty students entered the dean's office.

REVISED: At nine, thirty students entered the dean's office.

Exercise 7.1 — Commas That Separate Independent Clauses and Elements in a Series

In the following sentences insert commas where you think they are needed. If you must place one or more commas in a sentence, write *W* in the blank to the right; if the sentence is punctuated correctly, write *C* in the blank. If you are working on a separate sheet of paper, rewrite the sentences and insert commas when you think they are necessary. If the sentence is correct, simply write *C*.

EXAMPLES: Tom, Joe, and Jim went to the show together.   W

We saw him enter the store, but we did not see him leave.   C

1. Monica has taken up the game of tennis but she still plays golf regularly. _____
2. I cannot decide whether to have tea or coffee with my meal. _____
3. My favourite fruits are oranges and grapes. _____
4. Our team won the game but we also lost our star fullback. _____
5. My college is not large but it does have high academic standards. _____
6. Milo Gomez, Bill Granger and Gino Tezza all graduated with high honours. _____
7. Her plane arrived late but she was still in time for the graduation party. _____
8. The rock concert was sold out but we managed to get standing-room tickets. _____
9. Quincy mowed the lawn and then ate his lunch. _____
10. Jamal is both intellectually astute and emotionally stable. _____
11. The pharmacist recommended Aspirin and cough syrup for my head cold but he did not tell me to use an antibiotic. _____
12. No one knew who turned out the lights and slammed the door during the poker game. _____
13. Yesterday I painted the bathroom cleaned out the shed fixed the toaster and bottled the homemade wine. _____
14. Liam was selected as a candidate for student government but his brother was passed over. _____
15. Consuela does not own a motorcycle or drive a car. _____
16. Did your brother ever have chicken pox or whooping cough as a child? _____
17. Helene is either a business owner or a physician or a trial lawyer. _____
18. My house is almost twenty years old but my car is only one year old. _____
19. Calgary is not only where I work but also where I was born. _____

20. My father is a carpenter and my uncle is an electrician. _____

21. Our English teacher told us to read good literature to keep a daily journal and to try to add new words to our vocabulary by looking up word meanings in a dictionary. _____

22. Macy visited Edmonton and Calgary and Vancouver last summer during her school vacation. _____

23. Mario and Jack were partners in our annual golf tournament but they do not often play together during the week. _____

24. She is neither a cheerleader nor a member of the school band. _____

25. Zelda, Nora, Marisa and Melinda all play soccer for our college team. _____

26. Please eat sensibly and exercise every day. _____

27. She is, I am certain, an honours student and her brother is the captain of the football team. _____

28. Don't forget to feed the cat turn out the lights and lock the front door before you leave. _____

29. Neither wind nor rain nor sleet will keep us from attending the championship hockey game. _____

30. Carrie, my cat, and Edgar, my dog, are not good friends but they are not mortal enemies, either. _____

Exercise 7.2 — Commas That Separate Coordinate Adjectives and Confusing Sentence Elements

Insert the necessary commas in the following sentences. When you add commas, place *W* in the blank to the right of the sentence. If the sentence needs no further punctuation, write *C* in the blank. If you are working on a separate sheet of paper, rewrite the sentences and insert the necessary commas. If the sentence is already correct, simply write *C*.

> EXAMPLES: The dark, chilly room was shut off from the rest of the house. __W__
>
> The large brown dog was pulling the small red sled. __C__

1. Without Gloria Tess would not have gone on a European vacation. _____

2. Dimitri has a small European car not a large American car.
3. The rainy dreary depressing Monday afternoon seemed to last forever.
4. Down below the men were working on the sewer line.
5. Our new home is large airy bright and cheerful.
6. Outside the rain poured down in heavy sheets.
7. My father bought a used electric hedge trimmer and a new fifteen-inch chainsaw.
8. Before ten nineteen shoppers were outside, waiting for the department store to open.
9. The sleek jungle cat pounced on the small antelope.
10. Our black and white Dalmatian swam after the brown and white ducks in our village pond.
11. The frigid snowy gloomy winter afternoon was a good time to read by the fire.
12. After jogging the team had to do forty push-ups on the stadium grass.
13. Up above the swiftly moving clouds were threatening rain.
14. While Sarah was sewing her orange and white cat jumped on her lap.
15. The hot humid sultry summer day was not what we expected when we planned our class picnic.
16. Conchita purchased a pink and white golf shirt and two dozen long-distance golf balls.
17. Our powerful rugged expensive four-wheel-drive utility vehicle was just what we needed for our camping trips.
18. While Millie was dressing her pet parrot flew onto her shoulder.
19. The flat desert landing strip was large enough to land a 747.
20. The loud raucous smoke-filled rock concert was a financial failure.

21. Inside the crowd cheered wildly for Mark McGwire.

22. Our large furry docile tabby cat sleeps in front of our fireplace.

23. After nine fifty people rushed into the stadium to claim their free baseball caps.

24. Mai Ling made a green silk dress and light blue slacks for her sister.

25. With Drake her German shepherd Wilma feels safe and secure.

26. Your large expensive gas-guzzling car will cost you more than you think to run and maintain.

27. Before bathing, Vincent always trims his beard.

28. Sheila's black and white terrier puppy is still not housebroken.

29. His parents are young tall handsome and rich.

30. However hard it is to maintain Herman refuses to sell his twenty-foot yacht.

2. Commas That Set Off

Certain parenthetical words and word groups are set apart because they interrupt the normal rhythm of the sentence. Most of these parenthetical elements occur within the sentence and are therefore set off by two commas; others, however, occur at the beginning or the end of the sentence and are set off by only one comma. But wherever these parenthetical expressions occur, they are set off from the rest of the sentence because they interrupt the flow of ideas or contain information unessential to the meaning of the sentence.

(a) *Setting Off Non-restrictive Modifiers*

A non-restrictive modifier is a phrase or clause that adds non-essential information to the core of the sentence. It may be deleted without altering the meaning of the sentence:

> John Williams, who wears red ties, is my best friend.

The fact that your best friend has a preference for red ties is irrelevant information; it does not restrict or qualify the basic sentence statement. Now consider this sentence:

> The man who wears red ties is my best friend.

Now the modifier is restrictive because without its information the reader would not know which man is your best friend (the one with the red tie); therefore, you cannot delete the modifier and still maintain the sense of the sentence. Remember, only modifying phrases or clauses with commas around them can be safely removed from the body of the sentence; those that do not have commas cannot be removed without affecting the meaning of the sentence. Thus, one is restrictive (no commas) and the other non-restrictive (two commas). Consider the following examples.

NON-RESTRICTIVE: The traffic cop, *with a whistle in his mouth*, guided the school children across the street.

RESTRICTIVE: The traffic cop with the whistle in his mouth is the one who guided the children across the street.
(The modifying phrase points out which police officer.)

NON-RESTRICTIVE: Cliff Jackson, *who has a bearskin rug on his floor*, is a famous Canadian trapper.

RESTRICTIVE: The man with the bearskin rug on his floor is a famous Canadian trapper.
(The modifying clause identifies the man.)

NON-RESTRICTIVE: The British Museum, *where Karl Marx did most of his research on economic theory*, is prized by scholars from all over the world.

RESTRICTIVE: The museum where Karl Marx did most of his research on economic theory is prized by scholars from all over the world.
(The modifying clause identifies the museum.)

The same distinction can be made about adverb clauses that end sentences. If the clauses contain essential information, they are restrictive.

NON-RESTRICTIVE: I plan to visit Spain, *where the weather is pleasant and the prices are low*.

RESTRICTIVE: I plan to visit Spain if the weather is pleasant and the prices are reasonable.
(The weather and the prices will determine whether or not you visit Spain.)

NON-RESTRICTIVE: Martin will try out for the basketball team, *although he is not even 180 centimetres tall*.

RESTRICTIVE: Martin will try out for the basketball team if he is tall enough.
(His height will determine whether or not he tries out for the team.)

NON-RESTRICTIVE: We are moving to Vermont in the fall, *when the leaves change colour.*

RESTRICTIVE: We are moving to Vermont when the leaves change colour.
(The clause contains precise information about when you are moving.)

(b) *Setting Off Appositives*

An appositive is a noun, along with its modifiers, that is closely related to another noun as an explanation: Jacqueline, the student; Joe, the barber; Fred, the postal worker. Since an appositive can also be restrictive and non-restrictive, it obeys the same comma rule as phrases and clauses do.

NON-RESTRICTIVE: Ms. Price, *the dean of students,* has been promoted to vice-president.

Bertrand Russell, *the famous twentieth-century philosopher,* often demonstrated for nuclear disarmament.

Observe the difference in the appositives that contain essential explanatory information. They are more obviously restrictive and therefore do not take commas:

RESTRICTIVE: My sister *Peggy* is arriving by train.
(explains which sister)

The number *seven* is considered lucky by many people.
(explains which number is considered lucky)

(c) *Setting Off Sentence Modifiers*

Commas set off parenthetical words and phrases that modify whole clauses and sentences. These modifiers are used for summary, emphasis, or transition; they give direction to the writer's ideas and often reveal the precise tone he or she wishes to convey. A partial list of the most commonly used modifiers is shown in the box below.

It is true, *nevertheless,* that the price of oil will increase next month.

He is, *by the way,* a straight "A" student.

After all, nobody is perfect.

However, if you do not agree, we will revise our plans.

Some Sentence Modifiers

accordingly	by the way	however
after all	consequently	in addition
also	finally	in fact
as a matter of fact	first, second, etc.	in my opinion
as a result	for example	in other words
as a rule	for instance	in short
at any rate	furthermore	indeed
besides	hence	meanwhile
moreover	on the other hand	therefore
namely	on the whole	thus
naturally	otherwise	too
nevertheless	perhaps	well
no doubt	personally	without a doubt
obviously	still	without question
of course	that is	yes, no
on the contrary		

Remember, when these modifiers occur in the middle of a sentence, two commas are needed to set them off.

> WRONG: We are, *on the whole* fairly well off.

> CORRECTED: We are, *on the whole,* fairly well off.

(d) *Setting Off Absolute Constructions*
Absolute constructions are verbal phrases that, although set apart from the rest of the sentence, cannot stand alone as complete statements. Like other sentence modifiers, they interrupt the flow of thought and modify whole clauses or sentences. Many of these phrases are idioms that are often used in speech.

> *Weather permitting,* we shall arrive on time.

> *Times being what they are,* we are lucky to be able to afford a vacation.

> She is, *to be sure,* a first-rate scholar.

(e) *Setting Off Contrasting Sentence Elements*
Contrasting elements are normally used for clarification, and they usually begin with the words, *not, yet,* or *but.*

> He suffered, *but survived.*

> Paul is an electrical technologist, *not an electrical engineer.*

> The sprinter ran swiftly, *yet gracefully.*

(f) *Setting Off Long Introductory Phrases and Adverb Clauses*
To ensure clarity, long introductory phrases and adverb clauses are set off from the rest of the sentence by a comma.

> *When the customers arrived at the store,* the door was locked.
> (introductory clause)
>
> *As the crippled plane landed,* the firefighters sprayed foam on the runway.
> (introductory clause)
>
> *After leaving the classroom,* we played basketball in the gym.
> (introductory phrase)
>
> *With such an abundance of fresh fruit and vegetables,* we shall have no trouble finding customers.
> (introductory phrase)

Note: Short phrases and clauses are set off by commas only if the sentence may be misread without punctuation.

> UNCLEAR: While I was bathing the dog jumped into the tub.
>
> CORRECTED: While I was bathing, the dog jumped into the tub.
>
> UNCLEAR: After running a cold shower was what I wanted.
>
> CORRECTED: After running, a cold shower was what I wanted.

(See pp. 97-99, "Commas That Separate.")

(g) *Setting Off Names in a Direct Address*
When a name or a title is used to address someone, it is set off by commas.

> May we continue, *Mr. Bradley,* when you are finished talking?
>
> We have loaded the ship, *Captain,* and now it is ready to leave the harbour.
>
> Complete your answer sheet, *Tom,* before you turn in your test booklet.

(h) *Setting Off Speakers Directly Quoted*
The words that identify the speaker of a direct quotation are set off by a comma. When inserted in the middle of a quotation the words are set off by two commas.

> The hockey coach said, "If you miss one more practice, you're off the team."
>
> "Follow me," ordered the general.
>
> "I think," remarked the defendant, "the sentence is too harsh."

108 *Writing Fundamentals*

Note: The words specifying who the speaker is are not set off if the quotation is indirect.

> The defendant commented that he thought the judge's sentence was too harsh.
>
> The coach told me that if I miss one more practice I will be off the team.
>
> The general ordered us to follow him.

(i) *Setting Off Echo Questions*
Echo questions are parenthetical expressions, usually occurring in speech. They may occur in the middle or at the end of a sentence.

> You were elected, *weren't you*, to the local school board?
>
> You are aware, *aren't you*, that jackets and ties must be worn to the ceremony?
>
> You live at home, *don't you*?

(j) *Setting Off Mild Interjections*
These are expressions that, although parenthetical, are not really exclamatory and therefore require no exclamation point.

> *My word*, it certainly is a dismal afternoon.
>
> *Heavens*, I do not have a clue to what you mean.
>
> *My, my*, you certainly have grown during the past year.
>
> *Well, well*, you have started the job already.

Exercise 7.3 — Commas That Set Off Non-restrictive Modifiers, Appositives, and Introductory Phrases and Clauses

Insert the necessary commas within the following sentences that have elements that are not properly set off. Write *W* in the blank to the right of each sentence you correct or on a separate sheet; if the sentence requires no further punctuation, write *C* in the blank. Or, rewrite the sentences that require commas, inserting them where necessary.

> EXAMPLES: Farmers who purchase new tractors will be given government subsidies.   C
>
> Playing with intensity, our team rallied and finally won.   W
>
> Paul Baker, our team captain, was awarded the game ball.   W

1. My sister who is a long-distance runner has just won the annual marathon race. _____

2. The chainsaw that I bought yesterday was stolen from my car trunk this morning. _____

3. When my brother arrived in Ottawa from Halifax our entire family met him at the airport. _____

4. Stan Myers who is my accountant just won a new car in the hospital lottery. _____

5. Before you jump to conclusions we must discuss our new investment plan. _____

6. Friday evening's seminar Technical Report Writing was rescheduled for Tuesday evening. _____

7. Teachers who fail to take attendance before each class will be placed on report for disciplinary action. _____

8. My brother Tom has just left for Vancouver. _____

9. Our local butcher who just recently won the Father of the Year award is being investigated for failing to pay his back taxes. _____

10. When I first saw my future husband he was playing Frisbee with my best friend. _____

11. Without a second thought Paula spent her last thirty dollars on a new pair of shoes. _____

12. Nathan Kepler the famous bowling champion will visit our college next week. _____

13. The new camper that my father just bought has defective brake lights. _____

14. Brian my best friend is a trial lawyer. _____

15. Her cousin Rachel is a fashion model in Montreal. _____

16. During yesterday's baseball practice our star pitcher hurt her left elbow. _____

17. Sales personnel who ignore customers' requests will be immediately terminated. _____

18. Our mayor Sheila Berg will not hold a press conference until next week. _____

19. Students who want to try out for the lacrosse team must report to the gymnasium at 3:00 p.m. tomorrow afternoon. _____

110 *Writing Fundamentals*

20. After due deliberation we find that we cannot accept your proposal. _____
21. Our city's new curling rink which cost the taxpayers over half a million dollars had to be rewired for new lighting fixtures. _____
22. Attila the Hun was both respected and feared by his numerous enemies. _____
23. Without our lead actor the show cannot go on. _____
24. The man who fixed our water heater has just been arrested for grand theft. _____
25. My favourite singer Céline Dion is appearing in Toronto next month. _____
26. After Kathy Chung survived the airplane crash she vowed never to fly again. _____
27. Our parish priest who used to be an all-star baseball player has agreed to coach our Little League baseball team. _____
28. While searching for her sister's wallet Clare found her old coin purse. _____
29. My aunt Helen the family legal expert has just changed her last will and testament. _____
30. The printer that I ordered through the mail last month has not yet arrived. _____

Exercise 7.4 — Commas That Set Off Sentence Modifiers, Absolute Constructions, and Contrasting Elements

Insert the necessary commas within the following sentences that have elements that are not properly set off. Write *W* in the blank to the right of each sentence you correct; if the sentence requires no further punctuation, write *C* in the blank. Or, if you are working on a separate sheet, rewrite the incorrect sentences and insert commas in their proper places.

EXAMPLES: On the contrary, we approve of your actions.   W

To be certain of a seat on the train, arrive at the station at least thirty minutes early.   C

She was a model, not a dress designer.   W

1. Our health clinic is in fact associated with our general hospital. _____
2. I am certain that we will be on time weather permitting. _____
3. She will surely repeat her victory of last year. _____
4. The new city arena is without a doubt the most modern in our county. _____
5. The machinists' union unable to muster a strike vote returned to the bargaining table. _____
6. The high-school football coach was disappointed not devastated by his team's loss last week. _____
7. Our school counsellor is absolutely terrific. _____
8. All things considered we were lucky to have survived the sixteen-kilometre march. _____
9. She should change her diet not her dress size. _____
10. However hard we tried we still could not score the winning goal. _____
11. Harriet's flight was delayed not cancelled. _____
12. The camping trip was I am certain scheduled for a week from Thursday. _____
13. I cannot be certain that her first name is Zelda. _____
14. We absolutely will not under any circumstances tolerate your uncooperative behaviour. _____
15. Leniency not revenge is a far more humane solution. _____
16. Ottawa is I am almost certain the capital city of Canada. _____
17. Nellie is a seamstress not a quilter. _____
18. Enid Gooch is certainly the brightest student in our class. _____
19. However long it takes we will find the missing evidence. _____
20. The building was finished on time notwithstanding the carpenters' strike and the late delivery of roofing material. _____
21. Without a moment's notice the tornado hit the trailer camp. _____
22. However much you want to succeed you cannot continue to ignore self-sacrifice and hard work. _____
23. The basketball player was 6'9" not 7'1". _____

112 *Writing Fundamentals*

24. We are indeed fortunate to have such an understanding mathematics teacher. _____
25. Without realizing his mistake Pierre continued to wax his skis with car polish. _____
26. The correct spelling of the word is "advice" not "advise." _____
27. I am certain that Marc took the wrong personnel folder to work. _____
28. Our new fire engine is blue not red. _____
29. *Forever Young* is the title of the new movie that opened last night at the Rialto Theatre. _____
30. I cannot in principle agree to your outlandish proposal. _____

Exercise 7.5 — Commas That Set Off Names, Speakers, Echo Questions, and Mild Interjections

Insert the necessary commas within the following sentences that have elements that are not properly set off. Write *W* in the blank to the right of each sentence you correct or on a separate sheet. If the sentence requires no further punctuation, write *C* in the blank. Or, if you are working on a separate sheet, rewrite the sentences that need commas, inserting them in their proper places.

> EXAMPLES: "Pay attention, Vincent, or you will miss important information." __W__
>
> "I haven't decided what dress to purchase," replied Anne. __W__
>
> Tom made the team, didn't he? __C__

1. Tell me Donn what time did you get home last night? _____
2. "Please don't worry about your father" said my mother pleadingly. _____
3. "We will not lose our next game" said the coach forcefully "because we will all focus on not making any dumb mistakes." _____
4. Yes Lisa I have already purchased our theatre tickets. _____
5. The English teacher did not say that she was going to give us an in-class essay tomorrow. _____
6. Oh my what a mess you have gotten us into. _____
7. They are certainly a fine dance troupe aren't they? _____

8. "Stop right there" shouted the police officer "and place your hands on top of your head."
9. My aunt Flora and her partner won the bridge tournament this year.
10. Wow what an impressive air show our city has organized.
11. "Your jeans are filthy" complained my mother.
12. Our plane is leaving at 10:00 a.m. isn't it?
13. Please wax the car Fred before you go to the concert.
14. "Many people in the world do not have enough to eat" said our guest speaker "and many more do not have access to clean drinking water."
15. We did not say that you could smoke in the restaurant.
16. Well now aren't you ashamed of yourself for overeating?
17. I think you know by now don't you that lying to the school counsellor doesn't make any sense.
18. Stop shouting Kim; we can all hear you.
19. The conductor announced that our train would not arrive in Winnipeg for another hour.
20. "I can't help it" announced Lorna "the pollen in the air is making me sneeze."
21. Well well you finally passed your physics course.
22. "Leave your books and personal belongings behind" said the vice-principal "when the fire drill begins."
23. No sir the men will not be late for roll call tomorrow.
24. "Wait your turn" said the woman "I was in the queue before you arrived."
25. You returned before 1:00 p.m. didn't you?
26. Please return your library book Phyllis before you are fined by the librarian.
27. "Don't drive too fast" ordered the park ranger.
28. Uncle Bill didn't leave yet did he?
29. I think everyone realizes don't they that we have a school holiday tomorrow?
30. Oh well nothing ventured, nothing gained.

Exercise 7.6 — Comma Review Exercise

Insert the necessary commas in the following sentences that have elements that are not properly separated or set off; then write *W* to the right of each sentence you correct. If the sentence needs no further punctuation, write *C* in the blank. Or, if you are working on a separate sheet, rewrite the sentences that require additional commas, inserting them where necessary.

> EXAMPLES: May we sample your fudge, Helen, before we begin our diet?   ____W____
>
> I practised diligently but failed to qualify for the team.   ____C____
>
> Kirk Bennett, who wears loud ties, has just purchased a pink suit.   ____W____

1. My mother is a stockbroker and my father is a physics professor. _____
2. If you want to play football you must lift weights jog eight kilometres every day and eat a high-protein diet. _____
3. The calm cool collected poker player won steadily all evening. _____
4. We did not see the new Broadway musical but we did manage to attend the opening of the art museum. _____
5. Like clockwork the mail carrier comes every day at 8:00 a.m. _____
6. Before ten forty shoppers were waiting for the shoe store to open. _____
7. Our community college which is located near the St. Lawrence River is having a Founder's Day celebration. _____
8. Cynthia DeFalco my hairdresser is visiting Rome next fall. _____
9. The bus that was in an accident just last week is now back on the road. _____
10. Before we leave for our annual vacation we must notify the post office to hold our mail. _____
11. The lead actor I am certain is related to a famous concert pianist. _____
12. "Yes Virginia there is a Santa Claus." _____
13. My brother Phil works in a law office. _____
14. Now now don't cry over spilled milk. _____
15. Our bus leaves for Banff tomorrow not next Tuesday. _____
16. The house that has green shutters is the one that was burglarized last month. _____

17. "I cannot understand" announced the teacher "how any of you passed the chemistry test."
18. Curtis enjoys playing the trumpet and singing off-key.
19. Please don't touch the railing Mike it has just been painted.
20. We are community-college students not university students.
21. No one told us that we had to attend Professor Davis' lecture on African history.
22. "Stand still" commanded the drill instructor "or you will be on extra duty for the rest of the week."
23. My uncle Francis arrived late stayed for dinner watched television until midnight and then asked to be driven home.
24. I am certain that she is the one who bought the computer.
25. My family's cottage which is located near Georgian Bay is now up for sale.
26. Before eating Danny always takes an antacid pill.
27. You're playing tennis this afternoon aren't you?
28. Because of the minor earthquake last week the covered bridge is undergoing structural repair.
29. Oh dear another busload of tourists is arriving.
30. Fix the water leak Ted before our water bill grows any larger this month.
31. "Do me a favour" said Clemenza with irony "don't do me any more favours."
32. With friends like that who needs enemies?
33. We should be arriving in Edmonton in another twenty minutes shouldn't we?
34. He graduated from the University of Ottawa not the University of New Brunswick.
35. The team members entered the stadium without their coach.
36. Sophie the night bartender went back to school to finish her computer-science courses.
37. Up above the clouds looked threatening.
38. If we do not win our next game the coach will have a heart attack.

39. The Lotus Garden which is our new Chinese restaurant won the Restaurant of the Year award from our Chamber of Commerce. _____

40. Terry O'Sullivan is without a doubt the best baseball player I have ever coached. _____

B. EMPLOYING THE SEMICOLON

The semicolon may be thought of as a small period because it tells the reader to stop briefly before proceeding. It balances as well as separates. It balances related independent clauses, and it separates a series of complicated word groups that contain commas.

1. Semicolons are used between structurally related independent clauses *not* joined by a coordinate conjunction.

   > Manuel plays hockey for pleasure; his brother plays hockey for money.
   >
   > We will not meet this afternoon; we will meet tomorrow morning.

   Make sure both clauses are independent before you place a semicolon between them. Semicolons are never used to separate dependent from independent clauses.

   > WRONG: After the doctor delivered the couple's baby; he smoked a cigar with the baby's father.
   >
   > CORRECT: After the doctor delivered the couple's baby, he smoked a cigar with the baby's father.

2. Use a semicolon before a conjunctive adverb that connects two independent clauses.

   > I did not study for Friday's test; therefore, I shall probably fail.
   >
   > She was ill when the skating competition took place; nevertheless, she came in second.

   The comma after the conjunctive adverb is now optional. If you wish to emphasize the adverb, use a comma; otherwise you may leave it out.

   Note: Be certain that the conjunctive adverb does, in fact, connect two independent clauses before you place a semicolon before it. If it is used parenthetically within the sentence, it must be set off by commas.

WRONG: We are still optimistic, but we are; nevertheless, prepared for the worst.

CORRECT: We are still optimistic, but we are, nevertheless, prepared for the worst.

WRONG: Our guests are due to arrive at noon; we should; therefore, light the barbecue.

CORRECT: Our guests are due to arrive at noon; we should therefore light the barbecue.

Commonly Used Conjunctive Adverbs		
accordingly	indeed	nonetheless
besides	instead	otherwise
consequently	likewise	then
furthermore	meanwhile	therefore
hence	moreover	thus
however	nevertheless	

3. Use a semicolon between independent clauses connected by a coordinate conjunction when the clauses are long and contain internal punctuation.

   The financial section of the daily newspaper, where the stock quotations are located, is read diligently by my employer; but I prefer the sports section, since my son is a minor-league baseball player.

   When I first went away to college, my father gave me an electric typewriter; but my sister, knowing my communication difficulty, presented me with an Oxford dictionary.

4. Use a semicolon to separate items in a series when each item contains two or more pieces of information set off by commas.

   My second-semester instructors are Mr. Boyle, English; Dr. Rudenko, physics; Ms. Cheung, mathematics; and Dr. Priestly, psychology.

   I was interviewed for my job by Elizabeth Gray, vice-president, marketing; by Tibor Horvath, vice-president, manufacturing; and by Jack O'Neill, sales manager.

5. Use semicolons before independent clauses introduced by the expressions *namely, that is (i.e.), for example (e.g.),* or *for instance.*

You must be alert at all times; that is, when an opportunity arises, grab it.

We think that he is highly qualified for the chairman's position; for example, he has more than ten years' teaching experience.

Exercise 7.7 — The Semicolon

Supply semicolons wherever required in the following sentences. Write *W* in the blank to the right of each sentence that needs a semicolon. If the sentence is properly punctuated, write *C* in the blank. Alternatively, write out the corrected sentences on a separate sheet.

EXAMPLES: Our camping equipment did not arrive on time; therefore, we must delay our trip.   W

The director of marketing, the vice-president of finance, and the chairman of the board are now meeting in the president's office.   C

1. Some of us are playing tennis others, though, want to go swimming. _____
2. I can work on my computer for hours time seems to fly when I am on the Internet. _____
3. Yolanda is an excellent chess player she wins nearly all of her matches. _____
4. We missed the last train to Toronto fortunately there was a late bus that we managed to take. _____
5. Jack Daniels, our vice-president, William Frankel, our treasurer, Clara Stuben, our personnel director, and Son Ming Chu, our systems analyst, all attended the management meeting yesterday. _____
6. Drive carefully I don't want to have an accident on this lonely road. _____
7. Our college does not have a faculty lounge we have to use the same lounge as the students. _____
8. Doris, Janet, Chris, and Maureen, the hairstylist, are all going to the fashion show this afternoon. _____
9. The workers were not being paid the minimum wage, therefore they decided to sue the company. _____
10. The ship could not stay afloat, however fast the crew pumped water from the hold. _____
11. Carrie is a vegetarian, and so is her older brother. _____

12. "Don't touch the paintings," warned the museum guide, "or we will have to end our tour." _____
13. Try studying more efficiently, for example, turn off the stereo when you are preparing for a test. _____
14. "How many kilometres is it from Kingston to Toronto?" asked the tourist. _____
15. Count your blessings the tornado did very little structural damage. _____
16. We are almost out of firewood perhaps it is time for you to cut some. _____
17. Because she has chosen to ignore our warnings on missing practice, we are therefore considering banning her from the school basketball team. _____
18. Slim, Kurt, Chubby, and Sandy all failed the final examination. _____
19. Please tell everyone that I will be late I have to take my car to the garage. _____
20. The snowstorm was extremely severe for this time of year, for instance, we were without power for thirty-six hours. _____
21. "I cannot wait any longer," said the bus driver, "because the storm is getting worse." _____
22. I know how difficult it is to quit smoking, nevertheless, you must try. _____
23. Stay on your diet, however much you enjoy chocolate. _____
24. After we returned home, we found a message on our answering machine that said we had won money, but, of course, it was just another misleading scheme, like others we have received in the past, to get us to take a magazine subscription. _____
25. I think you are wrong, Scott, Melanie Snyder is not a Canadian citizen. _____
26. The fruit market is out of avocados, but you can buy some at the corner grocery store. _____
27. We could not understand Professor Clark's lecture, it was too obscure and was irrelevant to our present course of study. _____
28. Some people love to exercise others enjoy a sedentary lifestyle. _____
29. Notwithstanding your considerable influence with the school board, you will not be re-elected as treasurer. _____
30. Warn the others, I'll close the shutters and get out the candles. _____

C. USING THE COLON AND THE DASH PROPERLY

The colon and the dash are alike in that they both introduce explanations and items in series, but they are unlike in that one is more formal and the other more emphatic.

1. The Colon

Do not confuse the colon with a period or semicolon. It separates sentence elements but does not complete a thought. Rather, it has an introductory function, informing the reader that a piece of sequential information or an explanatory statement will follow.

(a) Use a colon to introduce a long statement that summarizes, amplifies, or explains a previous statement.

> The registrar told us everything we needed to know: he informed us of classroom locations, test schedules, and library hours.
>
> The job was not up to my expectations: the salary was too low and the working conditions were substandard.

(b) Use a colon to introduce an extended or a formal quotation.

> Professor Matthews was outraged when he made the following declaration: "I am not now, never have been, nor ever will be a Communist."
>
> One of the most significant statements on human love was made by Erich Fromm: "The love for my own self is inseparably connected with love for any other human being."

(c) Use a colon to introduce a series of words, phrases, or clauses.

> I was told to purchase the following items: a hammer, a wrench, a saw, and a pair of pliers.
>
> The requests she made were these: she wanted her lunch delivered, her mail opened, and her office reorganized.

Note: Be sure that an introductory antecedent such as *the following, these*, or *as follows* precedes the colon. Do not place a colon immediately after a verb or preposition.

> WRONG: The meal consisted of: bread, cheese, meat, and tea.
>
> The workers demanded: more money, better pension benefits, and extended health care.

To correct these sentences you must either include an antecedent or remove the colon.

> The meal consisted of bread, cheese, meat, and tea.
>
> The workers made the following demands: more money, better pension benefits, and extended health care.

(d) Use a colon after formal salutations in business letters and between figures separating minutes and hours.

> Dear Ms. Taylor: Volunteers: 10:15-1:05

2. The Dash

The dash is one of the least understood—and therefore one of the most abused—marks of punctuation. Unskilled writers tend to use it indiscriminately as a substitute for other marks of punctuation. The dash has two general characteristics: it is informal and emphatic. It can substitute for a colon when a less formal introductory break is required, and it can substitute for a comma when a greater stress is needed to set off a parenthetical element. However, for other reasons than these two, the dash is not a proper replacement for a colon or a comma.

(a) Use dashes to set off a parenthetical series that already contains commas.

> My favourite meal—roast beef, corn-on-the-cob, and home-fried potatoes—is being prepared right now.
>
> Snow, sleet, and rain—that is what we drove through last night.

(b) Use dashes to indicate a break in thought too abrupt and severe to be set off by commas.

> He said that he would meet us near the ticket counter—or was it the newsstand?
>
> The antique car—it was in mint condition—sold for almost twenty thousand dollars.
>
> Matthew already paid for our tickets—at least I hope he did!

(c) Use a dash to make single words more emphatic.

> Money—that is all he thinks about.
>
> Our citizens ask for only one thing—freedom!

(d) Use a dash in place of a colon when you wish to present an informal series or explanation.

> Our arrangement is simple—she handles sales, and I oversee production.
>
> He had an amazing variety of clutter on his desk—old pencils, worn erasers, bent paper clips, and elastic bands of different sizes.

Exercise 7.8 — The Colon and the Dash

Each of the following sentences requires either a colon or a dash. Insert the correct punctuation mark within the parentheses; then, in the blank to the right, indicate your choice by writing *CN* for colon and *DS* for dash. Alternatively, rewrite the corrected sentence on a separate sheet and write either *CN* or *DS* beside it.

EXAMPLES: Dan wanted the following items from the stationery store (:) envelopes, writing paper, memo pads, and ink erasers.   **CN**

Ellen's new dog(—)a black and white terrier(—)made friends with us almost immediately.   **DS**

1. Tracy bought the following items at the department store ( ) stockings, lipstick, note pads, towels, shampoo, and toothpaste. _____

2. Our mayor made the following statement before he left office ( ) "My opponent rigged the election." _____

3. Trout fishing, long hikes in the woods, horseback riding along picturesque mountain trails, and daily tennis games ( ) these are the things we did on our holiday. _____

4. In *Time* magazine ( ) or was it *Maclean's* ( ) I read that a civil war is likely to break out in Bangladesh. _____

5. I won't tell you again ( ) put away your toys and make your bed. _____

6. She wants only two things in life ( ) power and security. _____

7. Last Friday ( ) or maybe it was Thursday ( ) our history teacher resigned his position. _____

8. The ski trip was a total success ( ) the weather was perfect; the snow pack was free of ice; the group lessons were fun; and the food at the ski lodge was delicious. _____

9. I think you know who made this statement ( ) "There's a sucker born every minute." _____

10. Their scoutmaster ( ) I think his name is Andrew ( ) slipped and broke his ankle last week. _____

11. My uncle ( ) he is a high-school principal ( ) won the Father of the Year award. _____

12. My brother, who is a coach, made the following statement to his Little League baseball team ( ) "Winning is a state of mind; it takes desire, sacrifice, and hustle." _____

13. Her sister lives and works in Halifax, Nova Scotia ( ) or is it Moncton, New Brunswick? _____

14. Sports and girls ( ) they are all my brother thinks about. _____

15. The food that we need for the picnic ( ) bread, meat, pickles, mustard, catsup, cookies, and fruit ( ) is being purchased by Dave and Michelle. _____

16. The hockey announcer made this ludicrous statement on the air ( ) "Fighting is a part of the game." _____

17. Greed and selfishness ( ) these two vices are ruining our country. _____

18. I don't know which computer to buy ( ) the laptop or the desktop. _____

19. I was told how to get ahead in the company ( ) arrive early and leave late. _____

20. The Internet ( ) that's all she talks about. _____

21. Maury's two dogs ( ) Coco and Max ( ) won honourable mentions at our annual dog show. _____

22. The following statement was made by a famous author ( ) "I write because I am not qualified to do anything else." _____

23. The latest hurricane ( ) I think its name was George ( ) devastated the southeastern coast of the United States. _____

24. We have only two choices ( ) put up or shut up. _____

25. My Aunt Maude's antique store has everything ( ) old furniture, clocks, canes, jewellery, glassware, silver, and pottery. _____

26. We drove through three provinces on our trip to the East Coast ( ) Ontario, Quebec, and New Brunswick. _____

27. Carter's golf bag is made of cowhide ( ) or is it horsehide? _____

28. The discount store is having a huge sale on computers ( ) IBM, Macintosh, Hitachi, and Compaq. _____

29. Yesterday Mr. Yablonski made this surprising statement ( ) "Do as I say, not as I do." _____

30. Running three kilometres every day ( ) nothing is better for your heart and lungs. _____

D. WHEN TO USE QUOTATION MARKS

1. Quotation marks are used to enclose direct quotations—the precise words that someone else has spoken or written.

    "I am not yet ready to step down," said the vice-president.

    "Yes, I expect to be elected," said the candidate, "and by a wide margin."

    During convocation the main speaker told us to "improve that which we find lacking and to promote that which we find ignored."

2. Do not use quotation marks to set off indirect quotations—someone else's statements paraphrased in your own words.

    The vice-president said that she was not yet ready to step down.

    The candidate said he expected to be elected by a wide margin.

    At our convocation the main speaker told us to go out into the world and make our mark.

Note: Commas and periods are placed inside the final quotation marks; colons and semicolons are placed outside them. All other punctuation marks are placed outside unless they are part of the quotation.

    He said, "I am leaving now, and I shall not return."

    The football player said that he enjoys the game because "I love the physical contact"; however, he insisted in his private life he was "as gentle as a lamb."

    The man shouted, "Help! Help! I'm drowning!"; unfortunately, no one was near enough to save him.

3. Use quotation marks to enclose words and phrases with special or restricted meanings, such as technical or colloquial terms, names out of context, or humorous expressions.

    When I questioned the test schedules, the student agreed by saying, "right on."

    I could tell that he must have watched many Hollywood gangster movies when he called his pistol a "heater."

    His major "architectural" accomplishment was building a fence around his property.

Note: Do not use quotation marks to apologize for slang expressions or inappropriate language. If you have to excuse an expression, you probably should not have used it in the first place.

WRONG: He is "lousy" with money.

She is a "witch," and that's all there is to it!

4. Quotation marks are used to enclose the titles of short published material such as articles in magazines and newspapers, short poems and short stories, chapters from books, and essays in a collection.

The article, "A Program to Feed the Hungry," was written by Charles Gordon in the October issue of *The Atlantic* magazine.

"For Esme with Love and Squalor" is the title of a short story by J.D. Salinger.

The first chapter of the novel I am reading is entitled "The Way I See It."

5. Use *single quotation marks* to enclose a quotation within a quotation.

On the first day of class our instructor said, "Before I became a teacher my best friend, who used to be a teacher, told me, 'Do not try to mould students to fit one pattern; they are individuals, not faceless products.' I try to remember that advice at the beginning of every semester."

The article in *Time* quoted the major as saying, "When I arrived in Vietnam, I was told by my superior, 'If you can't save the town, destroy it!'."

E. WHEN TO USE ITALICS

In printed material italics are a special slanted typeface. In typing or handwriting, italics are indicated by underlining.

1. Italicize the titles of published materials of a considerable length: books, magazines, newspapers, pamphlets, and long poems.

The *New York Times* gave a favourable review to John Fowles' latest novel, *Daniel Martin*.

Harper's is one magazine I read every month.

Paradise Lost, by John Milton, is considered England's greatest epic poem.

2. Italicize names of motion pictures, television programs, plays, and works of art.

My sister has seen *Gone With the Wind* seven times.

I think *A Long Day's Journey into Night* is Eugene O'Neill's finest play.

Picasso's *Guernica* is a painting about death and destruction.

126 *Writing Fundamentals*

3. Italicize the names of ships, trains, airplanes, and spacecraft.

> The *Queen Mary* sailed from New York on Friday.
>
> *Apollo Nine* was placed in orbit exactly on schedule.

4. Italicize foreign words and phrases that have not yet become an accepted part of the English language.

> She is known and admired for her *savoir faire*.
>
> The chef proudly presented the *pièce de resistance*.

Note: Some foreign words and expressions are now considered a part of the English language; for instance, "a la carte," "vice versa," and "status quo" no longer require italics. If you are in doubt as to what expressions to italicize, consult your dictionary.

5. Italicize words, letters, and figures used specifically as words, letters, and figures.

> When writing contracts, you should cross all your *t*'s.
>
> You must not confuse the word *perfect* with the word *prefect*.
>
> His *5*'s look like *3*'s, and his *l*'s look like *7*'s.

Exercise 7.9 — Quotation Marks and Italics

Supply quotation marks or italics (underscoring) wherever required in the following sentences. Then write *W* in the blank to the right of each sentence you correct. If the sentence needs no further punctuation, write *C* in the blank. Alternatively, write out the corrected sentences on a separate sheet.

> EXAMPLES: Jane Austen's <u>Pride and Prejudice</u> is one of the most well-constructed novels ever written.   C
>
> The expression "crow's feet" is used to describe the wrinkles at the corners of someone's eyes.   W
>
> She said that she would protect the children.   C

1. The autobiography that Carol just published is entitled Just Me Again.   _____

2. Relax, she said, no one knows where we are.   _____

3. The computer teacher asked us if we wanted to download the prime minister's speech from the Internet.   _____

4. The musical Chicago is now playing in Vancouver.
5. Who Wants to Know? is the title of the scathing editorial in our local newspaper.
6. Who wrote the book of short stories entitled The Moons of Jupiter?
7. My brother refers to Sharon Stone, the movie actress, as a babe.
8. The Heritage is the name of our apartment building.
9. 60 Minutes is my favourite television news program.
10. Kay's expression for the latest fad in fashion is au courant.
11. How do you install word-processing software on your computer? asked Jefferson.
12. I finally told Paul what he needed to do in order to upgrade his computer memory.
13. Macaroni's is the name of our new Italian restaurant.
14. Are there one or two t's in your sister's name?
15. The play As You Like It is my favourite Shakespearean comedy.
16. Keep trying for the athletic scholarship, advised Abdul Jabbar, because you certainly have the talent to play on the university team.
17. Swish is our nickname for Clifford, our star halfback.
18. Who starred in the movie The Way We Were?
19. What was the name of the television show that had Spock as one of its main characters?
20. Does the word altar refer to a part of a church?
21. What does the Italian phrase buena sera mean in English?
22. The violin is a very difficult instrument to learn how to play, said my piano teacher, Mrs. Califano.
23. The Holiday Centre is the name of our newest shopping mall.
24. Madeline told Jiminez that her father does not approve of their relationship.
25. Sailing to Byzantium is one of William Butler Yeats' most famous poems.

128 *Writing Fundamentals*

26. The term birdie in golf means a score of one under par on any given hole. _____

27. The magazine article entitled Our Canadian Wilderness was both entertaining and informative. _____

28. Our committee spokesperson announced to the gathering of faculty members that we do not have enough money to build a new cafeteria. _____

29. My German girlfriend calls herself my frauline. _____

30. My father's speedboat is named Sandy's Dream. _____

F. WHAT SHOULD BE CAPITALIZED?

Your decision to capitalize will be determined, to a great extent, by your need to be specific; for only proper nouns, which give specific names to people, places, and things, take capitals.

> PEOPLE: Aunt Rosa, Jack Horner, Mrs. McDonnell, Professor Visconti, Captain Smith
>
> PLACES: Asia, Germany, Quebec, Montreal, California, Los Angeles, Dry Gulch
>
> THINGS: The National Arts Centre, Delta High School, Twinkles Cup Cakes

Other words and abbreviations require capitals simply because of English-usage conventions and can best be learned through simple exposure—by reading. There are specific capitalization rules, though, and here are some that may help.

1. Capitalize the first word in every sentence and in every direct quotation.

    We lived in Moncton for five years.

    As the doctor was leaving, he said, "*Call* me if there is any change in the patient's condition."

2. Capitalize the names of cities, provinces, states, countries, and specific avenues, streets, and highways.

    Our children live in *Vancouver, British Columbia*, but our parents live in *Tampa, Florida*, in the southern part of the *United States*.

    We moved from *Maple Avenue* to *Regent Street*, two blocks from the *Mackenzie Throughway*.

3. Capitalize names of buildings, ships, mountains, bodies of water, parks, or geographical locations.

> The *CN Tower* is the highest free-standing structure in the world.
>
> We sailed from *Halifax, Nova Scotia,* to *Hamburg, Germany,* on *The Bremen.*
>
> *Mount Madison,* near *Heron Lake,* is where the light plane crashed last weekend.
>
> *Banff National Park* in the *Canadian West* is one of the most scenic parks I have ever visited.

4. Capitalize major words in titles of publications, except for articles (a, an, the), prepositions (at, in, on, of, with), and minor connectives (and, as, but, or).

> I have just finished reading Edgar Allan Poe's *The Fall of the House of Usher.*
>
> Our teacher assigned us *A Jest of God* to report on in class.

5. Capitalize branches of government, political parties, religious groups, and names of organizations and nationalities.

> The *Department of Labour* is staffed by members of the *Conservative Party.*
>
> The *Knights of Columbus* is a *Catholic* organization.
>
> The city of Kitchener, Ontario, has a large *German* community.

6. Capitalize names of schools and businesses.

> Lucille transferred from *Bruce Secretarial School* to *Packenham Community College,* but her girlfriend decided to remain at the *University of Ottawa.*
>
> The *A.J. Peterson Company* is the major supplier of our drill bits.

7. Capitalize formal titles and terms of family relationships when they are used as parts of proper names or as substitutes for proper names.

> *Professor Ohashi* cancelled her classes on the advice of her physician, *Dr. Allison.*
>
> *Uncle Pat* and *Aunt Ruth* have just returned from their Mexican holiday.
>
> *Father* and *Mother* are flying to Europe next week.

8. Capitalize abbreviations of titles and academic degrees used after proper names.

> Guy Savard, *Ph.D.*, Peter Reynolds, *M.D.*, and David Phelps, *P.Eng.*, are all former members of our fraternity.

9. Capitalize days of the week and months of the year, but not names of seasons.

> The first *Monday* in *April* is when the lottery draw will take place.
>
> The fall season usually ends in *October*, and then winter sets in.

10. Capitalize names of civic holidays and names having historical or religious significance.

> *Christmas* and *Thanksgiving* are my favourite holidays; but *Remembrance Day* has a special meaning for my parents, for my uncle was a casualty of *the Second World War*.
>
> The feast of *The Nativity* is celebrated by Christians throughout the world.

Knowing when not to capitalize is just as important as knowing when to capitalize, for if your use of capital letters appears arbitrary and haphazard to your readers, they may very well lose interest in what you have to say. You will avoid misplacing capitals if you remember the following rules.

1. Do not capitalize the name of a subject in school unless it is the name of a language or a part of a course with a designated title.

> Helen is studying *physics, chemistry, math,* and *English*, but Ramiro has concentrated his studies in the *Romance* languages of *French, Italian,* and *Spanish.*
>
> *Sociology* 110 and *Psychology* 212 are being offered in the spring semester.

2. Do not capitalize general geographical locations used as points on the compass unless they designate a specific geographical region.

> To find our cottage you must drive *north* for twenty kilometres, then *east* for three kilometres; we are located just *south* of Bear Mountain.
>
> The *Far East* is no longer a mysterious part of the world.

3. Do not capitalize the second part of a hyphenated word unless it is a proper name.

> We walked all the way from Thirty-*second* Avenue to Forty-*fifth* Street.
>
> Last semester we studied the *Franco-Prussian War*, and this semester we will be assigned term papers on the *Pan-American* Peace Conference.

4. Do not capitalize general terms of family relationships, titles that are not used as proper names, and the word *the* when it is not a specific part of a proper name or title.

> It is obvious that *the* United States was instrumental in organizing *the* North Atlantic Treaty Organization.
>
> I believe that my *father* and your *uncle* are related.
>
> Our family *doctor* and her husband are visiting their son, who is a *captain* in the army.

5. Never capitalize for emphasis.

> I want you to do it *now*. (not "I want you to do it *Now*.")
>
> Jack told Ed to "*cool it*." (not "Jack told Ed to *Cool It*.")

Exercise 7.10 — Capitalizing Correctly

In each of the sentences below, find the capitalization mistake and write the word correctly in the blank space at the right or on a separate sheet. If there are no mistakes, write *C* in the blank.

> EXAMPLES: I was born in kingston, Ontario, and still live there.   *Kingston*
>
> My aunt has just finished her nursing diploma at our local community college.   *C*

1. The best seafood restaurant in our town is called squids. _____
2. My wife's birthday is next monday, February 17. _____
3. Donald's Cousin is arriving by train this evening. _____
4. Katy has just been hired as a waitress at Carl's Home-Style restaurant. _____
5. Last Sunday my mother reminded us that we should not forget our Father's birthday. _____
6. Our computer-science instructor made the following statement to the entire class: "your computer is an intellectual tool, not a physical plaything." _____
7. Next semester I will study math, history, English, and french. _____
8. The community college in our city has two more campuses in other Ontario cities. _____

9. The Grand Canyon in the state of arizona is awe-inspiring. _____
10. There are at least two hundred african students attending our university. _____
11. Reedy creek is the name of our local golf course. _____
12. The town council has decided to postpone building the new ice arena until next year. _____
13. Sayed Nawri has just been awarded his canadian citizenship. _____
14. "Yes, Yasmin," she said, "The carpet is handwoven." _____
15. Our vice-principal used to teach a computer-science course at the University of New Brunswick. _____
16. Last semester I took a course in american history. _____
17. We played golf last Summer on one of the Thousand Islands. _____
18. Milovik was born in croatia, which is a part of Yugoslavia. _____
19. My best friend, Marvin Shore, works for an electronics firm on the outskirts of our town. _____
20. We are building our manufacturing plant just west of the central post office. _____
21. Our imported carpet was made in afghanistan. _____
22. Sharon's little girl still believes in the Easter bunny. _____
23. My wife's best friend was born down east. _____
24. The health clinic is located on Thirty-First Street, near Cary Road. _____
25. One of our parish priests is named father Ryan. _____
26. The new pastry chef is Australian, not spanish. _____
27. We were told that Mr. Moray, our gym instructor, is a christian Scientist. _____
28. where is Saudi Arabia located? _____
29. The heart patient was released by Dr. Sidlowski yesterday afternoon at three o'clock. _____
30. Midlothian secondary school won the track and field competition last Saturday. _____

G. THE FUNCTIONS OF THE APOSTROPHE

Apostrophes have three major uses: (1) they form the possessive case of nouns and indefinite pronouns; (2) they indicate the omission of letters in contractions; and (3) they form plurals of letters and numbers and of words that do not normally take the plural form. These three uses are detailed below.

1. To Show Possession

(a) Add both an apostrophe and an *s* to nouns that do not end in *s*.

> Tom's hat is still on the rack.
> (the hat of Tom)
>
> The car's windshield was cracked.
> (the windshield of the car)
>
> Where is the men's locker room?
> (the locker room of the men)

(b) Add both an apostrophe and an *s* or an apostrophe only to singular nouns that already end in *s*. As a general rule, if the extra *s* makes pronunciation awkward, the apostrophe alone is sufficient.

> The Tomkins' (or *Tomkins's*) garage is on fire.
>
> The Jones' (or *Jones's*) party was a huge success.
>
> Jesus' (but not *Jesus's*) Sermon on the Mount is preserved in the New Testament.

(c) Add only an apostrophe to plural nouns already ending in *s*.

> The room is cluttered with the boys' gym equipment.
>
> Ladies' purses were selling for half price.
>
> Our parents' car would not start.

(d) Add both an apostrophe and an *s* to indefinite pronouns.

> Everyone's name is on the guest list.
> (the name of everyone)
>
> Somebody's headlights are still on.
> (the headlights of somebody)

Note: Personal and relative pronouns in the possessive case never take apostrophes: its, hers, his, ours, yours, theirs, and whose.

> The flower is losing its (not *it's*) petals.
>
> Whose (not *who's*) sweater is on the table?

2. To Indicate Omission

Apostrophes are used in contractions to indicate the omission of letters or numbers.

> We don't (do not) have our textbooks yet.
>
> It's (it is) almost time to get ready, for the race begins at ten o'clock (of the clock).
>
> She's (she is) a member of the class of '63 (1963).

Note: Be sure to place the apostrophe where the omission occurs.

> They're (not *Theyr'e*) the best of friends.
> (they are)
>
> Isn't (not *Is'nt*) it time for the game to start?
> (is not)

3. To Form Plurals

Add both an apostrophe and an *s* to form the plural of letters, numbers, and words.

> Your *t*'s look like *r*'s and your *v*'s look like *u*'s.
>
> You write your 7's much differently than I do.
>
> There are too many *and*'s in your sentences.

Exercise 7.11 — The Apostrophe

Find the word with the apostrophe error in each of the sentences below, and write it correctly in the blank to the right or on a separate sheet. If the sentence contains no error, write *C* in the blank.

1. Its the same magazine article that you read last night, isn't it? _____

2. Can you tell me whose supposed to present the basketball trophy? _____

3. I am not sure if the ballpoint pen is her's or yours. _____

4. Were we invited to the Harris luncheon this Tuesday? _____

5. James brothers are all Ontario scholars. _____

6. The next time you turn in an essay, Bruce, please make sure that you dot your *i*'s and cross you're *t*'s. _____

7. Who's your seventh-grade teacher this semester? _____

8. Is that used car you bought a 97 Plymouth or Buick? _____
9. I think its about time that your sister returns her library book. _____
10. Her dogs bone is under the kitchen table again. _____
11. The summer of 98 was the hottest on record. _____
12. I cannot understand they're position on abortion. _____
13. Let's surprise my brothers friends before they leave. _____
14. I hope your satisfied with your impressive performance onstage last night. _____
15. There was something I've wanted to ask you're father, but it has slipped my mind. _____
16. My truck looks new, but it's engine is almost worn out. _____
17. The United States foreign policy is confusing to us Canadians. _____
18. I think that he'd already gone to the mens room by the time their dinner companions arrived. _____
19. There not supposed to cross the yellow line outside the employees' locker room. _____
20. I hope we're not scheduled to go to the soccer game this afternoon. _____
21. Rachel insists that her mother's recipe isn't lost, just mislaid _____
22. The new computer is either her's or his—not theirs. _____
23. My business partners are developing next year's budget. _____
24. Our swim teams loss was a complete surprise. _____
25. My 94 Lincoln has been driven only thirty thousand kilometres; it's still like new. _____
26. Her children's toys are spread all over the tables surface. _____
27. Did someone's car keys' fall down the subway grate? _____
28. Is this book yours or mine? _____
29. Mr. and Mrs. Broderick's son owns three drugstores in our city. _____
30. The motorcycle is our's, not hers. _____

H. THE DISTINCT USES OF PARENTHESES AND BRACKETS

Both of these marks of punctuation have a very restricted use and therefore should be used sparingly. There are few occasions in formal writing when you will be required to use parentheses or brackets, but when you do use them be sure you know the precise function they serve.

1. Parentheses

Parentheses are employed only to set off non-essential and independent elements. The material enclosed within parentheses usually contains explanatory or clarifying information outside the main idea (thought) of the sentence. Remember, parentheses de-emphasize. Thus, if you want to stress a parenthetical sentence element, use dashes—not parentheses.

(a) Parentheses are used to enclose explanations or clarifications that are separate from, and irrelevant to, the essential meaning of the sentence.

> We are alarmed at the high addiction rate (75%) of the new tranquillizing drug.

> Our instructor told us that the results of our English examination were very promising (our test scores were among the highest in the province) and that he expects us to do even better next time.

> The city failed to live up to its agreement with the sanitary engineers (formerly known as garbage collectors), and now they are threatening to strike.

(b) Parentheses are used to enclose numbers or letters that enumerate items in a series.

> We asked for the following benefits in our contract negotiations: (1) flexible working hours, (2) a company dental plan, and (3) two more vacation days a year.

> When the new recruits arrived, they were told to (a) get their flu shots, (b) report to the testing room, and (c) turn in their civilian clothes.

(c) Parentheses are used to enclose dates of birth and death, and of significant historical events.

> William Shakespeare (1564-1616) is considered by many to be the greatest dramatist of any age.

> The American Revolution (1776) marked the beginning of a unique political vision of human freedom.

Chapter 7 / Punctuating Effectively **137**

Note: All the punctuation normally required for the sentence is placed outside the closing parenthesis.

> As soon as I arrived (late in the afternoon), I called a meeting of all the executives.
>
> I came as quickly as I could (I broke all speed limits); however, I was not in time to prevent the company takeover.

2. Brackets

Do not confuse brackets with parentheses. Brackets have only *one* use: they enclose editorial insertions.

(a) Brackets are used in quoted material to enclose editorial comments or corrections.

> "Our citizens can no longer tolerate a 10% unemployment rate. [The annual unemployment figures were 8.5%.] We must create jobs in the public sector of our economy."
>
> "We entered the city of Toledo [Spain] from the south."

Note: In quoting you may sometimes find it necessary to use *sic* (meaning *thus*) to inform the reader that a factual or spelling error belongs to the quotation, and not to you.

> "On December 8, 1941 [sic] Pearl Harbour was attacked by the Japanese."
>
> "There are no heroines or villians [sic] in our play."

Exercise 7.12 — Parentheses and Brackets

In the following sentences place either parentheses or brackets around the italicized expressions. Then, in the blank to the right, indicate your selection by writing *PR* for parentheses and *BR* for brackets.

> EXAMPLES: The anniversary of the dropping of the atomic bomb on Hiroshima (*August 6, 1945*) is still marked by the Japanese.   PR
>
> "We will never surrender; we will fight to the very last man!" [*The author surrendered to the enemy two days after making this statement.*]   BR

1. Mario Ben Venisti *the famous Italian hairstylist* was on the airplane that crashed into the sea last week.   _____

2. Jack Weston *1942-1998* was our town's mayor for twenty years. _____

3. Vanessa Massimini *she was a famous Italian movie star in the 1930s* was a member of the Italian resistance during the Second World War. _____

4. The Mafia don *also known as The Godfather* died yesterday of natural causes. _____

5. "The Sears Tower, just outside of Chicago, has been sold to a consortium of Japanese businesses." *The writer needs a geography lesson; the Sears Tower is in the heart of Chicago.* _____

6. "The Calgary Stampeders hockey team *sic* won its fifth game in a row last night." _____

7. Our company had a substantial increase *40 percent* in profits last year. _____

8. The text of one of Ernest Hemingway's most popular novels *The Sun Also Rises* is being read in its entirety on one of our local FM stations. _____

9. Don't forget that you have a series of errands to run before you leave for the cottage: *1* pick up the laundry, *2* buy grass seed and lawn fertilizer, *3* drop off the house keys to Aunt Rachel, and *4* fill up the car with gasoline. _____

10. "One should not go to the top of the CM Tower *sic* in Toronto on a foggy day." _____

11. My grandmother *1925-1990* worked as a nurse until she died. _____

12. "The Persian Gulf is where the American aircraft carrier is on patrol." *The more acceptable name for that body of water is the Arabian Gulf.* _____

13. Last Canada Day *July 1* we went on a picnic in St. Lawrence Park. _____

14. "The home-run race between Mark McGwire and Sammy Sossa *sic* was the most exciting sports competition of 1998." _____

15. "Our inflation rate last year was negligible." *It was actually 1.6 percent.* _____

16. Her instructions were explicit: *a* assemble in the college parking lot, *b* check to see that we have the necessary provisions for our hiking trip, *c* collect our lunches in the school cafeteria, *d* wait for the bus at the southeast corner of the lot. _____

17. Zeke Polonski *the famous hockey player* is now a sports announcer on the radio. _____

18. "Our unemployment rate is the lowest it has been for twenty years." *The speaker is mistaken; the actual number is twelve years.* _____

19. "Margaret Lawrence *sic* is one of my favourite Canadian novelists." _____

20. Our Riverfest celebration *July 8 and 9* this year was the most successful we have ever had—more than twenty thousand people attended. _____

I. THE USES OF THE HYPHEN

Hyphens are generally used to write compound words and to divide words between syllables at the end of a line. The conventions for using hyphens in forming compound words change quickly, and therefore no hard and fast rules exist for their use. The most prudent procedure is to consult a dictionary before deciding to use a hyphen for either compound words or syllable breaks.

Although hyphenation rules lack uniformity, there are some stable guidelines that will help you use hyphens with a high degree of consistency.

1. Use hyphens to join two- and three-word modifiers when they precede a noun.

    EXAMPLES: *well-dressed* woman, *warm-blooded* animal, *do-it-yourself* repair manual

    But omit the hyphen if the first word of the compound is an adverb ending in *ly*.

    EXAMPLES: a *frequently called* number, a *happily married* man, a *poorly done* essay

2. Use hyphens to avoid ambiguous expressions or an awkward combination of letters before and after root words.

    EXAMPLES: *four-week-old* or four *week-old* puppies; *twenty-odd* professors or twenty odd professors; *re-cover* or recover; *re-form* or reform; *re-elect, re-invent*

3. Use hyphens for compound numbers from twenty-one to ninety-nine. Also, hyphenate fractions that are spelled out.

    EXAMPLES: *thirty-eight, eighty-seven, one-third, three-fifths, one-sixth*

140 *Writing Fundamentals*

4. Use hyphens with written-out compounds when they indicate time.

   EXAMPLES: *twelve-thirty, five-fifteen, two-twenty*

5. Use hyphens with prefixes and suffixes under the following conditions:
(a) Hyphenate all words with the prefixes *self, all*, and *ex* (when *ex* means "former"); also with the suffixes *elect* and *designate*.

   PREFIXES: *self-serve* food counter, *self-appointed* treasurer, an *all-inclusive* financial report, an *all-familiar* situation, (*ex* as "former") e*x-partner, ex-wife, ex-parliamentarian*

   SUFFIXES: *secretary-elect, president-elect, ambassador-designate, chairperson-designate*

(b) Use hyphens between prefixes and proper nouns.

   EXAMPLES: *pre-Cambrian* shield, *all-Canadian* football player, *mid-January, anti-Christian*

6. Use hyphens between letters and numbers when they substitute for the prepositions "to" or "through."

   EXAMPLES: pages *73-67*, June *20-25*, *A-M* and *N-Z*, *Montreal-Windsor* rail corridor, *London-New York* air route

7. Use hyphens in some compound words that indicate family relationships.

   EXAMPLES: *sister-in-law, father-in-law, great-grandfather*; but not in words like "*grandmother*," "*grandchildren*," or "*stepfather*"

Exercise 7.13 — The Hyphen

Insert hyphens wherever required in the following sentences. Then write *W* in the blank to the right of each sentence you correct. If the sentence is already correct, write *C* in the blank. You may consult your dictionary if necessary.

1. The plumber told us that he had to realign our water pipes before he could install our new water heater. _____

2. We just discovered that the money in our pension fund had been misappropriated. _____

3. I think twenty six people out of forty voted to increase next year's budget. _____

4. Most gasoline stations today have self service pumps. _____

5. My twelve year old nephew has just joined a chess club. _____

6. Our first snowstorm this year occurred in mid October. _____

7. Her month old baby is already trying to crawl. _____

8. Farida's car is at least nine years old. _____

9. Yuri Ganikov has always been anti Fascist. _____

10. Charlene is an above average law student. _____

11. We are scheduled for the twelve thirty lunch period. _____

12. The annual trade show is scheduled for June 10 12 at the municipal auditorium. _____

13. Last year's Christmas decorations will have to be reused, since our budget for decorations has been cut again. _____

14. The food and clothing that we collected for the poor are more plentiful this year. _____

15. The hotel that we stayed in last night had in house movies. _____

16. Let's reestablish our position as the number one basketball team in our league. _____

17. The pollution control department did a better than average job this year. _____

18. Both my grandmother and grandfather are in their eighties. _____

19. The Toronto Vancouver flight was two hours late. _____

20. My stepbrother no longer lives at home. _____

J. END PUNCTUATION—THE PERIOD, QUESTION MARK, AND EXCLAMATION POINT

1. The Period
(a) Periods are most commonly used to mark the end of a sentence that makes a statement or issues a command.

> I purchased my notebook in the bookstore.
>
> Don't trip over the step.

142   *Writing Fundamentals*

(b) Periods are used to mark the end of an elliptical element that functions as a transitional expression or as a short answer to a question.

> Now, *to get down to business.*
>
> "You are going, aren't you?" "*Of course.*"
>
> "Do you want to rest?" "*Yes.*"

(c) Periods are used to mark the end of polite commands and requests that are phrased as questions.

> May we hear from you in the near future.
>
> Would you mail this letter for me after lunch.
>
> May I request your attention.

(d) Periods are used after most abbreviations.

> Mr.   Dr.   Ph.D.   a.m.   f.o.b.   mfg.

Note: Many abbreviations composed of capitals and representing single initials or organizations do not require periods.

> RCA   UAW   TWA   NATO   CBC   RCAF

(e) Three periods are used within quotations to indicate the omission of words; four periods are used to indicate word omissions at the end of a sentence either within the quotation or at the end of the quotation (the last of the four periods is treated as the end punctuation of the sentence).

> She replied, "Our last quarter's financial statement . . . reflects a loss of revenue over the previous quarter." (Omitted passage: "prepared by our accounting department . . . .")
>
> "We have not yet found the money. . . . " (Omitted passage: "that was lost yesterday.")
>
> "Events followed one after the other. . . . We were always kept busy." (Omitted passage: "with amazing frequency.")

Note: These series of periods, known as ellipsis marks, take one typewriter space between each period.

2. The Question Mark

(a) Question marks are used after all direct questions.

> What do you mean?
>
> The judge asked, "Are you ready to present your case?"

(b) Question marks are used after elliptical words and phrases expressed as questions.

> Where shall we meet you? *In front of the bank?*
>
> You managed to complete all the work. *How?*
>
> You want me to get you a wrench. *What for?*

3. The Exclamation Point
(a) Exclamation points should be used only to express strong feelings or surprise.

> Fire!   Help me!   Run for your life!

Note: Do not overuse exclamation points. When they are used too frequently for emphasis they lose their effectiveness.

> WRONG: Well! Well! You finally arrived!
>
> CORRECT: Well, well, you finally arrived.
>
> WRONG: Oh! I didn't expect you!
>
> CORRECT: Oh, I didn't expect you.

Your common sense will usually tell you how much emphasis an expression requires.

Exercise 7.14 — Periods, Question Marks, and Exclamation Points

Supply periods, question marks, and exclamation points wherever required in the following sentences. Then write *W* in the blank to the right of each sentence you correct. If the sentence is properly punctuated, write *C* in the blank. Alternatively, rewrite corrected sentences on a separate sheet.

> EXAMPLES: Will you please stop that noise?   W
>
> Look out for the falling rock!   W
>
> Why haven't you stopped smoking?   C

1. Please stop repeating yourself; it is an annoying habit!   _____

2. Would you please find the janitor? I forgot the key to my office door.   _____

3. 8:30 p m is too late to have dinner.   _____

4. Will you pick up the guest speaker this afternoon.   _____

144 *Writing Fundamentals*

5. I get all the world news from our national CBC station. _____
6. Mrs Parker thinks that her new IBM computer is wonderful. _____
7. Will you please be quiet while I am talking? _____
8. Well! Our team finally won its first game. _____
9. What time is she expected to arrive? At nine o'clock. _____
10. Clarence is enrolled in a Ph D program at the University of British Columbia. _____
11. Watch out; the scaffolding is falling. _____
12. Fitch Mfg and Bryson Inc are discussing a merger. _____
13. Please watch your step as you enter the elevator! _____
14. Is CTV broadcasting the hockey game at 8:00 p.m. _____
15. Marsha apologized to Evelyn, didn't she? _____
16. Watch out. The building is collapsing. _____
17. You should ask her if she is married, divorced, or single? _____
18. Mrs. Tonka, Mr. Bradley, and Dr Towndrow are meeting at 12:30 p.m. to discuss the new zoning laws for the medical centre. _____
19. Please be careful! You'll spill your coffee if you walk too fast! _____
20. Did the plumber ask if you had flood insurance. _____

Exercise 7.15 — Punctuation Review Exercise

Supply all necessary punctuation in the following sentences. Then write *W* in the blank to the right of each sentence you correct. (There are no comma errors, so do not add or subtract commas.) If the sentence needs no further punctuation, write *C* in the blank. Alternatively, rewrite corrected sentences on a separate sheet.

> EXAMPLES: My supervisor told me to purchase the following items: safety shoes, canvas gloves, and welding goggles.   *C*
>
> "No, Steve," said Helen," I cannot help you with your work; you must do it yourself."   *W*

1. Please find out when we should leave for the airport then call me at home with the answer. _____

2. Carlos and his partner her name is Jennifer came in second in the doubles competition at our annual tennis tournament. _____

3. Who was the person who said the following "You can't fight city hall"? _____

4. Tim was not fatigued, although the rest of us were exhausted. _____

5. The party organizers Ben, Connie, Eddie, and Karim did a wonderful job. _____

6. Hockey that's all my two sons think about. _____

7. Don't forget your dictionaries, said the English teacher, you will be able to use them for your test tomorrow. _____

8. The term for using cocaine in a cigarette, I think, is smoking crack. _____

9. The Toronto Star had a very interesting editorial page yesterday. _____

10. What prompted Fred to change his major from english literature to chemical engineering? _____

11. Tanya failed the Geography test; however, she will be given an opportunity to rewrite it next Tuesday. _____

12. Behave yourselves at the rock concert tonight! _____

13. The name of our new domed stadium is the Queen Dome. _____

14. I think NASDAQ is the name of a major stock exchange. _____

15. Danielle earned her M Sc in computer science. _____

16. So! You finally bought a luxury car! _____

17. Simon Granz, vice-president Graden O'Leary, treasurer Paula Carmichael, financial planner and Greta Schuman, personnel manager are now meeting with the company president, Doris Neil. _____

18. Do you think that its too late to make amends? _____

19. Jack Hunt asked the golf pro if he could have a putting lesson. _____

20. Ida's mother named her new compact car Martina. _____

21. The Taj Mahal is India's most famous tourist attraction. _____

22. When Summer Comes is the name of a short story in Martha's latest book, entitled *Summer Tales*. _____

23. "I will never leave my office because of a personal financial problem." The next day the mayor was charged with embezzlement and resigned.
24. Did Margaret Atwood write The Handmaid's Tale?
25. We have not been paid for our work to date, and therefore will not complete the job until we are paid in full.
26. Juan refers to large cigars as stogies.
27. Do you believe that theyre going to fulfill their part of the bargain?
28. Sam is strong and honest Reese is slim and sly.
29. My brother will study history, mathematics, sociology, and spanish next year.
30. The New York musical Rent is coming to the National Theatre in Ottawa next month.
31. "Keats is my favourite Irish poet." The writer has confused Keats with Yeats.
32. Sadler Inc and Tamarack Mfg both make aluminum products.
33. Why can't Cloris maintain a higher grade point average.
34. My three cats Mina, Claude, and Silvia have to be placed in a kennel for a week because my cat sitter is ill.
35. Did Dr Chang perform the heart surgery on your father?
36. "Last summer my family camped along the Cabbott Trail sic in Nova Scotia."
37. Keep away. Gas is leaking.
38. Two Gentlemen of Verona is my favourite Shakespearean comedy.
39. I think Morris asked Ellen if she would marry him?
40. The real estate agent recommended a pre inspection on the house.

CHAPTER EIGHT

Choosing the Right Words

To write clear, precise prose we must use the English language efficiently. That means our words and phrases should be properly positioned and should clearly denote our intended meaning. When we fail to write with precision, words lose their flavour, sentences fail to couch ideas, and the vitality of our thoughts dissipates into verbiage; invariably our written messages become boring, trite, pretentious, and even unintelligible.

Faulty diction is the term we use to describe language that is both inflated and inappropriate. Although many of our diction errors overlap, all faulty diction is either wordy or imprecise or both. Also, there are certain stock words and expressions that we tend to overuse. These problems can be discussed under the following headings: *clichés, jargon, wordiness,* and *redundancy*. A number of common usage mistakes, including grammatically incorrect words and phrases, are listed in the glossary of usage and diction on pages 158-171.

A. KEEPING YOUR LANGUAGE FRESH: CLICHÉS TO AVOID

Clichés, also referred to as trite or hackneyed expressions, are catchphrases that have lost their vitality from overuse. Some are dull litanies of dubious wisdom that substitute for fresher, more precise expressions, but all are excuses for originality that prevent us from expanding our vocabulary and refining our thinking. Think of a deflated balloon and you will understand how flaccid clichés appear to a literate reader. Unfortunately, they seem to be increasing each year. Here are some of the most awkward clichés; there are, of course, many more:

1. a chip off the old block
2. after all is said and done
3. all things being equal
4. any shape or form
5. apple of one's eye
6. at a loss for words
7. at the crack of dawn
8. bark up the wrong tree
9. better late than never
10. bite the bullet
11. blind as a bat
12. bolt out of the blue
13. bring to a head
14. burn the midnight oil

148 *Writing Fundamentals*

15. busy as a bee
16. call a spade a spade
17. cart before the horse
18. chip on one's shoulder
19. cool as a cucumber
20. diamond in the rough
21. different as night and day
22. doomed to failure
23. drop in the bucket
24. eager beaver
25. easier said than done
26. face the music
27. few and far between
28. fly off the handle
29. follow in the footsteps of
30. gentle as a lamb
31. get cold feet
32. get down to brass tacks
33. happy as a lark
34. hit the nail on the head
35. if and when
36. in the nick of time
37. it goes without saying
38. knows the ropes
39. last but not least
40. left holding the bag
41. let sleeping dogs lie
42. like talking to the wall
43. little bundle of joy
44. lock, stock, and barrel
45. long arm of the law
46. look a gift horse in the mouth
47. met his/her maker; passed away
48. nipped in the bud
49. on easy street
50. out on a limb
51. par for the course
52. pay through the nose
53. perfectly clear
54. piece of my mind
55. ripe old age
56. see eye to eye
57. see the light
58. ships that pass in the night
59. sight for sore eyes
60. skin of my teeth
61. slowly but surely
62. spill the beans
63. stick to your guns
64. strike while the iron is hot
65. take a rain cheque
66. take the bull by the horns
67. tale of woe
68. talk turkey
69. the last straw
70. this day and age
71. tighten our belts
72. time is money
73. toe the line
74. to make a long story short
75. to the bitter end
76. tough nut to crack
77. vicious circle
78. weather the storm
79. wet behind the ears

Exercise 8.1 — Detecting Clichés

Correct the following sentences by replacing the clichés with more precise and vigorous expressions of your own.

> EXAMPLE: It is as clear as night and day that we must bring our deliberations to a head.

> CORRECTION: It is obvious that we must conclude our deliberations.

1. We must take the bull by the horns and get down to brass tacks.

2. It goes without saying that she is planning to buy our company—lock, stock, and barrel.

3. Our crew escaped the fire by the skin of our teeth because the crew captain remained cool as a cucumber.

4. Just remember that time is money, so we should start our business trip at the crack of dawn.

5. I don't want to spill the beans, but Charles got cold feet when he was confronted by the long arm of the law.

6. Magda put the cart before the horse when she decided to give us a ballpark figure on her beachfront property.

7. The business partners did not see eye to eye, so they decided to bail out of their partnership agreement.

8. We nipped his proposal in the bud because it would have cost our company an arm and a leg.

9. Katya was a sight for sore eyes when she stepped off the plane.

10. Let's keep him at arm's length while we consider his job application.

11. The news came like a bolt out of the blue that our business venture was doomed to failure.

12. Jenkins received money under the table during the election campaign.

13. Erin's mother flew off the handle when she was told that Erin was going to have a little bundle of joy.

14. Our accountant knows the ropes, so let's give him a little elbow room.

15. Penelope's mother lived to a ripe old age because she always remained busy as a bee.

16. Donald is following in the footsteps of his successful father, who always worked like a dog.

17. If we tighten our belts we can weather this financial storm.

18. My father met his maker at the ripe old age of eighty-six.

19. Donna told us a tale of woe when she was asked to pay her debts.

20. His reluctance to strike while the iron is hot was par for the course.

Exercise 8.2 — Changing Clichés to Fresh Expressions

Fill in the blanks with ten more clichés from the media or from your daily conversations, then correct them by writing ten sentences with fresher, more original expressions. Alternatively, write your list of clichés and your improved sentences on a separate sheet.

1._____ 6._____
2._____ 7._____
3._____ 8._____
4._____ 9._____
5._____ 10._____

1._____
2._____
3._____
4._____
5._____
6._____
7._____
8._____
9._____
10._____

B. MAKING YOUR WRITING PRECISE: WATCH JARGON

We use clichés when we rely on time-worn expressions to convey our meaning, but we use jargon when we turn to unusual or technical language to impress or mislead. In the most literal sense, jargon is private language, usually developed within particular institutions, disciplines, or professions. Many jargon expressions have legitimate meanings within a restricted context. For instance, a computer "run" adequately describes a computational process within the computer industry, and the term "bottom line" may be a serviceable expression in an accounting office; but when those terms and others like them are used in everyday language, they lose their legitimacy and become awkward and overbearing:

> Would you *run through* your explanation once again so that we can come to the *bottom line* of your proposal?

In common English this sentence would look something like this:

> Please repeat your explanation so that we can understand the point of your proposal.

In short, when used outside their proper context, jargon expressions are occasionally wordy, often pretentious, and always imprecise. Here are some common jargon words and phrases we should try to avoid. (See pp. 158-171, the glossary of usage and diction, for others.)

1. address the issue
2. avail yourself of
3. ballpark figures
4. career path adjustment
5. cognizant of
6. connect with
7. consciousness raising
8. contact (to mean *speak* or *meet with*)
9. cross-fertilization
10. dialogue (as a verb)
11. downsize
12. effective and efficient
13. effectuate
14. egress
15. embark on
16. expertise
17. expose one's self to
18. feedback
19. field (to mean profession: *teaching field*, *medical field*)
20. guesstimate
21. identify with
22. image building
23. impact (as a verb)
24. input
25. interface
26. in the neighbourhood of
27. in the picture
28. liaise (as a verb)
29. low profile
30. meaningful relationship
31. misspeak
32. network (as a verb)
33. on stream
34. on track
35. opt out
36. ordinance (military)
37. output
38. posture
39. predisposed to
40. pre-owned
41. relate to (to mean *understand*)
42. running late
43. sanitary engineer
44. scenario
45. sensitize
46. share with
47. strategize
48. substantial number
49. surgical strike
50. talk shop
51. thrust
52. time frame
53. upcoming
54. upscale
55. wise (as a suffix attached to a noun: *timewise*, *weatherwise*)

Exercise 8.3 — Replacing Jargon

Correct the following sentences by replacing the jargon expressions with your own words and phrases.

> EXAMPLE: Pascal did not have enough *expertise* to fill the new management position.
>
> CORRECTION: Pascal did not have enough knowledge and experience to fill the new management position.

1. We must address the issue by contacting their legal representatives.
2. If our cost-cutting program is to be effective and efficient, we must embark on a quality control management plan.
3. I need to dialogue with your plant manager and get his feedback on our production figures.
4. Our political posture should sensitize our constituents to our stand on environmental issues.
5. Let's keep our discussions on track, so that we can meet the time frame set by our union negotiators.
6. The figures that I exposed you to were just a guesstimate
7. Can you relate to her position on our absentee policy?
8. We should clear the air before effectuating the proposed changes in our management structure.
9. Elvira did not misspeak; she merely stretched the truth.
10. Weatherwise, it couldn't have been a better autumn.
11. I think that she is predisposed to accept our business proposition.
12. Our marketing team networked with the software specialists and created a perfect strategy for selling our new product.
13. Mr. Yates was given a career path adjustment when his team's product line did not come on stream in time for our winter sales promotion.
14. The history professor could not understand the thrust of Andreas' argument on why the Second World War should not have been won by the Allies.
15. Please do not talk shop when we liaise with our union stewards about the Christmas party arrangements.
16. Moses Mobley manages a pre-owned car lot in Toronto.
17. The ordinance that was dropped by our bombers eliminated a substantial number of enemy troops.
18. Are you cognizant of your increased responsibilities as a supervisor?
19. Our upscaled department store will include a fashion coordinator and a beauty salon.
20. The mayor must be kept in the picture if we expect him to connect with representatives of our business community.

Exercise 8.4 — Alternatives to Jargon

Fill in the blanks with ten more jargon words and phrases, then correct them by writing sentences with clearer, more precise expressions. Alternatively, write out your jargon words and sentences on a separate page.

1. _____   6. _____
2. _____   7. _____
3. _____   8. _____
4. _____   9. _____
5. _____   10. _____

1. _____
2. _____
3. _____
4. _____
5. _____
6. _____
7. _____
8. _____
9. _____
10. _____

C. WRITING CONCISELY: AVOIDING WORDINESS

Because effective writing is always economical, there is a direct correlation between the number of words we use and the clarity of our message. Wordiness is a sure sign that we have failed to plan our sentences or to think through our ideas. The more we rely on certain inflated expressions, the more insensitive we become to the exact connotations of words and the more we ignore the principles of balance, coherence, and directness in constructing sentences. Consequently, we write, "I am not in a position to pay your tuition expenses due to the fact that I am currently financially embarrassed...," instead of "I cannot pay your tuition fees because I have no money." The following are some of the most commonly used inflated expressions; there are others in the glossary.

1. a small number of
2. absolutely nothing
3. afford an opportunity to
4. any apparent reason
5. as a matter of principle
6. at a later/earlier date
7. at this point in time
8. avail yourself of
9. because of the fact that
10. beyond a shadow of a doubt
11. by means of
12. by virtue of
13. come to realize
14. come to the conclusion
15. despite the fact that
16. for the purpose of
17. for the reason that
18. have to do with
19. I would like to say that
20. in a great many instances
21. in a position to
22. inasmuch as
23. in receipt of
24. in the first/second instance
25. in the nature of
26. in the near future
27. in the vicinity of
28. in view of the fact that
29. is of the opinion that
30. make the most of
31. on many occasions
32. on the occasion of
33. on the part of
34. on the whole
35. owing to the fact that
36. put in an appearance
37. similar in character to
38. subsequent to
39. take it up with
40. take it upon oneself
41. take something into consideration
42. the month of March, June, September, etc.
43. unless otherwise stated
44. until such time as
45. with a view to
46. with reference to
47. with regard to
48. without fail
49. without further ado
50. without further delay

Exercise 8.5 — Making Sentences Concise

Correct the following sentences by replacing the wordy expressions with clearer, more concise words and phrases.

> EXAMPLE: Did my sister's homemade pie meet with your approval?
>
> CORRECTION: Did you enjoy my sister's homemade pie?

1. I think that she has finally come to realize that her brother will not give up smoking.

2. In conclusion, I would like to say that our company is not in a position to comply with your financial demands.

3. Did you avail yourself of the opportunity to join our hiking group?

4. Our baseball team is not ready to compete for the league title at this point in time.

5. In view of the fact that the month of September is the month that Gertrude will deliver her baby, we will not oblige her to work on the weekends.

6. My geography teacher told me that he would take into consideration my request for a delay in submitting my term paper.

7. Willard's new sofa is similar in character to the sofa that my mother bought for our family room.

8. I cannot agree as a matter of principle to your stand on taxation.

9. I promised our student president that I would take his proposal up with the school principal next Monday.

10. We will be leaving by train for Vancouver in the near future.

11. All of us identified the perpetrator beyond a shadow of a doubt.

12. Our committee meetings will be closed to the public until such time as the information leaks to the news media are stopped.

13. Emory saw Felicity act onstage on many occasions.

14. I cannot think of any apparent reason why our students would have been in the vicinity of the closed hockey rink last Wednesday evening.

15. Sheila decided to put in an appearance at Martin's Halloween party last Tuesday.

16. Our hockey team members could have scored goals in a great many instances if their passing game had been more precise and timely.

17. Subsequent to the intense snowstorm, the city council decided to purchase two new snowplows.

18. Recently, our school came into receipt of three new computers from our local school board.

19. Pauline has cancelled her subscription to the drama society due to the fact that it will not consider showcasing young Canadian playwrights.

20. We will take into consideration your job application at a later date.

D. ONLY WHAT IS NECESSARY: AVOIDING REDUNDANCIES

A redundant expression is one that contains two or more words that convey the same idea. Thus it is both wordy and repetitious. Correcting redundancies is usually a matter of eliminating one or two words or of substituting one precise word for an entire expression.

156 *Writing Fundamentals*

We seem to write redundant phrases when attempting to emphasize a noun with an adjective that duplicates the idea—*exact* replica, *end* result, *new* innovation—or when using two similar words in a compound expression—first and foremost, each and every, fear and dread.

Basically, we write redundancies for the same reason we use wordy expressions: a failure to strive for precision and economy in constructing sentences and an insensitivity to the meaning of words. Here are some of the most obvious redundancies; more are in the glossary.

1. actual fact
2. adequate enough
3. agreeable and satisfactory
4. bound and determined
5. close/open up
6. cold shiver
7. collect together
8. complete and total
9. connect together
10. disappear from view
11. down below
12. end result
13. entirely eliminated
14. erode away
15. exact replica
16. expensive and costly
17. experienced veteran
18. fear and dread
19. firm and fixed
20. first and foremost
21. free gift
22. honest truth
23. hope and trust
24. human face
25. inexperienced rookie
26. join up
27. mental attitude
28. my personal opinion
29. necessary requirements
30. new beginner
31. new innovation
32. old antique
33. plain and obvious
34. red in colour
35. repeat again
36. same, identical
37. secret and covert
38. seldom ever
39. serious crisis
40. sincere and earnest
41. single, solitary
42. small in size
43. strict accuracy
44. surround on all sides
45. true facts
46. up above
47. use and apply
48. unexpected surprise
49. utter impossibility
50. very unique
51. visible to the eye

Exercise 8.6 — Removing Redundancies

Correct the redundancies in the following sentences by placing parentheses around unnecessary words and, if necessary, by changing the articles to suit the alteration (e.g., *a* to *an*). Alternatively, rewrite the sentences, eliminating redundancies.

> EXAMPLE: From where we were standing, the space shuttle was barely visible (to the eye) as it approached the coast.

1. Her old antique vase is an exact replica of the one in our museum.

2. The end result of his experiment was barely adequate enough to be included in our chemistry paper.
3. A cold shiver went down my spine when Raoul opened up the coffin lid.
4. Our tour guide gave us the true facts about the history of the Battle of Quebec.
5. Her car disappeared from view when it entered the fog bank on Carpenter Road.
6. Most students seldom ever concern themselves about the strict accuracy of their spelling on homework assignments.
7. The destruction of the village was complete and total after the terrifying hurricane hit the island.
8. Our town experienced a serious economic crisis last year, but our new mayor is bound and determined to turn things around this year.
9. Nora's black cocktail dress was very expensive and costly, but she swears that the money was well spent because the design is very unique.
10. As our plane soared up above the cloud bank, the clouds appeared red in colour as they reflected the setting sun.
11. The acid rain, throughout the years, has eroded away our city monuments.
12. Please ask our instructor to repeat again the instructions for writing the mid-term examination.
13. You cannot expect the inexperienced rookies to play like our experienced veterans.
14. The computer software company promised us a free gift if we would order its accounting package.
15. We tried to negotiate the sale, but the sales associate told us that the prices were firm and fixed.
16. There wasn't a single, solitary sale item left one hour after the store opened, and that's the honest truth.
17. The deplorable condition of our lake is plain and obvious.
18. We had to surrounded the enemy on all sides before they finally surrendered their armaments.
19. The printer and the computer have to be connected together with a special cable that we sell in our computer supplies store.
20. When Willard asked for my personal opinion of his new motor home, I told him that I thought it was too small in size.

E. PROPER USAGE

Usage mistakes result from spelling errors, words out of place, double negatives, and colloquial expressions that may not be used in formal English. We make usage mistakes because our bad habits in speech spill into our writing. Certain awkward and ungrammatical expressions take hold and are reinforced by our sometimes semi-literate environment. Thus it is difficult to stop writing "Between you and I" when you hear so many people using this expression in daily speech, or when your ear tells you to write *use to* instead of *used to*.

Habitual reading and familiarity with a dictionary will usually solve these usage problems. But if you read only sporadically and fail to confirm proper word use with a dictionary, your usage mistakes will be a constant source of irritation—both to you and to your readers. While literate people may overlook your occasional trite or wordy expression, they will not tolerate incorrect and illogical usage. Some of the most common—and most serious—usage errors may be found in this glossary.

Glossary of Usage and Diction

1. **ability/capacity** *Ability* means the power to or quality of being able to accomplish something; in formal writing *capacity* means the power or ability to hold or receive something, but it may be used informally as a synonym for ability.

    She has the *ability* to be a first-rate tennis player.

    Our holding tanks have a five-hundred-litre *capacity*.

2. **aggravate** To *aggravate* means to make worse; it should not be used in formal writing to mean to *annoy* or *irritate*.

    The football player *aggravated* his knee injury.

    His hostile questions *annoyed* (not "aggravated") the speaker.

3. **agree to/agree with** To *agree to* means to consent to something; *to agree with* means to be in accord with someone or something.

    We *agree to* the conditions in the contract.

    I completely *agree with* your proposal for increasing production.

4. **all-round** A misspelling of *all-around*.

    He is an *all-around* (not "all-round") athlete.

5. **allusion/illusion** *Allusion* means an indirect reference; *illusion* means a false idea or belief, a false perception.

The education study made an *allusion* to our poor library facilities.

Helen is under the *illusion* that she will not have to take mathematics next semester.

6. **along the lines of** A wordy and awkward substitution for *like* or *similar to*.

   We need a tool *similar to* (not "along the lines of") a socket wrench.

7. **alot** A misspelling of *a lot*.

   There are *a lot* (not "alot") of unfinished reports on my desk.

   Note: *A lot* is an overused expression; substitute expressions like *a great deal, very many,* or *a large amount* whenever you can.

   We have *a great deal* (not "a lot") to learn.

8. **already/all ready** *Already* means previously or before this time; *all ready* means completely prepared.

   The company has *already* met their financial demands.

   Our team is *all ready* for the big game.

9. **alright** A misspelling of *all right*.

   I had a headache last night, but I feel *all right* (not "alright") today.

10. **altogether/all together** *Altogether* means entirely or completely; *all together* means gathered in a group.

    They are *altogether* (entirely) too inexperienced to compete for this contract.

    The class of '62 were *all together* for the first time this year.

11. **am/are of the opinion** A wordy expression meaning *believe* or *think*.

    I *believe* (not "am of the opinion") that our office is understaffed.

12. **among/between** *Among* is used in connection with more than two persons or things; *between* is used in connection with only two persons or things.

    The prize money will be divided *between* Ralph and Dorothy.

    There are quite a few people from western Canada *among* the convention delegates.

Note: *Between* may be used with more than two persons or things when they are considered as pairs within a listing.

> There are many cultural differences *between* the United States, Canada, and Mexico.

13. **amoral/immoral** *Amoral* means indifferent to moral standards; *immoral* means contrary to moral standards.

    > The relentless pursuit of money and fame seems to be an *amoral* force in our society.
    >
    > Denying shelter to homeless refugees is *immoral*.

14. **anyone/any one** *Anyone* is used to refer to any member of a group; *any one* is used to refer to a specific person or thing within a group.

    > *Anyone* could pass this test.
    >
    > *Any one* of us workers could be fired tomorrow.
    >
    > *Any one* of these ballpoint pens will be sufficient.

15. **anywheres/nowheres/somewheres** Awkward misspellings of *anywhere*, *nowhere*, and *somewhere*.

    > You may sit *anywhere* (not "anywheres").
    >
    > They were *nowhere* (not "nowheres") to be found.
    >
    > I left my notebook *somewhere* (not "somewheres") near the water fountain.

16. **around** An inappropriate synonym for *nearly* or *approximately*; the word *about* is preferred in formal writing.

    > We are *about* (not "around") halfway through our work.

17. **argue with/argue against** You *argue with* someone, but you *argue against* something.

    > I intend to *argue with* the chairman about his committee's report.
    >
    > I intend to *argue against* the committee's report.

18. **as** *As* is inappropriate when used in place of words like *because, since, that, if, whether,* or *for*.

I cannot attend class tomorrow *because* (not "as") I have a dental appointment.

We are not certain *whether/that/if* (not "as") we can meet your sales deadline.

19. as to whether An awkward and wordy substitute for *whether*.

Whether (not "as to whether") we will change our present policy remains to be seen.

20. as yet A colloquial substitute for *yet*.

We have not *yet* (not "as yet") finished counting our receipts.

21. at the present time A wordy expression meaning *now*.

We are not accepting any more job applications *now* (not "at the present time").

22. awfully An awkward intensive when used in place of words like *very, greatly, extremely, immensely*.

The house was *very* (not "awfully") quiet.

She is *extremely* (not "awfully") shy.

23. basic fundamentals A severely redundant phrase for *basics* or *fundamentals*.

The *basics* (not "basic fundamentals") of electricity are taught by Professor Stevens.

24. be sure and Colloquial expression for *be sure to*.

Be sure to (not "be sure and") mail the letter on your way to work.

25. being as/being as how/being that Colloquial substitutes for *because* or *since*.

Since (not "being as" or "being that") you haven't had your lunch yet, we shall dine together.

I am still not satisfied with your performance *because* (not "being as how") you have not proven your determination to succeed.

26. **between you and I** A commonly misused expression for *between you and me*.

> Just *between you and me* (not "between you and I"), I think our company will be awarded the contract.

27. **bring/take** To *bring* means to carry towards (from the point of view of the speaker or writer); *to take* means to carry away from.

> Please *take* these slippers to your father.
>
> Will you *bring* my reading glasses when you return?

28. **but that/but what** Awkward and non-standard expressions for *that*.

> I do not doubt for a moment *that* (not "but that/what") the thief will be caught.

29. **cancel out** The *out* is redundant after *cancel*.

> I am afraid I will have to *cancel* (not "cancel out") our dinner engagement.

30. **can't hardly/can't scarcely** These expressions are ungrammatical double negatives for *can hardly* and *can scarcely*.

> I *can hardly* (not "can't hardly/scarcely") believe he is sixty years old.

31. **compare to/compare with** To *compare to* means to seek similarity; *to compare with* means to seek both similarities and differences.

> I often *compare* my grandfather *to* one of the Old Testament patriarchs.
>
> When I *compare* my lab results *with* Ivan's we shall know the most efficient method of approaching the problem.

32. **consensus of opinion** A redundant expression for *consensus*.

> The *consensus* (not "consensus of opinion") of the delegates was that the resolution should be adopted at once.

33. **continual/continuous** *Continual* means occurring at frequent intervals, repeated often; *continuous* means occurring without interruption.

> There were *continual* interruptions throughout the rock concert.
>
> There was a *continuous* flow of water through the sluice gates.

34. **continue on** The *on* is redundant after *continue*.

   Please *continue* (not "continue on") with your report.

35. **correspond to/correspond with** *To correspond to* means to be similar or equal to; *to correspond with* means to communicate by letter.

   This item in the manual of instructions *corresponds to* the part I need to repair my automobile.

   I often *correspond with* my uncle who is living in Europe.

36. **could of** A colloquial expression for the contraction *could've* (could have).

   We *could've* (not "could of") won first prize if we had bought a ticket.

37. **couple of** A colloquial expression for *a few* or *several*.

   We had *a few* or *several* (not "a couple of") friends over for dinner.

   Note: When referring specifically to two persons or things, do not use *couple of*.

   We each had *two* (not "a couple of") hot dogs while watching the baseball game.

38. **differ from/differ with** *Differ from* indicates that two things are not alike; *differ with* indicates a disagreement between two people or two groups of people.

   Our test results *differ from* yours.

   I *differ with* you over the interpretation of the test results.

39. **different than** In formal writing the preposition *from* is preferred after *different*.

   Canadian football is not too *different from* (not "different than") American football.

40. **disinterested/uninterested** *Disinterested* means impartial or unbiased; *uninterested* means indifferent to.

   A judge must keep an open mind so that he can remain *disinterested* during the trial.

   His students remained *uninterested* in the library assignment.

41. **due to the fact that** A wordy substitute for *because* or *since*.

   We were late for work *because* (not "due to the fact that") the commuter train was delayed by the snowstorm.

42. **each and every** A redundant expression for *each* or *every*.

   Each (not "each and every") rose on the bush was in bloom.

   Every (not "each and every") person in the room should contribute to the cancer drive.

43. **feature** A colloquialism when used to mean *to place emphasis on* or *to give prominence to*.

   Helen will be *given a prominent role* (not "featured") in our new play.

44. **fewer/less** *Fewer* means a small number of countable objects; *less* means smaller in amount, proportion, or degree.

   Mike used *fewer* words than Tom to express the same idea.

   We had *less* snow this week than last week.

45. **fix** *To fix* means to fasten in place, or to mend. It should not be used to mean a *difficult situation* or *to take revenge on*.

   When our car ran off the road in the middle of the night, we found ourselves *in a difficult situation* (not "in a fix").

   The next time he kicks sand in my face I will *take my revenge on* (not "fix") him.

46. **free of** A colloquialism for *free from*.

   We are finally *free from* (not "free of") debt.

47. **get** An incorrect synonym for *understand* or *irritate*.

   I explained the process carefully, but he did not *understand* (not "get") it.

   His constant arguing *irritates* (not "gets to") me.

48. **got** An incorrect synonym for *purchase, own,* or *must*.

   My sister just *purchased* (not "got") a new car.

Ira and Stan each *own* (not "have got") a stereo.

I *must* (not "I've got to") return my library books.

49. hadn't ought to A colloquial expression for *should not*.

Doug *should not* (not "hadn't ought to") have purchased so many expensive clothes.

50. half of a/a half a Both are non-standard for *a half* or *half a*.

Please purchase *a half* kilo (not "a half a kilo" or "half of a kilo") of butter when you go to the market.

51. hanged/hung *Hanged* is used for people; *hung* is used for objects.

We have just *hung* several paintings this morning.

Yesterday the murderer was sentenced to be *hanged*.

52. have got to A colloquial expression for *must* or *have to*.

We *must* (not "have got to") prepare dinner before our guests arrive.

53. healthy/healthful *Healthy* means having good health; *healthful* means causing good health.

We diet and exercise to remain *healthy*.

Fresh air and exercise are *healthful*.

54. hopefully An overworked adverb incorrectly used to mean *let us hope*.

Let us hope (not "hopefully") all of our financial problems will be solved by tomorrow.

55. identical with Colloquial for *identical to*.

My coat is *identical to* (not "identical with") the one that was on sale last week.

56. imply/infer *To imply* means to suggest; *to infer* means to conclude from evidence.

He *implied* that the meeting would be cancelled.

I have *inferred* from his comments that the meeting will no longer be necessary.

57. **in back of** A colloquial expression for *behind*.

> My golf ball is *behind* (not "in back of") the tree.

58. **in regards to** A colloquial substitute for *regarding* or *in regard to*.

> We shall take no further action *regarding* (not "in regards to") your memo of August 28.

59. **in terms of** A wordy and meaningless expression for the preposition *about* or *of*.

> I was thinking *of* (not "in terms of") baseball when I used the term "line drive."

60. **in the event that** A wordy substitute for *if*.

> *If* (not "In the event that") he doesn't agree to our plan, we will proceed without him.

61. **in the last analysis** A wordy and trite expression incorrectly used to mean *ultimately* or *conclusively*.

> We will *ultimately* (not "in the last analysis") agree to the terms.

> I have decided *conclusively* (not "in the last analysis") to abandon the project.

62. **initiate/instigate** *To initiate* means to begin or originate; *to instigate* means to incite or urge on.

> We *initiated* our new program last week.

> Emma was responsible for *instigating* the workers' rebellion.

63. **inside of** A redundant phrase for *inside*.

> Please place the parcel *inside* (not "inside of") the container.

Note: *Inside of* should never be used as a synonym for *within* when referring to time.

> Patrick will arrive *within* (not "inside of") a week.

64. **irregardless** Colloquial for *regardless*.

> We shall carry on *regardless* (not "irregardless") of the consequences.

65. is when/is where Clauses beginning with *when* or *where* never follow the verb *to be* when an action is implied.

> In golf a par *occurs when* (not "is where") a player puts the ball in the hole in the required number of strokes.
>
> A comma splice *happens* when (not "is when") a comma is substituted for a period or a semicolon between two independent clauses.

66. it stands to reason A wordy cliché used vaguely to mean *obvious* or *apparent*.

> It is *obvious* (not "It stands to reason") that quality control is our highest priority.

67. -ize A perfectly legitimate English suffix that has been relentlessly abused by jargon-makers who create verbs like maximize, finalize, prioritize, utilize, formalize, and other such gobbledygook words.

> Make your maximum effort (not "*maximize* your effort").
>
> Our plans will be made final (not "*finalized*").
>
> Make your presentation prior to the meeting (not "*prioritize* your presentation").
>
> Make use of your athletic ability (not "*utilize* your athletic ability").
>
> Please write your remarks in a formal manner (not "*formalize* your remarks").

68. kind of a/sort of a The *a* in both expressions is superfluous.

> A certain *kind of* (not "kind of a") lubricant should be used.

Note: *Sort of* or *kind of* should never be used to mean *rather* or *somewhat*.

> It was *rather* (not "sort of") pleasant sitting in the rocking chair on the back porch.

69. lay/lie *Lay* is a transitive verb (taking an object) meaning to put; *lie* is an intransitive verb (taking no object) meaning to recline or remain.

> Please *lay* my briefcase on my desk.
>
> I think I will *lie* down until my headache goes away.

70. learn/teach *Learn* means to acquire knowledge; *teach* means to impart knowledge.

I shall *teach* him all I know.

Unfortunately, he *learns* very slowly.

71. **lend/loan** In formal writing *loan* is preferred as a noun, *lend* as a verb.

    I haven't any money to *lend* you.

    You will have to apply for a *loan* at the bank.

72. **let/leave** *Let* means to allow to; *leave* means to depart.

    Would you please *let* the cat go out before you come to bed?

    We shall *leave* in an hour.

73. **like** *Like* is incorrectly used in place of *as* or *as if* in making comparisons or contrasts.

    The machinery performed *as* (not "like") we expected.

    He behaved *as if* (not "like") he were already president of the company.

74. **likely/liable** *Likely* suggests probability; *liable* suggests an undesirable risk, the probability of something unpleasant taking place.

    We are *likely* to be promoted this year.

    If Kathy is not careful she is *liable* to hurt herself on that swing.

75. **maybe/may be** *Maybe* means perhaps; *may be* is an expression of possibility.

    Maybe we should study for our test tomorrow.

    There *may be* an increase in our taxes next year.

76. **might of** A colloquial expression for *might have*.

    She *might have* (not "might of") won the race if she had trained harder.

77. **most/almost** *Most* means greatest in amount, quality, or degree; *almost* means very nearly.

    She is the *most* unselfish person I ever met.

    Caleb ate *almost* a kilo of chocolate last week.

Chapter 8 / Choosing the Right Words **169**

78. **nowheres near** A colloquial expression for *not nearly*.

> He is *not nearly* (not "nowheres near") as talented as his sister.

79. **off of** The *of* after *off* is redundant.

> Take the casserole *off* (not "off of") the stove.

80. **on account of** An undesirable and awkward substitute for *because*.

> Mara missed her finance class *because* (not "on account of") her car had a flat tire.

81. **on condition that** A wordy expression meaning *if*.

> I will accept the prize money *if* (not "on condition that") I can share it with my teammates.

82. **outside of** The *of* after *outside* is redundant.

> Please place the lawnmower *outside* (not "outside of") the tool shed.

> Note: *Outside of* should never be used as a substitute for *except for* or *beside*.

> *Except for* (not "outside of") his tendency to be slow, Dave is a dependable worker.

83. **over with** A colloquial expression for *finally finished*.

> I am relieved that our examinations are *finally* or *completely finished* (not "over with").

84. **plan on** Colloquial for *plan to*.

> All of us *plan to attend* (not "plan on attending") a rock concert this Friday.

85. **practical/practicable** *Practical* means useful or sensible; *practicable* means feasible or able to be put into practice.

> His observations were *practical* and to the point.

> Your suggestions for redesigning the assembly line are simply not *practicable*.

86. **prior than** Incorrect for *prior to*.

> Please submit your term essay *prior to* (not "prior than") the final examination date.

87. **rarely ever** The word *ever* is redundant.

> We *rarely* (not "rarely ever") eat dinner before seven o'clock.

88. **reason is because** An undesirable substitute for *the reason is that*.

> I cannot attend your party; *the reason is that* (not "the reason is because") I have to meet my parents at the airport.

89. **reason why** The *why* after *reason* is redundant.

> The *reason* (not "reason why") I phoned was to ask you about our homework assignment.

90. **refer back/return back** The word *back* is redundant in both these phrases.

> Please *refer* (not "refer back") to the introduction in your textbooks.
>
> I must *return* (not "return back") the shovel I borrowed from my neighbour.

91. **sit/set** *Set* is a transitive verb meaning to place or position; *sit* is an intransitive verb meaning to be seated.

> Please *set* the dial on the oven.
>
> You may *set* the glass on the table.
>
> Because we arrived late, we had nowhere to *sit*.

92. **so** An overworked word incorrectly used to mean *because* or *therefore*.

> *Because* Frank pitched faultlessly, he was given the game ball.
>
> not
>
> Frank pitched faultlessly, *so* he was given the game ball.

93. **sure and** *Sure to* is the preferred phrase in formal writing.

> Be *sure to* (not "sure and") call me the minute you arrive.

94. **tasty/tasteful** *Tasty* means flavourful; *tasteful* means showing good taste or judgement.

Your beef stew was very *tasty*.

Her living room was *tastefully* decorated.

95. that there/this here Both are colloquial phrases for *that* and *this*.

Will you open *that* (not "that there") can of peaches with *this* (not "this here") can opener?

96. use to Colloquial for *used to*.

We are all *used to* (not "use to") physical labour.

97. wait on A colloquial substitute for *wait for*.

I suppose we should *wait for* (not "wait on") Sally.

98. ways Colloquial for *way* or *distance*.

Toronto is a long *way* (not "ways") from Ottawa.

99. where at The *at* is unnecessary in phrases beginning with *where*.

I do not know *where* the telephone directory *is* (not "is at").

100. with respect to A wordy substitution for *about*.

We have some reservations *about* (not "with respect to") our present salary scale.

Exercise 8.7 — Revising for Effective Diction

Rewrite the following paragraphs, correcting the usage and diction errors.

The strategies for teaching the basic fundamentals of writing on the post-secondary level should be used and employed in a variety of contexts, and emphasis should be placed on both the process and the end product of their writing. Students should be given the necessary requirements in order to write expository essays, creative pieces, reports, and research papers; they should also be able to describe and interpret diagrams, tables, and graphs. And, if humanly possible, their writing should be done on computers and stored together in electronic portfolios.

It is of the utmost importance that students develop an awareness of the various stages of writing, irregardless of their proficiency or grade level. In the first and foremost initial planning stage, for instance, the students should focus and concentrate on generating and organizing ideas. They should also be obliged to take into consideration the importance of determining readership when selecting the content of their essays and reports. During the drafting and evaluation stages, they should concentrate and focus on critiquing their writing so that they can write and produce further drafts to improve accuracy and syntactical quality.

Teachers should also be sure and make students aware of the logic and coherence in written texts. Utilizing sample reading texts can provide useful models for analysis. And the planning strategies in the form of outlining, which focusses on main and supporting ideas, can aid and help students develop a coherent framework for their writing.

Teachers also need to provide a great deal of substantial support for students in order to help them develop the high-level skills embodied in research and report writing. For example, students will need alot of practice in paraphrasing, summarizing, and avoiding plagiarism; they will also need instruction in converting the visual information contained in diagrams, tables, and graphs into readable prose. Furthermore, they need to be learned how to supply in-text or bibliographic references in an acceptable format.

Last but not least, the students must be provided with appropriate and realistic contexts for their writing. These should include a substantial number of topics that are relevant, meaningful, and motivating—ones that the students can easily identify with and find or access through library or Internet research.

CHAPTER NINE

Preparing an Outline

A. WHAT IS AN OUTLINE?

An outline is an instrument for organizing ideas and information. It is almost a step-by-step procedure of the way we think when we write. And since all good writing stems from clear thinking, the outlining process can be an invaluable tool for attaining the mental discipline needed for effective prose organization.

However, the outlining process is not an end in itself; that is, it is not a skill that can be set apart from any other skill related to written expression. It is simply one of the mental steps we must take in order to write clearly and efficiently.

B. THE BENEFITS

Whether you are writing a few short paragraphs, a major essay, or a formal report, the benefits derived from the skill of outlining will be immediate:

1. Outlining will help you focus on your main ideas and work out the pattern of their development. It will enable you to anticipate organizational problems before they occur, thus permitting you to keep your ideas in perspective.

2. Outlining will help you seek out the logical connection between your principal and subordinate topics. Your ideas will be expressed in parallel form because you will be more sensitive to the skill of coordination; your transitions between paragraphs will be smoother and more efficient because you will be more aware of the pattern of sequential development (subordination) that leads logically to a summary conclusion. Thus your writing will become more proportionate and selective, enabling you to separate the major from the minor, the relevant from the irrelevant, the abstract from the concrete, the direct from the indirect, and the emphatic from the bland.

3. Your topic statements and your supporting evidence will be clear, direct, and comprehensive because you will be better able to spot weaknesses in your arguments. Strict attention to the principles of development will ensure that your data will be complete, containing no gaps in logic or sequence. And as you become more adept at penetrating the organization of written expression, your reading will become more thoughtful and critical.

4. Finally, your sentences will grow forceful and expressive, and your paragraphs controlled and coherent, for you will have a better visual image of your essay's structure and a more precise idea of how to frame your thoughts. In short, you will be working from a structured plan that has its roots in deductive and inductive logic, enabling you to think more intelligently about length, transition, emphasis, tone, precision, and coherence.

In summary, then, we may say that the skill of outlining is directly related to the logic of prose organization. It teaches us how to control our language and order our thoughts so we can give clear and effective expression to our ideas.

C. TYPES OF OUTLINES

There are three common types of outlines representing different levels of thought organization: the scratch outline, the topic outline, and the sentence outline.

1. Scratch Outline

The scratch outline is composed of a tentative and random list of topics and ideas. In this outline you write down, almost in a stream-of-consciousness process, everything that you can think of about a given topic. This exercise provides you with an important, though rudimentary, framework for testing your ideas before attempting to organize them. Thus a scratch outline of an essay on environmental pollution might look like this:

> Industrial waste
> Automobile exhaust
> Lakes are dying
> Soil becomes non-productive
> Factory smoke
> Smog in Montreal
> Bad for lungs: cancer and emphysema
> Acid rain
> Fish die
> Cities are too noisy
> People have nervous disorders
> Noise levels in factories

Air pollution is dangerous to the elderly
Mercury found in fish
Drinking water full of bacteria
Municipal garbage
Poisonous chemicals in rivers and streams
Something must be done

2. Topic Outline

The topic outline is the most common type. This outline arranges the random ideas of the scratch outline into headings and subheadings, according to their levels of significance. It is here that you must pay strict attention to the principles of coordination and subordination, as well as to the logic of parallel construction: words with words; phrases with phrases; clauses with clauses. It is here, too, that the topic is refined into a thesis statement.

(a) *Thesis Statement*

The key word here is "focus," for that is precisely what a thesis statement does. It narrows or limits the topic so that it can be discussed in clearly definable steps. It may also convey your point of view, aligning you closely with one specific section of the topic. (See pp. 198-200 for a detailed discussion of point of view in relation to the topic sentence.) A good thesis statement, then, can show you the direction you should be heading and indicate how far you will have to travel to get there. Here are a few examples of how thesis statements refine and develop topics:

TOPIC: Television Advertising

THESIS STATEMENT: *Television advertising that deals with feminine hygiene products is both tasteless and insulting.*

Here the writer has focussed on a specific type of advertising and will demonstrate his or her position under two major headings.

TOPIC: Keeping Pets

THESIS STATEMENT: *It need not be difficult to housetrain dogs if three major points are kept in mind.*

Here the writer has limited the topic to a specific kind of pet—dogs—and has chosen three major headings to instruct the reader how to housetrain them.

TOPIC: Living in Large Cities

THESIS STATEMENT: *There are certain cultural advantages to living in a large city.*

Here the writer has chosen to talk about city living from only one point of view. The main headings will consist of a number of cultural advantages that may be discussed in detail or simply listed and exemplified.

As you can see from the above examples, the thesis statement implicitly reveals the length and organization of the essay by embodying the central idea governing sequential development.

(b) *Sequence of Symbols*

In the topic outline a set of conventional outline symbols is used. Starting from the largest headings and working downward to the smallest, you use alternate numbers and letters to indicate major and minor topics and subtopics. The largest sections are indicated by upper-case Roman numerals (I, II, III); then subheadings take, in descending order of importance, capital letters (A, B, C), Arabic numbers (1, 2, 3), small letters (a, b, c), and then, if needed, lower-case Roman numerals (i, ii, iii). Major headings are placed at the margin, and then subheadings are uniformly indented so that they fall neatly under each other in columns. The skeleton of a topic outline might look like this:

I. _____
   A. _____
      1. _____
      2. _____
         a. _____
         b. _____
      3. _____
   B. _____
      1. _____
      2. _____
      3. _____
II. _____
   A. _____
      1. _____
      2. _____
      3. _____
         a. _____
         b. _____
           (i) _____
           (ii) _____
   B. _____
      1. _____
         a. _____
         b. _____
         c. _____

                    2. _____
                    3. _____
        III. _____
            A. _____
            B. _____
            C. _____
                1. _____
                2. _____
                3. _____
                    a. _____
                    b. _____

Most topic outlines you write, however, will rarely go past the third level of indentation. The length of the topic is usually determined by the range of the thesis statement. Here is the way a topic outline on environmental pollution might appear after being converted from the scratch outline (on p. 174). Observe how some of the ideas in the scratch outline are rephrased and refined, and how some are placed logically into headings and subheadings.

TOPIC: Our Endangered Environment

THESIS STATEMENT: *We are making our environment unfit for human habitation.*

I. **Air Pollution**
    A. Automobile exhaust
        1. Contributes to lung cancer and emphysema
        2. Causes smog in cities
            a. Montreal
            b. Eastern seaboard of U.S.
    B. Factory smoke
        1. Kills vegetation near factory towns
        2. Kills lakes and poisons soils
            a. Acid rain kills marine life in lakes
            b. Heavy concentrations of lead make fertile soil barren

II. **Water Pollution**
    A. Industrial waste
        1. Pollutes estuaries along sea coasts
            a. Oyster beds become contaminated
            b. Wildfowl lose feeding grounds
        2. Pollutes rivers and streams, and poisons fish
            a. Toxic chemicals in streams and rivers eliminate recreational swimming and boating
            b. Mercury compounds make fish inedible

B. Municipal waste
    1. Uses up oxygen in freshwater lakes
    2. Causes high bacteria count in drinking water
III. **Noise Pollution**
  A. Airplane noise
  B. Factory noise
  C. Traffic noise in congested cities
    1. Causes nervous disorders in animals
    2. Causes high blood pressure and hypertension in people

Notice that the thesis statement is written as a complete sentence and that it effectively focusses the essay topic. Notice also that every division and subdivision is equally balanced—for every A a B, every 1 a 2—and that each heading is logically and grammatically parallel. Finally, notice that the first word in each heading is capitalized and that there is no end punctuation after phrases or dependent clauses.

3. Sentence Outline

In the sentence outline you write headings and subheadings as complete sentences. This outline is especially useful when you are composing a long essay or a formal report, for it forces you to think through your major sections more thoroughly and to locate the logical relationships of their parts. In fact, a comprehensive sentence outline could be your final organizational step before the first draft of your essay. The sentence outline of the environmental pollution essay might look like this:

TOPIC: Our Endangered Environment

THESIS STATEMENT: *We are making our environment unfit for human habitation.*

I. Air pollution adversely *affects* our health and *destroys* the beauty of our countryside.
  A. Automobile exhaust *is* indirectly *related* to lung cancer and emphysema and directly *related* to smog in our cities.
  B. Factory smoke *destroys* vegetation, *kills* lakes, and *pollutes* soil.
    1. Sulphur compounds *denude* vegetation near factories.
    2. Acid rain *kills* marine life in lakes.
    3. Heavy lead concentrations *destroy* the fertility of topsoil.
II. Water pollution *releases* toxic chemicals into our rivers and streams, *poisons* our fish, and *taints* our drinking water.
  A. Industrial wastes *are responsible* for removing rivers and streams from recreational use and for the high concentrations of mercury found in our freshwater fish.

B. Municipal wastes *are responsible* for the high bacteria count in our drinking water and for the oxygen starvation of our freshwater lakes.

III. Noise pollution *causes* nervous disorders in animals, and high blood pressure and hypertension in humans.

Notice that each sentence effectively sums up a key idea implicit in the thesis statement and that each is expressed in proper parallel form.

D. ORDERING THE OUTLINE

Outlines are usually arranged in one of three ways: analytically, chronologically, or spatially. Depending upon the nature and scope of your topic, you will most likely use one of these three methods of arrangement to organize your essay.

1. Grouping by Ideas or Analysis

The analytical outline is one in which the topic and thesis statement are divided into manageable parts according to the logic of your argument. Ideas are grouped into related sections so that each section has a pattern of development. This pattern may take many forms: it may be a simple classification by rank, purpose, or degree; or it may be structured according to cause and effect, or statement and example. But no matter which pattern is chosen, it must be used consistently throughout the outline. In the following examples you can see how attention to these principles—manageability of topic divisions, logical development, and consistency of structure—leads to clear, useful outlines.

Simple Classification

THESIS STATEMENT: *Our Canadian educational system is both comprehensive and flexible.*

I. Elementary Schools
 A. Public
 B. Private

II. Senior Elementary Schools

III. Secondary Schools
 A. Public
  1. Composite schools
  2. Vocational schools
  3. Academic collegiates
 B. Private
  1. Non-denominational

2. Denominational
    a. Catholic
    b. Protestant
    c. Jewish

IV. Post-secondary Education
    A. Universities
    B. Community colleges
    C. Technical institutes

Statement and Example

THESIS STATEMENT: *Movies are better than ever.*

I. **Better Actors and Actresses**
   A. Robert De Niro
   B. Dustin Hoffman
   C. Al Pacino
   D. Meryl Streep
   E. Jodi Foster
   F. Katharine Hepburn

II. **Better Directors**
    A. Francis Ford Coppola
    B. Sidney Lumet
    C. James Cameron
    D. Steven Spielberg

III. **Better Scripts**
     A. *The Godfather*, Parts I and II
     B. *Schindler's List*
     C. *Shakespeare in Love*

IV. **Better Cinematography**
    A. *The Titanic*
    B. *Butch Cassidy and the Sundance Kid*
    C. *Saving Private Ryan*

Cause and Effect

THESIS STATEMENT: *Our dependence on foreign energy is leading us into a major recession.*

I. **Balance of Payments Deficits**
   A. Increase in interest rates
   B. Devaluation of the dollar

II. **High Utility Costs**
    A. Increase in cost-of-living index
    B. Decrease in consumer spending

1. Less business investment
2. More unemployment

2. Arranging Chronologically

A chronological outline is one in which events are arranged according to a logical time sequence. This type of arrangement is used to write narration, to describe a process, and to write evaluation reports. Time order is the key to this outline.

TITLE: *How to Plan a Child's Birthday Party*

I. Send invitations
II. Arrange transportation if needed
III. Decorate party room
IV. Buy food and beverages
V. Prepare party games
VI. Purchase plenty of Aspirin for the adults

TITLE: *Technical Report Evaluation Procedure*

I. **Purpose of the Report**
   A. Who requested it and why?
   B. Is it for external or internal circulation?

II. **Form of the Report**
   A. Is the format appropriate to its function and readership?
   B. Are all required formal components included?
   C. Are format and substance complementary?

III. **Substance of the Report**
   A. Is the factual information accurate and complete?
   B. Are relevant and authoritative sources cited?
   C. Does the sequence of the facts justify the conclusion?
   D. Are the recommendations reasonable?
   E. Are there logical transitions between ideas?
   F. Is the style clear and grammatical, and is it appropriate to the occasion and purposes of the report?
   G. Is the tone sufficiently technical?
   H. Is the visual material completely integrated with the textual information?
   I. Does the appendix contain supplementary material unessential to the body of the report?

3. Arranging by Location and Situation

In this type of outline the writer organizes things as they appear in space, or as they relate to a specific location. This arrangement usually follows a line of movement in one direction, whether from left to right, top to bottom, north to south, or east to west. This type of arrangement provides a very simple and straightforward way of organizing material, as may be seen in the examples below.

>TITLE: *Post-secondary Education in Canada*
>
>   I. Universities in British Columbia
>   II. Agricultural and Technical Colleges in the Prairie Provinces
>   III. Community Colleges in Ontario
>   IV. CEGEPs in Quebec
>   V. Colleges of Art in the Atlantic Provinces

>TITLE: *Decorating a Study Room*
>
>   I. Gold rug on floor
>   II. Rust-coloured wallpaper on three walls
>   III. Off-white paint on south wall
>   IV. Recessed lighting in ceiling

E. THE ELEMENTS OF A CONSTRUCTIVE OUTLINE

To determine whether your outline will effectively organize your essay, ask yourself the following questions listed under the headings of balance, unity, and completeness.

1. Balance
(a) Are my headings and subheadings properly coordinated and subordinated?
(b) Are my headings logically and grammatically parallel?
(c) Are there at least two subheadings under each heading, and are they properly indented?
(d) Is the first word in each heading capitalized?

2. Unity
(a) Have I established a consistent pattern of arrangement?
(b) Do my ideas fall into a logical sequence?
(c) Is my language clear and concise?

3. Completeness
(a) Does my thesis statement properly focus my topic?
(b) Do my headings and subheadings fully develop my thesis statement?
(c) Have I used any irrelevant or unrelated material?

Exercise 9.1 — Preparing an Outline

#1 In the blanks to the right, or on a separate sheet, arrange the following terms in a logical outline sequence.

(a) Types of Food
    Apples
    Potatoes
    Meat
    Grapes
    Broccoli
    Peaches
    Vegetables
    Steak
    Fruit
    Beans
    Poultry
    Wax beans
    Turkey
    Bananas
    Lima beans
    Citrus fruit
    Veal
    Grapefruit
    Chicken
    Oranges

(b) Professions
    Civil
    Doctor
    Trial
    University
    Electrical
    Surgeon
    Aeronautical
    Family
    Heart
    High school
    Tax

Brain ———
Teachers ———
Ears, nose, and throat ———
Community college ———
Urologist ———
Psychiatrist ———
Secondary ———
Labour ———
Post-secondary ———
Engineer ———
Lawyer ———

(c) Rivers of the World

Mississippi
Africa ———
Colorado ———
North America ———
Rhine ———
St. Lawrence ———
Amazon ———
Seine ———
Germany ———
Europe ———
South America ———
Orinoco ———
Italy ———
Moselle ———
Volga ———
Yangtze ———
France ———
Asia ———
Russia ———
Loire ———
Tiber ———

#2 Place the proper outline symbols next to the following lists of terms, or write this outline on a separate sheet and insert the proper symbols. Begin with Roman numerals.

(a) Famous World Cities

Central America _____
Panama _____
Panama City _____
North America _____
United States _____
East Coast _____
New York _____
Boston _____
Philadelphia _____
West Coast _____
Los Angeles _____
San Francisco _____
Golden Gate Bridge _____
Chinatown _____
Canada
Ontario _____
Toronto _____
Ottawa
Alberta _____
Calgary _____
Calgary Stampede _____
British Columbia _____
Vancouver _____
Europe
Western Europe _____
Germany _____
Berlin _____
Munich _____
France _____
Paris _____
The Eiffel Tower _____

The Louvre _____
Italy _____
Rome _____
The Colosseum _____
Venice _____
Eastern Europe _____
Russia _____
Moscow _____
St. Petersburg _____
The Hermitage Museum _____
Poland _____
Cracow _____
Warsaw _____

(b) Shakespearean Plays I Have Seen throughout North America
United States _____
New York _____
New York City _____
Comedies _____
As You Like It _____
All's Well that Ends Well _____
Tragedies _____
King Lear _____
Othello _____
Illinois _____
Chicago _____
Comedies _____
Twelfth Night _____
Histories _____
Richard II _____
King John _____
Canada _____
British Columbia _____
Vancouver _____
Tragedies _____

Hamlet _____
Macbeth _____
Alberta _____
Edmonton _____
Histories _____
Richard III _____
Henry IV, Parts 1 & 2 _____
Ontario _____
Ottawa _____
Tragedies _____
Julius Caesar _____

(c) My Favourite Ethnic Restaurants in Our City
North Side _____
German _____
Stengel's _____
Town Haus _____
Italian _____
Faragetti's _____
Milano's _____
Greek _____
Athena _____
West Side _____
Eastern European _____
Russian _____
Tatiana's _____
Polish _____
Pulaski's _____
South Side _____
Middle Eastern _____
Lebanese _____
Kalba's Bistro _____
Hassan's Pearl _____
Egyptian _____
The Nile Café _____

#3 Rewrite the following outlines by correcting the parallel construction errors; make sure the terms within each section are similarly expressed.

(a) *I visited several famous Museums while I was an exchange student in Europe.*

I. **Western Europe**
   A. Paris in the spring of 1976
      1. The Louvre
         a. I saw a great collection of Impressionist painters.
            i. Monet
            ii. A special exhibit of Manet's paintings
            iii. Cezanne was also represented.
         b. Italian Renaissance paintings
            i. Titian's works were most impressive.
            ii. I saw da Vinci's Mona Lisa
            iii. Tintoretto

   B. I visited Madrid in October, 1976
      1. The Prado Museum
         a. A magnificent collection of religious art
            i. Rafael
            ii. Fra Angelico's most famous paintings were on exhibit.
            iii. Rubens
            iv. Velàzquez

II. **Eastern Europe**
   A. Russia
      1. The beautiful city of St. Petersburg
         a. The Hermitage Museum
            i. French painters from the nineteenth and twentieth centuries
            ii. Byzantine art from fifth to twelfth centuries was on special exhibit.
            iii. Superb collection of carved stones and Assyrian reliefs from the ninth century BC

(b) *Global warming will be one of the most serious problems of the twenty-first century.*

I. **The Causes**
   A. Emissions of carbon monoxide from gasoline-burning vehicles
      1. Very little effort by advanced Western countries to reduce pollutants from vehicle exhaust systems.
         a. The major automobile manufactures building more vans and utility vehicles that burn more fuel per kilometre.
         b. Very little effort by the three major North American automobile companies to build and sell compact and subcompact cars that burn less fuel.
         c. There is little or no interest by automobile companies to manufacture electric cars that would eliminate exhaust emission.

B. Emissions of carbon and sulphur dioxide from industrial smokestacks.
      2. Little effort by industry to seek alternative fuels.
         a. Large manufacturing companies still relying heavily on fossil fuels such as coal and oil.
         b. Utility companies have done very little research on alternative sources of energy such as wind and wave power.
   C. Burning of major rain forests
      1. Brazil and Indonesia
         a. Trees and foliage burned to open more land for farming
         b. Governments not providing leadership or financial incentives to stop the devastation.
         c. The United Nations does not consider the burning of rain forests a high priority.

II. Results
   A. Ice caps melt, causing oceans and rivers to rise.
      1. Seaside cities, villages, estuaries, and resorts flood.
         a. Low-lying countries like Bangladesh and Sri Lanka lose living space and farmland.
         b. The disappearance of millions of hectares of farmland and estuaries throughout the world.
         c. Hundreds of billions of dollars are lost due to the worldwide floods.
   B. World climates radically change
      1. Temperate climates become tropical
         a. Crops die and billions of people suffer famine and disease
         b. Rainfall increasing dramatically
      2. Cold climates becoming temperate
         a. The melting of ice and snow
         b. Arctic tundra disappears
      3. The tropical countries to become arid.
         a. Deserts expanding and increasing
         b. Tropical grasslands disappear
         c. Animals and plants die

#4 Organize the following list of terms into a topic outline; use conventional outline symbols and uniform indentation to indicate coordinate and subordinate relationships.

   (a) TOPIC: *My Experience as a tourist during the last ten years*

   Europe
   France
   Paris
   Nightclub tour
   Seine River cruise
   Notre Dame Cathedral visit
   Eiffel Tower visit

Germany
Berlin
Munich
Attended Oktoberfest
The Hofbrauhaus
Festival Biergarten
Denmark
Copenhagen
Little Mermaid
Tivoli Gardens
British Isles
London
Changing of the Guard at Buckingham Palace
Shopping at Harrods department store
Cruising on the Thames River
Middle East
Egypt
Cairo museum visit
Nile cruise
Tour of the pyramids
Persian Gulf
United Arab Emirates
Dubai City tour
Camel rides in the desert
Indonesia
Jakarta
City tour
Bali
Shopping
Golfing
Scuba diving

(b) TOPIC: *Checklist for developing a collaborative learning environment*

Classroom
Are traffic patterns to storage areas, large tables, printers, doorways, and black- or whiteboards clear and unfettered?

Can they seek resources to assist their own learning?

The physical organization

Do I use multiple techniques, and are they consistent with the desired goals of my lesson plan?

Does the classroom organization allow for cooperation, sharing, and group work?

Do they practise assessing their own strengths and weaknesses?

Teacher

Is the lighting flexible enough to allow for overhead projections and computer displays?

Students

Do my evaluation techniques reflect the interactive learning process?

Teaching strategies

Do I use a variety of group activities that encourage new and diversified group formations?

Are students involved in decision-making, planning, organizing, and evaluating classroom activities?

Do they use peer evaluation techniques?

Do I implement interactive skills that generate a learning environment conducive to self-directed learning?

Do they learn through a variety of class, group, and individual activities?

(c) TOPIC: *The personal essay revision process*

Content

Have you used a consistent pattern of development?

Are all words spelled correctly?

Does your introduction inform the reader what the essay is about?

Do you have all the information you need to make your argument?

Are your arguments properly sequenced?

Is your essay properly punctuated?

Are your paragraphs unified and connected with transitional words and phrases?

Are the main ideas stated clearly?

Do you have a conclusion that summarizes the development and that restates the topic idea?

Have you enclosed all direct quotes in quotation marks?

Diction and Grammar

Are the general statements supported by evidence?
Have you avoided jargon and clichés?
Did you use the correct bibliography and citation format?
Have you used precise words to convey your meaning?
Is your thesis statement logical and complete?
Have you avoided sentence structure errors?
Are all typographical errors neatly corrected?
Mechanics
Organization

#5 Check the following outline for errors in coordination, subordination, and parallel structure, and then rewrite it correctly on a separate sheet of paper.

Members of my family who are attending and who have attended universities and colleges across Canada

I. **Alberta**
   A. University of Edmonton
      1. My brother Phil studied history
      2. My nephew Edgar just received his B.A. in English literature.
         a. My sister Francine is studying mathematics
         b. My cousin Dennis
            i. Studied geography
            ii. Played football

II. **The Province of British Columbia**
    1. Simon Fraser University
       A. My niece Phyllis is majoring in physics
       B. My brother Cliff studied chemistry
    2. British Columbia Institute of Technology
       a. My nephew Morris
          i. Computer Science

III. **Ontario**
     1. Universities Attended
        A. University of Toronto
           i. My mother earned her law degree
           ii. My uncle
              a. played hockey
              b. studied Electrical Engineering
        B. Attended Queen's University
           2. My sister Claudia
              a. Mechanical Engineering
              b. My aunt Betty also studies there
                 i. B.A. in history
                 ii. M.A. in English literature

3. Colleges
    a. St. Lawrence College
        A. Kingston
        B. My cousin Flora studied to be a child-care worker
    b. Algonquin College
        A. Located in Ottawa
            i. My niece Jeannette is studying nursing
            ii. My nephew Roland studied early childhood education and played baseball.

#6 Convert the following outline into a sentence outline; compose a thesis statement that is effectively developed by the outline.

The dramatic increase in fast-food restaurants in our city

THESIS STATEMENT: _____

  I. **Pizza Restaurants**
      A. Drive-through Service
          1. Pizza Hut
          2. Domino's Pizza
      B. Free Delivery
          1. Tombstone Pizza
          2. Pizza, Pizza
          3. Don Corleone's Pizza
 II. **Hamburger Restaurants**
      A. Charbroiled
          1. Burger King
          2. Hardy's
      B. Fried
          1. McDonald's
          2. Wendy's
          3. Wimpey's
III. **Chicken Restaurants**
      A. Takeout
          1. KFC
          2. Swiss Chalet
      B. Opened Last Year
          1. Chicken Lickin'
          2. Southern Delight
 IV. **Seafood Restaurants**
      A. Opened Last Year
          1. Dockside Restaurant
          2. Squidd's
      B. Free Delivery
          1. Trident Sea Food
          2. The Chowder House

V. **Steak House**
   A. Family Restaurants
      1. Outback Steakhouse
      2. Sid's Steakhouse
   B. Takeout Restaurants
      1. Ponderosa
      2. Steak Express

VI. **Chinese Restaurants**
   A. Opened Last Year
      1. Golden Leaf
      2. Lotus Blossom
      3. China Moon

#7 Use three of the following topics to construct an analytical outline, a chronological outline, and a spatial outline. Use no more than three major headings for each outline.

1. How to study for an examination
2. Religions of the world
3. My favourite subjects in school
4. Administering artificial respiration
5. Learning how to drive an automobile
6. How to lose weight
7. Setting up a classroom
8. Married people have more fun
9. Skiing in Canada
10. I would rather have a dog than a cat for a pet
11. Sightseeing in Canada
12. English is my best subject
13. Learning how to ski
14. Our school library is well organized
15. Evaluating a research essay

CHAPTER TEN

Constructing Effective Paragraphs

The paragraph is an essential unit of written expression, for it allows the writer to focus on the development of a single idea within the larger context of an essay or a report. Mastering the organization of a paragraph is the first important step towards mastering practically any piece of expository prose.

A. WHAT IS A PARAGRAPH?

The single paragraph may be defined as a series of related sentences that develops one major idea. Each sentence is logically and structurally joined to the one before it. It is, in effect, a unified whole, with a beginning, a middle, and an end. Each paragraph (in an extended essay) is indented to indicate a shift in thought.

B. MAKING PARAGRAPHS UNIFIED

The key term in the paragraph definition above is "related sentences," because without a unified sentence structure the paragraph would fall apart. Like the outline pattern, the formal paragraph structure enables you to place ideas into sequential groups that ensure their logical progression. Here is an example of a poorly constructed paragraph:

> My younger brother's room is always a mess. He never learned to be neat. Instead of straightening up his room when he returns from school, he'd rather go to the schoolyard and play basketball. Even though he is a pretty good basketball player, he should try to be a little less sloppy.

There is no sentence continuity in this paragraph, for it is composed of a series of unrelated and disconnected ideas. The sentences wander aimlessly without coming to a point, making it impossible for readers to focus on a unifying idea. Now consider the following paragraph:

> My younger brother's room is always a mess. His bed is never made, and there are parts of model airplanes all over his desk and bureau. Dirty clothes are invariably piled in a corner, and chewing gum wrappers are usually scattered beneath his desk. If he doesn't clean up his act soon, my father will discontinue his allowance.

The sentences join together to form a unified and coherent paragraph because only one idea is developed—the messy room. Each sentence demonstrates and proves the topic idea, and each leads logically to the concluding statement.

If you think of the paragraph as a delicate structure containing interrelated pieces of information that answer a general question or develop a formal statement, you will realize how irrelevant information disturbs its balance and thereby frustrates your readers.

Exercise 10.1 — Paragraph Unity

Rewrite the following paragraphs by eliminating unnecessary and unrelated ideas and details and by tightening the sentence structure.

1. My dog and cat have become fast friends. When I purchased a tabby kitten to provide company for my dog, Max, I did not expect them to be so dependent upon each other. Now they do everything together. My best friend, Marvin, also has a dog and two cats as pets, but they ignore each other and go their separate ways. Max and Barney—my cat's name—sleep and play together: they take turns chasing each other throughout the house, and then, when they become exhausted, take naps with their paws on each other's body. I did not think that dogs sleep as much as cats, but apparently their sleeping habits depend on the environment they are in. They even, occasionally, eat each other's food, which doesn't seem to annoy either of them. And when one of my pets is ill, the other broods and mopes around the house until the illness passes. My dog Max gets sick much more than my cat Barney. I have never seen anything as strange or affecting as their close relationship. I hate to think what would happen if one of them should pass away.

2. Our city has many recreational opportunities for both young and old. Other cities that I have visited do not compare with ours. There are, of course, baseball fields, soccer fields, and hockey rinks for our youth, and tennis and squash courts, curling rinks, cross-country ski trails, and jogging paths for the physically active of all ages. But we also have several fine golf courses that cater to an older group who cannot participate in physically demanding sports. Cross-country skiers use our golf course in the winter. Our senior citizens also enjoy walking and bicycling. Furthermore, in our parks we have hiking trails, bicycle paths, and ice-skating ponds that can be enjoyed by the whole family. The ponds, though, do not always freeze solid enough for skating. In addition, picnic areas abound throughout our city. A lot of

these picnic areas are too noisy, though, because there always seems to be a slow-pitch game or a soccer match being played nearby. We are indeed fortunate to have a city council that cares so much for recreation and sports opportunities for all of our citizens.

3. My sister is the busiest person I know. I have a brother, too, but compared to my sister he is a couch potato. Besides working part-time in our college library, she also does volunteer work in our psychiatric hospital. The patients love her, and are always asking her to read to them. In addition, she is an active athlete: she golfs at least twice a week, belongs to a local tennis club, and curls for a team in our women's league. I am also an active athlete, but I am not as dedicated as she is. She is also taking a quilting course in the evening at our community college and is serving on a parent-teacher committee at the school her daughter attends. Her energy, it seems, is inexhaustible.

4. My college is not keeping up with the information age and the computer revolution. We have only four computer labs to service over two thousand students and most of these computers do not even have Pentium processors. A few of our administrators wanted to purchase Apple Macintosh computers, but they were voted down. Also, our printers are old ink-jet types, not laser printers, and they are always breaking down. Furthermore, the only computers with Internet access are in the library, and they are always in use. I think Internet access is essential today if one has to do significant research. Nor do we have an internal network that enables us to use e-mail to converse with our teachers. Everyone knows that e-mail is essential in today's information environment. Because of this lack of computers in our school, very few students know how to use the latest word-processing and spreadsheet programs. I think that the administrators at our college all need to take professional development courses in managing a computer-based learning environment.

5. The Christmas season has become too commercial. It didn't used to be that way; when I was a child, I always related Christmas to church attendance. The department stores start advertising "Christmas specials" in the middle of November, and gift giving has become an unfortunate substitute for the Christmas spirit. I hate shopping in crowded stores with harried and overworked salespeople. Santa Claus has become nothing more than a conduit between a child and a department store. There is no longer any religious significance in Christmas trees or Christmas music: "Rudolph the Red-Nosed Reindeer," cheap tinsel, and coloured bulbs are now the order of the day. My family does not adorn our Christmas tree with tinsel or multicoloured balls. Everyone goes on a buying frenzy, and liquor stores always do a booming business because of all the office parties where prodigious amounts of liquor are consumed. I think that Christ has permanently gone out of Christmas and has been replaced by the gift catalogue.

C. THE TOPIC SENTENCE: POINT OF VIEW

One of the most important parts of the expository paragraph is the topic sentence, for it contains the controlling idea. And because the controlling idea is the one discussed by the rest of the sentences in the paragraph, the topic sentence must not only state the idea clearly and succinctly but also determine its pattern of development.

A good topic sentence, then, places certain expectations in the minds of readers by focussing their attention on a specific attitude or position that you have assumed. It thus informs readers how you feel, as well as what you think, about the topic idea.

1. An Effective Topic Sentence

An effective topic sentence must fulfill two essential requirements: it must be specific enough to convert the topic statement into an idea, and general enough to be broken down, explained, and defended by the rest of the sentences in the paragraph.

(a) If the topic sentence is too general, your paragraph will be loose and unwieldy, and readers will have trouble distinguishing it from the thesis topic of your essay. Consider the following statements:

> Democracy is the political philosophy governing North America.
>
> The highest mountain in the United States is Mount McKinley.
>
> Oil exploration off Canada's east coast is taking place.

These sentences lack direction because they contain no specific idea or point of view. They are merely statements of fact, revealing no sense of purpose and placing no questions in the minds of the readers. They may therefore be dismissed as inert statements, too general and insubstantial to be contained in a single paragraph. Observe how much more solid and interesting they become when given a specific focus:

> Democracy in North America is being eroded by special interest groups.
>
> Climbing Mount McKinley can be extremely hazardous.
>
> Oil exploration off Canada's east coast is absolutely essential for the economic health of the Atlantic provinces.

Now each of these topic statements has been given a clear direction. You now know the precise idea you will stress throughout the rest of the paragraph: the first topic sentence focussed on the harmful influence of special interest groups; the second, on the hazards of climbing; and the third, on the promotion of east-coast oil exploration. This conversion of the general topic statement into a specific topic idea is illustrated below.

TOPIC:	Democracy	TOPIC IDEA:	Hurt by special interest groups
TOPIC:	Mount McKinley	TOPIC IDEA:	Hazardous to climb
TOPIC:	East-coast oil exploration	TOPIC IDEA:	Important to the economic health of the Atlantic provinces

(b) If the topic sentence is too specific, it will be self-explanatory and therefore static. It will leave no room for you to expand it into a unified paragraph. Here are a few examples:

> My chair is made of wood.
>
> I completed my math test yesterday.
>
> This orange was grown in Florida.

Because these sentences are too narrow and restricted, they literally have no place to go. They cannot be expanded and explored because they lack a general point of view. Now consider these sentences:

> Wooden chairs are more decorative than metal chairs.
>
> We are given too many math tests.
>
> Florida oranges are better tasting than California oranges.

You can develop these sentences because they contain a general point of view. The initial statement can be justified by giving reasons, examples, and specific details. Adequate arguments can be developed because a clear position has been taken. In short, there is a solid foundation on which to build a unified and coherent paragraph.

Exercise 10.2 — Selecting the Topic Sentence

From the lists below, select the number of the sentence that you think would best serve as a topic sentence and write it in the space to the right or on a separate sheet.

EXAMPLE: 1. My pet cat is named Herman.
                 2. Many people have cats as house pets.
                 3. I swear my cat Herman has a distinct sense of humour.   __3__

(a) 1. My car is being repaired again.
     2. Since I bought my car, it has never run properly.
     3. I had problems with my brakes and transmission and had to purchase a new muffler and radiator.   _____

(b) 1. Basketball is my favourite sport.
2. Five players must play as a cohesive team.
3. The three-point shots are exciting to watch. _____

(c) 1. The picnic food was delicious.
2. Our school picnic was a great success.
3. The weather was perfect and the lake was not too cold for swimming. _____

(d) 1. My brother lifts weights and jogs for an hour every day.
2. My sister teaches an exercise class for the YWCA.
3. All members of my family are physically active. _____

(e) 1. Many American companies have manufacturing plants in Canada.
2. General Motors makes cars in the province of Quebec.
3. Black and Decker has a plant in Brockville, Ontario. _____

(f) 1. Handguns are used in domestic quarrels.
2. Concealed handguns are often used in bank robberies.
3. Why aren't handguns outlawed in the United States? _____

(g) 1. Why do people still smoke?
2. The evidence that smoking causes cancer and heart disease is irrefutable.
3. Smoking is now socially unacceptable. _____

(h) 1. Toronto is an attractive city for tourists.
2. Many tourists visit the CN Tower.
3. Tourists also enjoy eating at the many ethnic restaurants. _____

(i) 1. It takes me about five days to read a good book.
2. Reading good literature is both enjoyable and intellectually rewarding.
3. I learn a great deal from reading historical novels. _____

(j) 1. I enjoy Shakespearean drama.
2. I saw *King Lear* performed in Stratford, Ontario.
3. Shakespeare's tragic characters are fascinating. _____

(k) 1. I am losing my taste for red meat.
2. The diet I am following is very difficult.
3. I have to eat fruits and vegetables every day. _____

(l) 1. She gives too much homework.
2. She gives a mini test every week.
3. My English teacher expects too much from her students. _____

(m) 1. Our bus system is a mess.
2. The buses are always breaking down.
3. The seats are all ripped, and the buses are always late. _____

(n) 1. Salespeople won't take no for an answer.
2. Salespeople exaggerate and bend the truth.
3. Telephone sales are both annoying and misleading. _____

(o) 1. My new automobile is dark blue.
2. The car burns too much gasoline.
3. I will never again buy a luxury car. _____

2. Position of Topic Sentences

Although the topic sentence is most often placed at the beginning of the paragraph, it can also appear at the beginning and the middle, the beginning and the end, or at the end only. Writers position topic sentences in these different ways according to the way they wish to organize their ideas, the emphasis they wish to place on them, and the tone they wish to convey. However, the developmental details must be clearly arranged so that the reader can follow the logic of the sequence of thoughts, either before or after the topic sentences.

(a) *Topic Sentence at the Beginning*

This type of paragraph structure, which is the most common, introduces the topic idea in the first sentence, so that the reader will know immediately how the rest of the paragraph will be developed.

> *The central symbol for Canada—and this is based on numerous instances of its occurrence in both English and French-Canadian literature—is undoubtedly survival, la Survivance. Like the Frontier and The Island, it is a multi-faceted and adaptable idea.* For early explorers and settlers, it meant bare survival in the face of "hostile" elements and/or natives: carving out a place and a way of keeping alive. But the word can also suggest survival of a crisis or disaster, like a hurricane or a wreck, and many Canadian poems have this kind of survival as a theme; what you might call "grim" survival as opposed to "bare" survival. For French Canada after the English took over it became cultural survival, hanging on as a people, retaining a religion and a language under an alien government. And in English Canada now while the Americans are taking over it is acquiring a similar meaning. There is another use of the word as well: a survival can be a vestige of a vanished order which has managed to persist after its time is past, like a primitive reptile. This version crops up in Canadian thinking too, usually among those who believe that Canada is obsolete.[1]

In this paragraph the writer uses examples in the body to define precisely what she means by the term "survival" and its relevance as a Canadian symbol.

(b) *Topic Sentence at the Beginning and End*
In this type of paragraph organization the topic idea is restated in the last sentence so that the reader will clearly understand the writer's position before going on to the next paragraph. You will find this paragraph structure used most often in textbooks or educational journals, where the flow of ideas may be sophisticated and difficult to grasp.

> A child who is made to read, "Nan had a pad. Nan had a tan pad. Dad ran. Dad ran to the pad," and worse nonsense can have no idea that books are worth the effort of learning to read. His frustration is increased by the fact that such a repetitive exercise is passed off as a story to be enjoyed. The worst effect of such drivel is the impression it makes on a child that sounding out words on a page—decoding—is what reading is all about. If, on the contrary, a child were taught new skills as they became necessary to understand a worthwhile text, the empty achievement "Now I can decode some words" would give way to the much more satisfying recognition "Now I am reading something that adds to my life." *From the start, reading lessons should nourish the child's spontaneous desire to read books by himself.*[2]

By describing the failure of reading lessons in the opening sentence of this paragraph, the writers implicitly tell us what they think the most important goal of such lessons is. Then they explicitly state this goal in the concluding sentence.

(c) *Topic Sentence at the Beginning and in the Middle*
This type of paragraph structure is used when the topic idea can be discussed in two parts. First one idea is introduced and developed, and then its opposite or complementary idea is introduced and developed. Paragraphs organized in this manner are usually quite lengthy.

> *The future of literacy is ultimately in the hands of the teachers of English.* If they are well enough trained, determined enough, and dedicated enough to the cultivation of literacy, no one can actually stop them from making their students literate. Not every student can be educated to the same degree of literacy, though my own long experience taught me what a great deal can be achieved with what might seem to be unpromising material. But the teacher must have a clear notion of what he is trying to do, and of how to do it, and be constantly imaginative and inventive in his methods. *English is by no means an obsolete industry.* It is an industry which has been suffering from a great deal of confusion about what products it is trying to make and about what its workers are supposed to be doing. Its genuine and proper products should be as valuable and as necessary as ever.[3]

Under the general heading of the future of literacy, the writer first discusses the function and qualities of English teachers; then he goes on to discuss the relevance of English as a subject taught in schools.

(d) *Topic Sentence at the End*
This type of paragraph may be organized in one of two ways: it may contain a series of details or minor statements that are brought together by the final sentence, which serves as the conclusion of the paragraph. Or it may be composed of a number of rhetorical questions that are answered by the final sentence of the paragraph.

> The assumption that budget cuts should be made in our social service programs needs careful consideration. In 1978 there were three halfway houses for the needy in our city; in 1982 there were two, and today we have only one. Furthermore, in 1981 we had four daycare centres; today we have only two and both are overcrowded. And finally, the hours our chest x-ray clinic is available to the public have been severely curtailed, while our home for abused women must now rely on private donations. These facts seem to indicate that instead of reducing our social welfare budget, we should significantly increase it.

In this paragraph the writer provides the reader with figures and statements of fact that lead logically and inevitably to his topic position in the last sentence.

> How long must we endure an increasing debt burden that fuels inflation year after year? How much longer can we go on paying off our mortgages when mortgage rates go up every six months? How much longer do you think our elderly will survive on fixed incomes in a climate of runaway inflation? And how long before our unemployed revolt over the lack of jobs in our sick economy? If action isn't taken soon to halt our high inflation and unemployment, we should call for another election and then vote in leaders who will take decisive political action.

The suggestive questions in this paragraph lead logically to the last sentence which, as a drawn conclusion, functions as the topic idea.

There are also paragraphs that do not contain unifying sentences with specific topic ideas. Instead, they gather together enough detailed information to suggest the topic idea without actually stating it. These paragraphs, however, are difficult to write and should be avoided, especially in a closely reasoned essay or report.

> In existing capitalisms at any definite time, profit may not be guaranteed for all capitalists but only for a certain number. But this number may be sufficient to keep production up to a level where most workers are employed while those who are temporarily unemployed receive social benefits. Marx was indisputably right in anticipating periodic economic dislocations where the market still operates in an unplanned economy.[4]

This paragraph contains no topic sentence because it is not organized around a single central idea. Rather, it is composed of a series of statements which, when read together, add up to a single thought—that full employment is not a prerequisite for a capitalist economy.

The point to remember about topic sentences is that no matter where they occur, they must serve as the focus of the paragraph; that is, they must contain the ideas around which the other sentences in the paragraph are organized.

Exercise 10.3 — Position of the Topic Sentence
In the space to the right or on a separate sheet, place the number of each sentence that contains the topic idea. There may be more than one topic sentence in each paragraph.

(a) 1. The plot is dull and convoluted. 2. The characters are flat and uninteresting. 3. The settings are unrealistic and artificial. 4. The writing style is full of clichés and jargon. 5. The novel that we were assigned to read is boring and poorly written.

(b) 1. Our mayor has not performed well in office this year. 2. Our city went over budget for the second year in a row. 3. There was not enough money to pay our road crews to repair the many potholes in our streets. 4. The wife of the mayor was given a supervisory position in the city accounting office. 5. Our city auditor was accused of taking bribes and is awaiting trial. 6. I think it is about time that we select someone more honest and more competent in the next election.

(c) 1. My putting stroke is still jerky and uneven. 2. I slice my drives from the tee. 3. I tend to pull my long irons to the left. 4. I often scuff my pitches to the green. 5. My golf game is still very weak. 6. My chip shots are almost always too short.

(d) 1. We had rain for seven straight days. 2. Our van broke down twice and we had to have it towed to a garage. 3. My mother contracted food poisoning, and we had to take her to the emergency room at a hospital in Halifax. 4. One of our motel rooms flooded one night from the heavy rain, causing four of us to have to sleep in one room. 5. My father lost his credit card and had to wire our bank in Ontario for money. 6. Our family vacation in the Maritimes last summer was a colossal failure.

(e) 1. I can walk to work. 2. There are no large traffic jams. 3. We know all of our neighbours. 4. Our recreation facilities are not overcrowded. 5. There are many advantages to living in a small town. **6.** Our crime rate is low. **7.** Our pollution level is one of the lowest in the province.

D. THREE PARAGRAPH TYPES

Besides the expository or developmental paragraph found in the body of essays, there are other types of paragraphs that, although not independent units of thought, are important for the smooth development of any extended paper. These are the introductory, transitional, and concluding paragraphs.

1. The Introductory Paragraph

This paragraph prepares readers for the body of the essay. It arouses their interest and whets their curiosity. It may also project your attitude towards your subject and thus set the tone for the rest of the essay. In short, it places readers in a proper frame of mind to accept what you have to say. Here are a few examples of introductory paragraphs:

> If we are going to develop a sensible approach to the encouragement of talent, we shall have to dispose of a good many myths surrounding the talented individual.[5]

> The arguments in favour of a great deal of freedom in education are derived not from men's natural goodness, but from the effects of authority, both on those who suffer it and on those who exercise it. Those who are subject to authority become either submissive or rebellious, and each attitude has its drawbacks.[6]

> There are still no satisfactory answers to many of the general questions which anyone interested in the early eighteenth-century novelists and their work is likely to ask. Is the novel a new literary form? And if we assume, as is commonly done, that it is, and that it was begun by Defoe, Richardson, and Fielding, how does it differ from the prose fiction of the past, from that of Greece, for example, or that of the Middle Ages, or of seventeenth-century France? And is there any reason why these differences appeared when and where they did?[7]

In the above paragraphs the authors clearly define what they intend to write about in their essays. They introduce the statements to be examined and the questions to be answered, so that their readers are able to anticipate how the rest of the essay will be developed.

2. The Transitional Paragraph

This type of paragraph allows readers to move from one section of material to another in an easy and smooth progression. It functions as a signpost that reminds readers where they have been and where they will go next. These paragraphs are usually brief—sometimes no more than a sentence or two—and are often highlighted by transitional words and phrases that reflect different thought relationships. Here are some examples of transitional paragraphs:

> Having identified four components of a teacher's intellectual and emotional equipment, I would now like to consider a question pertaining to them that has been much debated: Is there a science of education?[8]
>
> So far I have spoken from my own experiences as a teacher in high school, college, and university. But you need not take my uncorroborated word for the deplorable failure of American education. There are many other witnesses who can be called to the stand.[9]
>
> So far so good. But now we must return to the distinction between reading for information and reading for understanding. In the previous chapter, I suggested how much more active the latter sort of reading must be, and how it feels to do it. Now we must consider the difference in what you get out of these two kinds of reading.[10]

These paragraphs remind readers what was previously covered and what is still to be covered, leading them from one idea to another without an abrupt break in thought. They may be thought of as mental handholds that assist readers to maintain their balance through the stacked paragraphs of an essay or a report.

The transitional expressions in these paragraphs alert readers to the change in the direction of thought. A partial list of such expressions appears on p. 207.

3. The Concluding Paragraph

This paragraph sums up the point of the essay by restating the thesis topic. By summarizing some of the development and re-emphasizing topic ideas, you provide your readers with a concise statement of your position.

Concluding paragraphs should maintain the same tone as the rest of the essay and refrain from introducing any ideas that were not already discussed in the body. Here are some examples of concluding paragraphs:

> Let us sum up again. The majority of young people are faced with the following alternative: Either society is a benevolently frivolous racket in which they'll manage to boondoggle, though less profitably than the more privileged; or society is serious, but they are useless and hopelessly out. Such thoughts do not encourage productive life.[11]
>
> The language of individuality overpromises, and we see the wreckage of its illusions all around us. Only when this happens is individualism's seductive message doubted. It is an insufficient guide to the pursuit of happiness. I suspect we will eventually make our peace with the reality, while, in familiar American fashion, stubbornly continuing to extol the illusion.[12]
>
> The bonuses of "less is more" are vast. The choice facing the American people is not between growth and stagnation, but between short-term and long-term disaster. We can continue to pursue the growth policies of the

past and let urban decay, exorbitant prices, and risks to our national security dictate stringent remedial policies a few years from now. Or we can exercise restraint and learn to live comfortably, within our means.[13]

Each of these paragraphs brings the essay of which it is a part to a close. By reviewing some of the ideas that were discussed in the body, and by restating and sometimes redefining the thesis topic, the writer allows the reader to follow the logic of the conclusions drawn from the body of the essay.

Transitional Thought Relationships

1. **Addition**
   again
   also
   and, and then
   besides
   further
   furthermore
   in addition
   moreover
   too

2. **Emphasis**
   above all
   as a matter of fact
   certainly
   chiefly
   doubtless
   indeed
   in fact
   in point of fact
   to be sure
   unquestionably
   without doubt

3. **Similarity**
   in like manner
   in the same way
   similarly

4. **Contrast**
   although
   but
   conversely
   however
   in contrast
   nevertheless
   nonetheless
   on the contrary
   on the other hand
   otherwise
   still
   unlike
   while
   yet

5. **Example**
   for example
   for instance
   in particular
   in this case
   namely
   to illustrate

6. **Reason**
   as
   because
   for
   for that reason
   since

7. **Result**
   accordingly
   as a result
   consequently
   hence
   so, so far
   then
   therefore
   thus, thus far

8. **Time**
   at present
   afterwards
   at last
   before
   immediately
   in due time
   in the meantime
   meanwhile
   once
   shortly
   shortly after
   soon
   until
   while

9. **Chronology**
   finally
   first, second, third, etc.
   next
   then

10. **Conclusion**
    in brief
    in conclusion
    in other words
    in short
    to conclude
    to sum up

Exercise 10.4 — Paragraph Types
A. Write a brief introductory statement for each of the following developmental paragraphs. Make sure that your statement is broad enough to introduce the ideas discussed in the body of each paragraph.

> EXAMPLE: We exercise not only to lose weight but also to improve our muscle tone and strengthen our heart and lungs. Exercise makes us feel physically vital and mentally alert; it is, literally, a life saver.
>
> INTRODUCTORY STATEMENT: The advantages of daily exercise are many and varied, and they cannot be overestimated.

1. My brother Salvatore's batting average was .344, and he hit 28 home runs. He also had the best fielding percentage among all the infielders, and he was second in stolen bases. Moreover, he never missed a game all season due to injury or sickness.

   INTRODUCTORY STATEMENT: _____

2. I write my letters and term papers with WordPerfect, and I do my accounting homework with a spreadsheet called Quicken. I also do some of my research with Encarta, and Multimedia Encyclopaedia. For my relaxation I play computer games like Dungeons and Dragons and Space Cadet.

   INTRODUCTORY STATEMENT: _____

3. I read daily newspapers for provincial and city news. I read weekly newsmagazines for national and international news, and I read *The Economist* and the *Wall Street Journal* for financial news. My bedtime reading consists of collections of short stories—usually by Alice Munro—and my longer fiction reading consists mainly of historical novels. I also enjoy reading biographies of famous people for pleasure.

   INTRODUCTORY STATEMENT: _____

4. Many of the side streets were not blocked off by the police, which resulted in minor traffic jams. Several of the Disney characters' balloons were not properly inflated and fell on the marching band. The clowns ran out of candy for dispensing to the crowds of people lining the street, and the rain started just as the first float approached the viewing stand. And to top off the disastrous morning, Santa Claus' beard blew off and sailed down the street.

   INTRODUCTORY STATEMENT: _____

5. My father refinishes old furniture, and my mother is an accomplished quilter and potter. My sister collects stamps, and my brother is a bird watcher. Furthermore, I recondition antique automobiles.

INTRODUCTORY STATEMENT: _____

B. Connect the following paragraph fragments with brief, transitional statements. Make each statement serve as a logical bridge between each pair of fragments.

> EXAMPLE: Therefore, I think that the shocking obsolescence of our military hardware can be directly traced to the lack of military planning by our government.
>
> TRANSITIONAL STATEMENT: (But the obsolescence of our equipment is not the the only problem, nor is it the most serious. There is also the human factor.)
>
> The quality of our military personnel is lower than it has ever been. Recruits are inadequately trained, poorly motivated, and physically unfit.

1. So our hockey team seems to have a solid foundation of talented players and should therefore be in contention for the league championship next season.

   TRANSITIONAL STATEMENT: _____

   Our baseball team does not have a top-quality pitcher, and our best long-ball hitter is on academic suspension. Two of our infielders are first-year students, and our schedule this year is tougher than last year's. Furthermore, our coach, who is new this year, has never coached a college team.

2. In summary, the cottage that my father just bought is an ideal vacation home for the entire family.

   TRANSITIONAL STATEMENT: _____

   My uncle's cottage is in a location that is accessible only by a four-wheel-drive vehicle. It has no electricity and no phone. It is not winterized and is heated by only a wood stove. Moreover, the lake is fed by mountain streams and is invariably too cold for swimming, even in July.

3. We all agreed that our bus tour through the French countryside was outstanding.

   TRANSITIONAL STATEMENT: _____

   The train we took through Germany and Holland was noisy and overcrowded. The cars were full of cigarette smoke and the food was tasteless. The engine broke down outside of Hamburg, Germany, and we had to spend four hours on a siding waiting for a new one to be hooked up to the passenger cars.

210 Writing Fundamentals

4. It is obvious, then, that poultry products can be included in every sensible diet.

   TRANSITIONAL STATEMENT: _____

   Red meat is full of saturated fat and high in cholesterol. It is difficult to digest and has been linked to colon cancer. Also, it is certainly more expensive than poultry. Even lean cuts of steak, like filet mignon and New York strip, are rarely recommended by any dietitian for weight loss.

5. Therefore, our skiing holiday in the Canadian Rockies was thoroughly enjoyable.

   TRANSITIONAL STATEMENT: _____

   The airport bus had an accident and we missed our return flight. When we finally arrived at the airport it was crowded with students on mid-term break, and we had to wait in a queue for more than an hour to arrange alternate flight connections. When our plane finally took off, we were told that the Toronto airport was closed because of a severe snowstorm, and were therefore diverted to Winnipeg, where we had to spend the night at an airport hotel.

C. Write a concluding statement that logically sums up and completes the ideas and information in each of the following paragraphs.

> EXAMPLE: Our city is one of the most progressive cities in Canada. It has an enlightened mayor, a dynamic city council, an abundance of parks, an efficient transportation system, a new arts centre, and light industry that does not pollute the environment.
>
> CONCLUDING STATEMENT: Because of all these recreational, cultural, and commercial advantages, I would not choose to live anywhere else—unless, of course, another Canadian city could duplicate these attractions.

1. Our university is in serious financial trouble. The student tuition rate was raised three years in a row. The classroom buildings are all in disrepair, and the library building has had a leaky roof for the last two years. Furthermore, the professors are disputing their salary scale and are threatening to strike. Moreover, the athletic department has discontinued our baseball and soccer teams.

   CONCLUDING STATEMENT: _____

2. What must we do to convince our company to pay more attention to air and water pollution? Last week three employees had to be hospitalized because of a toxic-fumes leak in one of our testing laboratories. Last month our city filed a lawsuit against the company, claiming that it is releasing sulphur

dioxide from its smokestacks. Furthermore, the neighbouring community claims that water the company releases into the river is not properly treated and is causing numerous fish deaths.

CONCLUDING STATEMENT: _____

3. Our citizens cannot afford the new sports facilities planned for our city. The new football and baseball stadium will cost over one hundred million dollars. The new basketball arena and Olympic-size swimming pool will cost the taxpayers over thirty million dollars, and the cost of the new hockey rink is projected to be sixty million dollars. Furthermore, it is not yet certain that our city will attract a major-league baseball team or a professional football team.

CONCLUDING STATEMENT: _____

4. Where have all the good paying jobs gone? What happened to the shopping centre that was supposed to open last spring? Why has the largest industry in our city laid off one third of its workforce? Why are so many of our citizens moving to other provinces? And why has our city closed two of our public schools and cut its workforce by twenty percent?

CONCLUDING STATEMENT: _____

5. Our graduation day left a lot to be desired. The ceremony had to be moved inside because of the inclement weather—there were intermittent downpours all day. Not enough caps and gowns of the same colour were ordered, so we had to improvise. The guest speaker was late and there were not enough seats for the parents and guests. Furthermore, we had to have recorded music because several key members of the school band were participating in a concert out of town.

CONCLUDING STATEMENT: _____

E. CREATING PATTERNS OF DEVELOPMENT: THE EXPOSITORY PARAGRAPH

Since the expository or developmental paragraph controls the direction and flow of the essay, we must pay particular heed to how expository paragraphs are developed.

Although there are numerous ways to develop a paragraph, some are more common and, for our purposes, more relevant than others. Here are eight of the most useful patterns of development:

1. Classification
2. Comparison and Contrast
3. Narration and Description
4. Example
5. Enumeration by Details
6. Cause and Effect
7. Process Description
8. Definition

These are the patterns that you, as a student, will most often have to write. They each serve specific functions, and each has a definite organizational scheme. Your use of one or more of these developmental patterns in your writing will depend upon a number of considerations: (1) What precisely you want to say about a given topic; (2) how you want to arrange your ideas; (3) what effect you want to create in the mind of your reader; (4) how much emphasis you wish to place on certain ideas; (5) how forceful you wish your topic idea to be.

Ninety percent of the time your opening sentences will contain the topic idea that determines how the rest of the paragraph will be developed. This is illustrated below.

Topic Sentence	Pattern of Development
The term "behaviour" can be misleading.	Definition
Many factors contributed to the outbreak of the Second World War.	Cause and Effect
A cruise ship has numerous unexpected amenities.	Enumeration by Details
I remember my first date.	Narration and Description
Our history course was broken into four historical periods that were almost mini-courses.	Classification
Nineteenth-century capitalism, although theoretically the same as that of the twentieth century, functioned quite differently.	Comparison and Contrast
Some baseball teams have better facilities and more fan support than other teams.	Example
There is only one way to operate a forklift truck.	Process Description

Of course, some lengthy paragraphs, or a series of paragraphs, will use a combination of these patterns to develop a topic idea adequately; nevertheless, in most of your expository writing you will have to focus on one pattern at a time in order to write a unified and coherent essay.

1. Classification

This type of paragraph may not only place its subject term into a class or group to which it belongs but also divide it into its constituent parts. This pattern of development gives readers a more precise and comprehensive understanding of the thing or idea being examined, as you can see in the examples below.

Topic Sentence *In the earlier epochs of history, we find almost everywhere a complicated arrangement of society into various orders, a manifold gradation of social rank.* In ancient Rome we have patricians,

Classification by Social Rank	knights, plebians, slaves; in the Middle Ages, feudal lords, vassals, guild-masters, journeymen, apprentices, serfs; in almost all of these classes, again, subordinate gradations.[14]
Topic Sentence	*A useful rhetorical classification divides sentences into those which make a major point near or at the beginning of the sentence and then add to that point—the loose sentence—and those which delay, by interruption and qualification, the major point 'til the end of the sentence—the periodic sentence.* The basis for this division is essentially grammatical. The loose sentence will usually begin with a complete simple sentence and add phrases, clauses or more sentences. On the other hand, the periodic sentence will usually not complete the central grammatical structure until the end of the sentence.[15]
Classification by Function	

2. Comparison and Contrast

In this type of paragraph the idea in the topic statement is related both to terms that are similar and to those that are distinct. The comparison terms, which are usually more obvious and concrete, place the topic statement in a familiar context; the contrasting terms emphasize the uniqueness of the topic statement.

These developmental terms are usually examined point by point: either all the comparison details are presented and then all the contrasting details—AAA—BBB (as seen in the first example below)—or the contrasting and comparing details are presented alternatively—ABABAB (as seen in the second example). But whatever organizational scheme is used, a closely reasoned relationship must exist between the subject term and its supporting details.

Topic Sentence	*Historically, the engagement of craftsman and professional was analogous.* A craftsman was accepted into the guild of his peers by making a masterpiece and, just as with the professional, this achievement signalled a long growth, by apprenticeship, into a career that had become second nature. Usually he would have a prior disposition to the craft, by family, or locality, or personal talent. Thus, induction into a job was a process of personal engagement, not unlike the doctor's ring and kiss. It must be said, however, that unlike the humane professions, attachment to a craft or mechanic trade could easily produce a craft-idiot or drudge. Up to a point, "alienation" from this situation was liberating both from narrow ideas and long hours.[16]
Comparison Details	
Contrasting Details	
Topic Sentence	*Consider our lives. All other activities we share with the other inhabitants of the planet.* Animals, birds, reptiles, fish and insects also struggle for power, as we do. They organize themselves into social groups. Many build. Some control their own environment by ingenious inventions. Some of them, like some of us, collect wealth. They fight. They make love. They play games. Some have powers we shall never possess and can scarcely comprehend.
Comparison Details	

Contrasting Details	Cunning and skillful, that they are. Yet collectively they learn little that is new, and individually almost nothing. Their skills are intricate, but limited. Their art, though charming, is purely decorative. Their languages consist of a few dozen signs and sounds. Their memory is vivid but restricted. Their curiosity is shallow and temporary, merely the rudiment of that wonder which fills the mind of a human scientist or poet, or historian or philosopher. They cannot conceive of learning and knowledge as a limitless activity administered by the power of will. Only human beings really learn, and know, and remember, and think creatively as individuals far beyond the limitations of any single group or the dominance of any single need. Knowledge acquired and extended for its own sake is the specific quality that makes us human. Our species has the hair and the lungs of animals, reptilian bones, and fish-like blood. We are close indeed to the beasts; often we are more cruel.
Contrasting Details and Conclusion	But we are fundamentally different from them in that we learn almost infinitely, and know and recollect. We are *Homo Sapiens:* Man the Thinker.[17]

3. Narration and Description

These two developmental patterns almost always go together. A narration tells a story or relates an event, and a description provides a sensory impression of that story or event.

In this type of paragraph the reader is made to stand at the elbow of the writer, to see and feel what the writer sees and feels. That is why the sensory quality of the language is so important here—it conveys to the reader not only what happened but also what it looked, sounded, and felt like.

To enhance the sensory dimension of the narrative, you will often need to employ similes and metaphors that exemplify what you are describing. A *simile* is a direct comparison of two essentially different things or ideas, usually joined by the words "like" or "as":

> Hearing him relate his boring and repetitious foreign travel experiences is like listening to the eternal dripping of a leaky faucet.

> This knife is as sharp as a gust of winter wind.

A *metaphor*, on the other hand, is a figure of speech that makes its comparison by transferring the qualities of one thing directly onto another thing:

> Jack is a tiger when he is angry.

> Her mind was a vast treasury of historical knowledge.

In narrative or descriptive writing your task is to convey experiences precisely and, in the process, to make them vivid, meaningful, and dramatic. The following two paragraphs exemplify these qualities.

Chapter 10 / Constructing Effective Paragraphs   **215**

Opening I set about gaining Piquette's trust. She was not allowed to go
Narrative swimming, with her bad leg, but I managed to lure her down to the
Statement beach—or rather, she came because there was nothing else to do.
      The water was always icy, for the lake was fed by springs, but I
Descriptive swam like a dog, thrashing my arms and legs around at such speed
Details and with such an output of energy that I never grew cold. Finally,
      when I had enough, I came out and sat beside Piquette on the
Narrative sand. When she saw me approaching, her hand squashed flat the
Details sand castle she had been building, and she looked at me sullenly,
      without speaking.[18]

Opening The beach is a vast and preternaturally clean and simple land-
Descriptive scape. It is like a piece of the moon. The surf had pounded the
Statement floor solid, so it was easy walking, and everything left on the sand
      had been twice changed by the waves. There was the spine of a
Descriptive shell, part of a broomstick, and part of a brick, both of them milled
Details and broken until they were nearly unrecognizable, and I suppose
      Lawrence's sad frame of mind—for he kept his head down—went
Narrative from one broken thing to another. The company of his pessimism
Details began to infuriate me, and I caught up with him and put a hand on
      his shoulder. "It's only a summer day, Tifty," I said. "It's only a
      summer day. What's the matter? Don't you like it here?"[19]

4. Example

Paragraphs that use examples as their pattern of development usually expand and support an explanation in the topic sentence. These paragraphs narrow down general and abstract statements into concrete sections that enable the reader to focus clearly on the writer's argument, as in the following examples.

Topic   *And yet poverty, even the poverty of an entire society, is not an*
Statements *insurmountable barrier to education if people are determined to*
      learn and prepared to sacrifice. An entire society can raise its
      standards within fifty years by a concerted effort, or maintain
First   *them for centuries against persistent discouragement.* Finland is
Example one of the poorest nations in Europe, but it has splendid schools,
      and its citizens are far more cultivated than many a richer nation.
Second Scotland was never wealthy; yet she has supported four universities
Example ever since the Renaissance, and the annals of each of them are
      filled with tales of peasant boys reared in grinding poverty and
      scarcely able to buy a suit of clothes, still winning their way to
      college, living there on a sack of oatmeal and a few salt herring
      brought from their cottage homes, and rising to distinction as
Third   scholars and inventors. Most astonishing of all, perhaps, is the
Example tenacity with which the Jews, living for many generations in the
      poor ghettoes of Eastern Europe, kept up their own school sys-
      tem, transmitted their books faithfully through the centuries, and
      added to them a mass of explanation, symbolism, and decoration
      which is a monument to the power of the human mind as well as
      an act of homage to God.[20]

Topic Statement	Technological modesty, fittingness, is not negative. It is the ecological wisdom of cooperating with nature rather than trying to master her.
First Example	A well-known example is the long-run superiority of partial pest control in farming by using biological deterrents rather than chemical ones. The living defenders work harder, at the right moment, and with more pin-pointed targets.
Second Example	But let me give another example because it is so lovely—though I have forgotten the name of my informant: A tribe in Yucatan educates its children to identify and pull up all weeds in the region; then what is left is a garden of useful plants that have chosen to be there and now thrive.[21]

5. Enumeration by Details

In this type of paragraph the topic sentence is always placed at the beginning, and is broad enough to be supported by a substantial number of details, which may be statements of fact, statistics, examples, or minor definitions. The topic sentence states an idea or affirms an opinion, and the following sentences develop and support it. When using this pattern of development, you must be certain that your supporting information adequately develops your topic idea.

Topic Statement	When I finally brought my 1987 automobile to my mechanic for a thorough checkup, he told me that the motor was still in good shape but that I needed a number of parts and services if I expected to drive it for another ten years.
A Series of Development Details	He told me that I needed new brakes, a new battery, a new muffler and tailpipe, all new belts and hoses, new wheel bearings, and two new tires. He also advised me to change my spark plugs and air filter and to have my radiator flushed. Furthermore, he said that I should have my rusted left front fender replaced and my emissions-control converter repaired. Finally, he said that he would give me a special price on an engine tune-up and an oil change.
Concluding Statement	After he finished his litany of my mechanical problems, I offered to sell him my car for what it would cost me to have it repaired. He wisely refused.

6. Cause and Effect

In this type of paragraph the writer demonstrates in a causal sequence how one event is necessarily the result of another event. The reader is shown why something has occurred in the past and may occur in the future. Each step in the sequence depends upon a preceding step, and the developmental details must logically follow from the topic sentence when it occurs at the beginning of the paragraph, or lead up to it when it falls at the end of the paragraph.

This cause-and-effect pattern of development may be organized around a statement of fact or an opinion, and its causal sequence may vary: one cause may have one or more effects, several causes may have a single effect, or in a long paragraph there may be an involved sequence of causes and effects.

At the end of the paragraph, however, the reader must be convinced that every term in the cause-and-effect sequence has satisfactorily demonstrated the topic idea.

> *Topic Sentence* — *The perfection of gene splicing, as one offshoot of biological engineering, could cause dangerous social changes in the twenty-first century.* For instance, it may lead to a biological class system in which, say, blond hair and blue eyes would indicate a certain socio-economic group, and heavy upper-body musculature another socio-economic group. I.Q. levels may be intentionally reduced so that certain people could be matched with repetitious, low-level occupations. And the ability to *grow* new organs would dramatically increase life expectancy which, in turn, would spur population growth and place intolerable burdens on food production and energy consumption.
>
> *Sequence of Causes and Effects*

> *Topic Sentence* — *On balance, one is compelled to say that the advances in technology already made and to be made promise that mankind's future, with effective population control, can be much brighter than its past.* If technology makes highly destructive world wars possible for the first time in this century, it is also true that for the first time in this century the technological conditions are such that world government has become a practicable project. If technology results in uncontrollable industrial expansion and sometimes wasteful affluence, it is also true that our power to produce consumable wealth has reached the point that for the first time in this century, the elimination of poverty is even conceivable; more than that, this is the first century in which any steps have been taken to reduce its extent.[24]
>
> *First Effect*
>
> *Second Effect*

7. Process Description

This paragraph pattern describes a series of successive events that lead to a specific result. Each step in the series must necessarily lead to the next, and the final results must be the logical outcome of the series. Also, the specialized terms used in describing the process must be adequately defined.

This type of development is most often used in a report that explains how a given task is accomplished by following a number of procedural steps in chronological order.

> **How to Saw a Board** There is only one correct way to saw a board. First, measure carefully with a ruler or a tape and then use a pencil and a square to draw your line across the top edge of the board. Second, place the board on two sawhorses, keeping the pencil line on the outside, but allowing a few centimetres of clearance for the saw. Third, start the cut near the handle of the saw at the far end of the board, and when you have a groove, saw towards yourself at a 45° angle. Remember to saw outside the line, because if you saw on the line the kerf (the width of the cut) will cause the board to be too short.

Cleaning a Paint Brush Cleaning a paint brush can be easy if you follow the correct procedure. After you finish using the brush remove excess paint with a scraper. Then soak the brush in a can of paint thinner, working it back and forth against the bottom of the container so that the thinner soaks through. Next, squeeze the bristles between your thumb and forefinger to loosen the paint in the centre of the brush. Rinse it again in the thinner to make sure that all the paint has been removed. After rinsing thoroughly, press out the water with a stick, and then comb the bristles carefully with a wire comb. Allow the brush to dry by suspending it from the handle or by laying it on a clean, flat surface. Finally, wrap the dry brush in heavy paper to keep the bristles straight and store suspended by its handle. If you follow this simple procedure, your brush will be clean and ready to use when you need it again.

8. Definition

This type of paragraph is the most flexible, for it may follow more than one pattern of development. Because the developmental details supporting the topic sentence must be simpler and more concrete than the term defined, a writer will often use examples, comparisons, analogies, or synonyms to convert general and abstract ideas into specific and concrete information.

The definition of the subject term should be comprehensive, containing all the necessary details that not only place it into a specific category but also distinguish it from any other term in its class. It should tell readers what something is and how it differs from anything else with which it might be confused. An orange, for example, may be defined as a citrus fruit, but its difference from other citrus fruits, such as grapefruit, can be described in terms of its colour, size, and taste.

Ideally, then, at the end of a paragraph readers should know precisely the important and unique characteristics of the defined term and be familiar with the context in which it was defined.

Topic Sentence	*I think that what we mean in practice by reason can be defined*
First Definition Detail	*by three characteristics.* In the first place, it relies upon persuasion rather than force; in the second place, it seeks to per-
Second Definition Detail	suade by means of arguments which the man who uses them believes to be completely valid; and in the third place, in form-
Third Definition Detail	ing opinions, it uses observation and induction as much as possible and intuition as little as possible.[25]

Topic Sentence	*The term "class" in Marx is used in various senses, not at*
Sequence of Definition Details	*all strictly derivative from each other.* Sometimes its defining feature is the role a group plays in production, sometimes it is their common mode of life, including culture and traditions, sometimes the source of their income or the level of their income, sometimes their vocation or, in the case of the unemployed, their lack of any.[26]

Exercise 10.5 — Topic Sentence and Patterns of Development

From the list below select the pattern of development that you think most logically develops each topic sentence; then write it in the space to the right or on a separate sheet. Choose only one pattern for each topic sentence.

Classification
Comparison and/or Contrast
Cause and Effect
Narration and Description

Example
Enumeration by Details
Definition
Process Description

EXAMPLE: There is only one logical method of organizing an essay. <u>Process Description</u>

1. I am required to travel to Montreal this winter for pressing business reasons. _____
2. Paco's experience with the customs officials was very amusing. _____
3. Our store sells different kinds of chainsaws for a variety of jobs. _____
4. My brother and sister share many of the same personality traits. _____
5. The skills involved in ice-skating and downhill skiing are different in many respects. _____
6. My new car cost more money than my old one, but it has many safety features that make it a better value for the dollar. _____
7. Canadian and American football have different rules, each of which has advantages and disadvantages for the offensive team. _____
8. Stockbrokers are often under a great deal of stress. _____
9. There are many advantages to having a personal Web page on the Internet. _____
10. Learning how to play golf can enhance your leisure time as you grow older. _____
11. There are major differences between the games of cricket and baseball. _____
12. I will never forget my first date. _____
13. The definition of the word *terminal* depends entirely upon the context in which it is used. _____

14. Organizing a camping trip with preteens can be a harrowing experience. _____

15. Our ski school is second to none when it comes to organizing ski lessons for all levels of skiers—novice, intermediate, and advanced. _____

16. Tess's new apartment is much larger and more comfortable than our apartment. _____

17. Sayed's return to Cairo, Egypt, will depend on his family's willingness to pay his tuition to graduate school. _____

18. The employment clearinghouse at the teachers' conference this year offered both secondary and post-secondary teaching positions in different parts of the world. _____

19. My English teacher taught us not only how to read literature but also how to write creatively. _____

20. Who among us will ever forget our wild graduation party? _____

Exercise 10.6 — Selecting Topic Sentences and Constructing Patterns of Development

Select four topic sentences from the list below, or use four similar topic sentences of your own, and write four paragraphs that use the following patterns of development: Classification, Comparison and/or Contrast, Cause and Effect, and Narration and Description.

1. The two Shakespearean tragedies that I saw last week in Stratford, Ontario, used different tragic themes and took place in different settings.

2. Clarence, the "organizer," has divided his work into three different categories—home work, office work, and volunteer work—and he devotes different amounts of time to each category.

3. My sister's birthday party was a huge success.

4. We lost the league championship because of a number of factors, both physical and motivational.

5. Abdel Razzak has collected an impressive variety of oriental carpets.

6. I do not know what I dislike most: cleaning out the attic or washing our two dogs.

7. The bank's refusal to lend my father money to start his own business will have dire consequences for the whole family.

8. Knowing when to say "no" can save you a great deal of grief and turmoil.

9. I don't know which habit is more detrimental to your health—smoking cigarettes or eating fatty foods.

10. Watching too much television can seriously affect your ability to read, write, and think clearly.

11. Yasmin's fascinating tour of Pakistan will be the subject of our next Explorers meeting.

12. Both computer-based instruction and class lectures are used by our faculty for different reasons to teach business administration courses.

13. Drug abuse is directly related to the increase of crime in our city.

14. I am not sure which author I like most, Margaret Atwood or Mordecai Richler.

15. Our ski trip to Banff, Alberta, was a memorable experience.

Exercise 10.7 — Selecting Topic Sentences and Constructing Patterns of Development

Select four topic sentences from the list below, or use four similar topic sentences of your own, and write four paragraphs that use the following patterns of development: Example, Enumeration by Details, Process Description, and Definition.

1. Our summer vacation at the seashore was a major disappointment.

2. The word *palimony* came into our language because of people's willingness to live together without getting married.

3. Organizing a tour of Ottawa for U.S. tourists takes a great deal of planning, especially if the tourists know little about Canada and its government.

4. Driving while intoxicated has become a major problem for our city.

5. Our store carries numerous Christmas decorations for both inside and outside the home.

6. Putting up wood panelling in a recreational room is not complicated if you have the proper power tools.

7. Our neighbours are all involved in volunteer work for different charities.

8. What does the word *incognito* mean?

9. How does one set up a Neighbourhood Watch program?

10. Our regional hospital's emergency room is poorly equipped and understaffed.

11. The recreation area in our nursing home has numerous board games and computer games for the elderly.

12. *Software* seems to be a term that covers different computer programs, both educational and entertainment.

13. Knowing how to search the Internet for the cheapest airplane fares can save you both time and money.

14. Ernestine's new computer has many interesting features that mine does not have.

15. The trip we took to Vancouver was filled with surprises—some good and some bad.

NOTES

1. Margaret Atwood, *Survival: A Thematic Guide to Canadian Literature* (Toronto: House of Anansi Press, 1972), p. 32. Reprinted by permission of House of Anansi Press Limited.
2. Bruno Bettelheim and Karen Zelan, "Why Children Don't Like to Read," *The Atlantic* (November 1981), p. 26. Excerpt from *On Learning to Read* published by Alfred A. Knopf. Reprinted with permission.
3. F.E.L. Priestly, "English: An Obsolete Industry?" in *In the Name of Language*, ed. Joseph Gold (Toronto: Macmillan of Canada, 1975), p. 145. Copyright © The Macmillan Company of Canada Limited, 1975. Reprinted by permission of Macmillan Company of Canada, a Division of Gage Publishing Limited.
4. Sidney Hook, *Marx and the Marxists* (New York: Van Nostrand, 1955), p. 42. Reprinted by permission of the Wadsworth Publishing Company.
5. John Gardner, *Excellence: Can We Be Equal and Excellent Too?* (New York: Harper and Row, 1962), p. 58.
6. Bertrand Russell, "Education and Discipline," in *In Praise of Idleness* (London: Unwin Books, 1960), p. 127. Reprinted by permission of George Allen & Unwin Ltd.
7. Ian Watt, *The Rise of the Novel* (Pelican Book, Chatto and Windus, 1974), p. 9. Reprinted by permission of Chatto & Windus Ltd.
8. James B. Conant, *The Education of American Teachers* (New York: McGraw-Hill, 1963), p. 117. Reprinted by permission of McGraw-Hill Book Company. Copyright © The McGraw-Hill Book Company, 1963.
9. Mortimer J. Adler, *How to Read a Book* (New York: Simon and Schuster, 1967), p. 54. Copyright © 1940, 1967 by Mortimer J. Adler; Copyright © 1972

by Mortimer J. Adler and Charles Van Doren. Reprinted by permission of Simon & Schuster, a Division of Gulf & Western Corporation.

10. *How to Read a Book*, p. 35. Reprinted with permission (see above).

11. Paul Goodman, *Growing Up Absurd* (New York: Vintage Books, Random House, 1960), pp. 33-34. Reprinted with permission.

12. Thomas Griffith, "Party of One," *The Atlantic Monthly* (1979), p. 32. Copyright © 1979 by The Atlantic Monthly Company, Boston, Mass. Reprinted with permission.

13. Stewart Udall, "The Last Traffic Jam," *The Atlantic Monthly* (1972), p. 65. Copyright © 1972 by The Atlantic Monthly Company, Boston, Mass. Reprinted with permission.

14. Hook, *Marx and the Marxists*, p. 134. Reprinted with permission (see above).

15. Tom E. Kakonis and James C. Wilcox, *Forms of Rhetoric: Ordering Experience* (New York: McGraw-Hill, 1969), p. 222.

16. Paul Goodman, *People or Personnel* (New York: Vintage Books, Random House, 1968), p. 132. Reprinted with permission.

17. Gilbert Highet, *Man's Unconquerable Mind* (New York: Columbia University Press, 1954), pp. 7-8. Reprinted by permission of Columbia University Press.

18. Margaret Laurence, "The Loons," in *Double Vision: An Anthology of Twentieth-Century Stories in English*, selected by Rudy Wiebe (Toronto: Macmillan of Canada, 1976), p. 21. Reprinted by permission of The Canadian Publishers, McClelland and Stewart Limited, Toronto.

19. John Cheever, "Goodbye, My Brother," in *The Stories of John Cheever* (New York: Alfred A. Knopf, 1978), p. 18.

20. Highet, *Man's Unconquerable Mind*, pp. 72-73. Reprinted with permission (see above).

21. Paul Goodman, "Can Technology Be Humane?" in *Technology and Man's Future*, ed. Albert H. Teich (New York: St. Martin's Press, 1972) p. 186. Reprinted with permission.

22. Michael Shifter and Peter Hakim, excerpted from the Foreign Policy Association's *1999 Great Decisions, Topic 7*, "Latin America: A Broad Overview." Published by and reprinted with permission from FPA, 470 Park Ave., SO., NY, NY 10016.

23. Goodman, *People or Personnel*, p. 4. Reprinted with permission (see above).

24. Mortimer J. Adler, *The Time of Our Lives* (New York: Holt, Rinehart and Winston, 1970), p. 215. Copyright © 1970 by Mortimer J. Adler. Reprinted by permission of Holt, Rinehart and Winston, Publishers.

25. Russell, "The Ancestry of Fascism," in *In Praise of Idleness*, pp. 55-56. Reprinted with permission (see above).

26. Hook, *Marx and Marxists*, p. 39. Reprinted with permission (see above).

CHAPTER ELEVEN

Composing an Expository Essay

The skills involved in organizing and writing an expository essay are precisely those needed to organize and pattern sentences, construct topic outlines, and compose unified and coherent paragraphs. The pattern of organization may be broader and more complex, and the ideas more involved and segmented, but the thinking process is essentially the same. The primary difference is that, in organizing the essay, you must use a number of different skills to achieve a specific result.

A. WHAT IS AN EXPOSITORY ESSAY?

Because the word "exposition" means to point out or explain something, the essay should answer a specific question or questions about its subject. Therefore, as soon as you construct a thesis statement, you must justify that statement by responding to questions like these: What is it? How does it work? What is its significance? What values does it convey? Why is it important? Why should someone find it interesting? If you fulfill this purpose, readers should leave the essay quietly, with their curiosity satisfied and their imagination inspired.

B. PREPARING TO WRITE

Because a number of important planning decisions must be made before you begin writing your essay, you can divide your preparation time into a series of specific planning steps. These steps involve outlining, subject focus, thesis statement, tone, method of development, and summary conclusion.

Step One: Make a Scratch Outline
Whether you choose your topic or are assigned one by an instructor, your starting point is the same: write down everything you know or think you know about your topic; do not be concerned about relevance or logical sequence. That you are jotting down words and phrases that bear some relationship—however distant—to your topic means you have already begun the necessary process of organizing your essay. At this initial planning stage your most important concern is getting started, and the scratch outline format can serve as a useful crutch.

Step Two: Focus Your Subject
Assuming that you already have an essay topic, and that you have written down everything you know about it, you must now start thinking about the length of your paper. Remember, your subject must be narrow enough to be handled in a given space and within a given time; do not overextend yourself.

You may begin the process of narrowing the subject by eliminating ideas that are too broad or too vague from your scratch outline. This process of elimination will help you think about point of view and allow you to pose questions that give your subject more substance: "What can I draw from my own reading and experience that will help me develop this topic? What portion of it should I stress? How do I want my reader to respond? How much outside reading must I do to adequately cover my topic?" These questions and others like them will enable you to develop your outline as the functional skeleton of your essay. And as you eliminate some ideas and include others, you will gradually bring the subject of your essay clearly into focus.

Step Three: Write a Thesis Statement
After choosing—even tentatively choosing—the aspect of the topic you wish to stress, you must attempt to state the central idea or theme of your essay in one or two sentences. Nothing you write during these preparatory stages will be more important than your thesis statement; for, like the topic sentence in a paragraph, it will serve as the framework on which everything else in your essay will hang. It is essential not only because it defines more clearly your essay's limits but also because it keeps your mind fixed on its central theme. Therefore, once your statement is formulated, the rest of the essay will begin taking shape in your mind. Gradually the weak skeleton of random thought fragments that you started with will give way to a more substantial structure of logically sequenced ideas.

Step Four: Plan the Body and Prepare a Topic Outline
The functional question you will ask yourself in planning the body of your essay will be this: "How can I break down, define, and exemplify my thesis statement?" In posing this question, you will use your outline to list your major points, because at this stage you will be thinking of your essay as a series of topics and subtopics. The following list of questions should occur to you as you begin the process of expanding your thesis statement: "How many major sections will my essay require, and what will be the approximate length of each section? How many examples or illustrative details will I need to fully develop my central idea? What method of development should I use to successfully exploit the implications in my thesis statement, and what tone should I properly employ?" As your essay begins taking shape in your outline, you will be thinking more clearly about the organization of your ideas: how they should lead into one another, and how they should begin and end. You will also be thinking about the structure of your paragraphs—their length, unity, and coherence. At this point you will be well into the final planning stages of your essay and in firm control of its direction.

Step Five: Plan Your Conclusion
Ideally, your concluding statements should flow easily and naturally from the ideas in the body. In reality, however, this process often works in just the reverse manner. Your progress in developing the ideas in the body of your essay may well depend upon how carefully you have planned your concluding statements. Thus, even when still in the process of organizing your essay, you should have some idea of how you wish to end it. Here are a few questions that may help you formulate your final remark: "How can I summarize the main sections of my essay so that the logic of my conclusions will be explicit? How can I restate my central idea so that it has a conclusive impact on my reader? And in what frame of mind do I want my reader to leave the essay?" Even though you have only a vague idea of how you want your essay to end, jot down some ideas or a few phrases you may wish to use. This exercise will keep you working towards a goal, so that by the time you are ready to write your conclusion, you will be better able to summarize your major ideas and rephrase your thesis statement.

Step Six: Write and Revise
After you have composed the first draft of your essay from your topic outline, read aloud what you have written. Try placing yourself in the mind of your reader by asking yourself the following questions: "Have I a well-articulated thesis statement? Do my ideas hold together? Is my tone consistent and my word selection adequate? Does my introduction clearly prepare the reader for the discussion in the body of the essay, and is my conclusion a logical extension of my development? Can I express any of my ideas more clearly and emphatically?" And finally, "If I were the reader, would I be interested in the content of the essay?" Once you have answered these questions to your satisfaction and made the proper structural revisions, reread your essay for grammar, spelling, and mechanics. Remember, one of the keys to good essay writing is an orderly process of revision; if you do a thorough job, your first and last drafts should be quite different.

C. THE PARTS OF THE ESSAY

One of the most common prescriptions for a well-constructed essay is that it must have a beginning, a middle, and an end. At first glance this statement may seem obvious and simplistic, but upon further reflection we realize that its importance cannot be overemphasized; for each of these divisions serves a specific function, and without all of them our essays would almost certainly be unreadable. Here is a brief description of what each section of the essay should accomplish.

1. The Introduction

The introduction has one primary function: it persuades your reader to read the rest of your essay. It does this by arousing interest in its purpose and significance and by informing readers, in clear, precise prose, of the central idea that will organize it. Unless they have specific knowledge of what you intend to say and how you intend to say it, they may not be inclined to read further. The introduction, then, in sales vernacular, is "the grabber."

2. The Body

The body of the essay develops the central idea in your thesis statement. It is written in sections, with each section dealing with one aspect of your central idea. If you are discussing, say, the future of nuclear energy as a power source, you might devote one paragraph to operating costs, one to safety procedures, and one to waste disposal. In this way the main idea in the introduction is broken down and discussed in separate but related developmental paragraphs.

3. The Conclusion

The conclusion should simply restate the central idea (or ideas) in the introduction and briefly summarize the major points in the body. But it should not, under any circumstances, contain anything new. Nothing is more frustrating to the reader than finding ideas in the conclusion that were not suggested in the introduction and discussed in the body. It may also contain several general remarks designed to ease the reader out of the essay. These remarks may suggest other areas and other circumstances where your discussion may be relevant, or they may simply restate a general point made in the introduction.

D. THE WELL-CONSTRUCTED STUDENT ESSAY

The following writing sample illustrates the organizational characteristics of the brief expository essay. Its three sections are obvious and well defined. It has a clear introduction with a central thesis idea, a body that breaks down and exemplifies different aspects of the idea, and a conclusion that sums up and restates the idea.

The Various Skills and Responsibilities of Executive Secretaries

1. After observing the daily activities of three different executive secretaries, I have come to realize that these secretaries must possess a wide variety of skills to do their jobs effectively. Among their most essential skills are the ability to communicate, an acute sense of organization, and an intimate knowledge of different types of office equipment.
2. Communication skills include both oral and written communication, for executive secretaries must represent their supervisors in many different business situations. Orally, for instance, they are required to speak effectively on the telephone, which means using

proper diction and an effective tone. They must also be able to greet and converse intelligently with each of their supervisors' clients and transmit his or her instructions accurately and concisely. Their written skills comprise a detailed knowledge of the rules of grammar and a familiarity with syntax. Duties in this area would include taking minutes of meetings and translating rough notes into accurate and readable prose. Correcting improper English in any outgoing correspondence and writing letters from bare outlines may also be part of their communication responsibilities. It is obvious, then, that executive secretaries must master a broad range of oral and written communication skills before they can represent their supervisors properly.

3. Another important skill that executive secretaries must have is a keen sense of organization. The day-to-day responsibilities that test this skill would be arranging transportation and accommodations for their supervisors' out of town visitors, keeping his or her appointment calendar up to date, and arranging staff meetings and conferences, both inside and outside the building. But perhaps their most important skill, which comes under the general heading of organization, is the ability to set priorities. Since they are given a number of various duties, some requiring immediate action, they must make judgements that provide for their supervisors' time restrictions. In this way they ensure that their supervisors do not waste time dealing with unessential information. *(Transitional Statement)*

4. Finally, because modern business offices use the latest audio-visual and electronic equipment, executive secretaries must have "hands on" knowledge of this equipment. Making overheads, setting up projectors, and using electronic calculators are some obvious examples, but they must also be familiar with video display equipment and word processors. Their skill in accessing and transmitting information effectively will depend on their keeping abreast of the latest electronic information technology which, in turn, will increase productivity and lower costs.

5. Therefore, it is obvious that executive secretaries do much more than simply type and take dictation. Rather, they should be thought of as executive assistants who keep the office running smoothly by controlling the working environment. And this control is directly related to their ability to communicate, to organize, and to use modern office equipment.

Analysis of Paragraph Development
1. In the introductory paragraph the student sets up her thesis, which explicitly informs the reader that the essay will be divided into three parts—communication, organization, and office equipment.

2. Under communication she makes a further breakdown into oral and written, and provides specific examples of each skill. Notice also that in this paragraph two topic sentences are used—one at the beginning and one at the end.
3. Under organization she not only discusses the daily external duties of secretaries but also their internal judgement in setting priorities. Here the student uses a transitional sentence to link the two ideas.
4. The third section talks about executive secretaries having to use modern office equipment to save time and money.
5. Her conclusion restates her thesis idea and sums up the three-part analysis in the body of the essay.

Exercise 11.1 — Essay Assignment

Write a brief expository essay of at least five paragraphs on *one* of the following topics. Try breaking the essay into three topic ideas that are each developed by one paragraph. Make sure that your concluding paragraph restates the theme and sums up the development.

1. Selling online through the Internet has become a billion-dollar business.
2. Attending a small university has quite a few advantages over attending a large urban university.
3. New and different vacation opportunities in Canada are being offered in tourist brochures this year.
4. The novels that I enjoy reading most are the ones that deal with moral choices.
5. Selecting the right college or university is an important process, one that will determine both your intellectual and employment future.
6. Our summer vacation in the Finger Lakes in upstate New York was one of the best vacations that we have ever had.
7. There are a number of reasons why our basketball team has had such a poor season.
8. Students today cannot function properly without home computers and access to the Internet.
9. The company I work for has decided to sponsor the Special Olympics in our city and is calling for volunteers to help plan the various sports activities.
10. Being a mentor for disadvantaged children is not an easy job.

E. EXAMPLES OF EFFECTIVE ESSAYS

The following examples of the expository essay are written for different audiences and therefore each has a slightly different pattern of organization. One deals with an abstract human quality, one with concrete observation, and one with personal speculation. But although each has a different level of formality, all have an identifiable organization that permits the reader to follow the writer's thoughts.

The first example, which is by Bertrand Russell, is personal and speculative.[1] In it, he wanders easily through history, giving us facts of survival and extinction. He discusses insects as a possible threat to mankind to get us thinking about man's vulnerability. We are given the impression that he is thinking aloud, wondering how much longer the human race will survive with its rage and lust for power. He ends by suggesting that man, through his irrationality and penchant for war, may forfeit the earth to the insects and micro-organisms.

Men versus Insects

1. Amid war and rumours of wars, while "disarmament" proposals and non-aggression pacts threaten the human race with unprecedented disaster, another conflict, perhaps even more important, is receiving much less notice than it deserves—I mean the conflict between men and insects.
2. We are accustomed to being the Lords of Creation; we no longer have occasion, like the cave men, to fear lions and tigers, mammoths and wild boars. Except against each other, we feel ourselves safe. But while big animals no longer threaten our existence, it is otherwise with small ones. For many ages dinosaurs ranged unconcerned through swamp and forest, fearing nothing but each other, not doubting the absoluteness of their empire. But they disappeared, to give place to tiny mammals—mice, small hedgehogs, miniature horses no bigger than rats, and suchlike. Why the dinosaurs died out is not known, but it is supposed to be that they had minute brains and devoted themselves to the growth of weapons of offence in the shape of numerous horns. However that may be, it was not through their line that life developed.
3. The mammals, having become supreme, proceeded to grow big. But the biggest on land, the mammoth, is extinct, and the other large animals have grown rare, except man and those that he has domesticated. Man, by his intelligence, has succeeded in finding nourishment for a large population, in spite of his size. He is safe, except from the little creatures—the insects and the micro-organisms.
4. Insects have an initial advantage in their numbers. A small wood may easily contain as many ants as there are human beings in the whole world. They have another advantage in the fact that they eat our food before it is ripe for us. Many noxious insects which used to live only in some one comparatively small region have been unintentionally transported by man to new environments where they have done immense damage. Travel and trade are useful to insects as well as to micro-organisms. Yellow fever formerly existed only in West Africa, but was carried to the Western hemisphere by the slave trade. Now owing to the opening up of Africa, it is gradually travelling eastward across the continent. When it reaches the east coast it will become almost impossible to keep it out of India and China, where it may be expected to halve the population. Sleeping sickness is an even more deadly African disease which is gradually spreading.

5. Fortunately science has discovered ways by which insect pests can be kept under control. Most of them are liable to parasites which kill so many that the survivors cease to be a serious problem, and entomologists are engaged in studying and breeding such parasites. Official reports of their activities are fascinating; they are full of such sentences as: "He proceeded to Brazil, at the request of the planters of Trinidad, to search for the natural enemies of the sugar-cane froghopper." One would say that the sugar-cane froghopper would have little chance in this contest. Unfortunately, so long as war continues, all scientific knowledge is double-edged. For example, Professor Fritz Haber, who just died, invented a process for the fixation of nitrogen. He intended it to increase the fertility of the soil, but the German government used it for the manufacture of high explosives, and has recently exiled him for preferring manure to bombs. In the next great war, the scientists on either side will let loose pests on the crops of the other side, and it may prove scarcely possible to destroy the pests when peace comes. The more we know, the more harm we can do each other. If human beings in their rage against each other, invoke the aid of insects and micro-organisms, as they certainly will do if there is another big war, it is by no means unlikely that the insects will remain the sole ultimate victors. Perhaps, from a cosmic point of view, this is not to be regretted; but as a human being I cannot help heaving a sigh over my own species.

Analysis of Paragraph Development
1. Introduction suggesting potential conflict between humans and insects.
2. Discussion of how large mammals have disappeared and how humans have
3. managed to survive.
4. List of the many advantages insects have over humans.
5. Lengthy conclusion observes that modern science will continue to control insects and micro-organisms unless, through war, we unleash them and wipe out the human species.

Exercise 11.2 — Essay Assignment

Write a personal and speculative essay on *one* of the topics below. Be sure that your ideas are logical and fully developed, and that you use a consistent pattern of development.

1. How can we help prevent the spread of AIDS throughout Africa and Southeast Asia?

2. I wish I knew more about reducing crime in the cities throughout our country.

3. I cannot understand how our country can tolerate industrial air and water pollution.

4. I wonder how our university would react if our province obliged it to offer ESL courses to the ever-increasing number of foreign students enrolled each year.

5. I think that the drug problem in Canada will get worse if nothing is done to control the illegal drug trafficking across the border with the United States.

John Gardner's essay deals with the fairly abstract idea of human motivation, how it is encouraged and frustrated.[2] As an example he uses the American post-secondary educational system; he discusses its positive and negative effects and how it meets or fails to meet the requirements of individual motivation. His examples are meant to persuade us that a problem exists and that a solution should be found. (Please note that italics have been used to emphasize particular sentences; these italics do not belong in the original text.)

Motivation

1. Dan, who was twelve years old and the best ballplayer in his school, was undergoing a psychological interview. The psychologist said, "What is the thing you feel you need to change to be the kind of person you'd like to be?" Dan replied, "Learn to spell. Learn to throw a knuckler that hops."*
2. If all young people were as capable as Dan of putting first things first, some of the perplexing problems facing American education would resolve themselves.
3. *Everyone agrees that motivation is a powerful ingredient in performance.* Talent without motivation is inert and of little use to the world. Lewis Terman and Catherine Cox found that historical geniuses were characterized not only by very high intelligence but by the desire to excel, by perseverance in the face of obstacles, by zeal in the exercise of their gifts.†
4. Some people may have greatness thrust upon them. Very few have excellence thrust upon them. They achieve it. They do not achieve it unwittingly, by "doing what comes naturally"; and they don't stumble into it in the course of amusing themselves. *All excellence involves discipline and tenacity of purpose.*
5. *The problem of motivation raises some questions of social strategy which are extremely perplexing*—so perplexing that Americans have never been willing to face them squarely. Consider, for example, the presence in our colleges of large numbers of boys and girls who really "couldn't care less" about higher education but are there because it's the thing to do. Their presence creates problems which, if honestly faced, would be

---

*P.S. Sears, "Problems in the Investigations of Achievement and Self Motivation," *The Nebraska Symposium on Motivation*, University of Nebraska Press, 1957.

† Catherine M. Cox et al. *The Early Mental Traits of Three Hundred Geniuses*, Genetic Studies of Genius, vol. 2, Stanford University Press, 1926.

the grounds for genuine concern. We avoid that unpleasantness by the simple expedient of not facing the problems honestly. This is to be commended on grounds of comfort, but it is not the path that leads on to wisdom. *Let us explore some of the issues.*

Transitional statement

6. *Over the past thirty years, we have made it easier and easier for young people to enter our colleges and universities.* We have scattered colleges so liberally that no student need go far for an education. We have lowered the financial barriers in the hope of easing the way for the qualified boy or girl who could not possibly pay for higher education. Many of our institutions have held academic requirements as low as possible in order to salvage talented young people from poorer secondary schools, and in the hope that able youngsters who loafed through high school would "wake up" in college.

7. Now that we are entering a period of overcrowding in our colleges, the trend toward lowered barriers to higher education appears to have reversed itself—at least temporarily. But over the past three or four decades—for the country as a whole—the trend has been clear.

8. Important social benefits have flowed from these policies. They have brought into the colleges a considerable number of bright and ambitious youngsters who might not otherwise have continued their education. *But with every step we took along this path we also increased the flow into the system of youngsters with little or no real concern to educate themselves....*

Transitional statement

9. Anyone who has ever taught could comment on the vivid differences between *eager* and *apathetic* students. A Chinese proverb says, "To be fond of learning is to be at the gate of knowledge." It is almost impossible to prevent the interested student from learning. He meets the teacher more than half-way—all the way if necessary. He seeks out the situations in which he can learn. He gets an education in the most active sense of that term.

10. The apathetic student, if he is at all affected by schooling, receives an education. To say that teachers must meet him more than half-way understates the case: they must block all exits and trap him into learning. They must be wonderfully inventive in catching his attention and holding it. They must be endlessly solicitous in counselling him, encouraging him, awakening him and disciplining him. Every professor has observed what Lounsbury once described as "the infinite capacity of the undergraduate to resist the intrusion of knowledge...."

11. *The flow of languid and indifferent youngsters into the colleges is not wholly indefensible.* In many instances, lack of interest in education is traceable to handicaps of home

background that the school and college must try to remedy. Bright youngsters with low motivation do represent a potential national resource, and it is important to discover whether that resource is recoverable. It is our obligation to salvage those who can be salvaged. Furthermore, there are social reasons why a society might wish to provide higher education even for those youngsters who care little about it. *But we should be aware of the consequences of what we are doing. Education of the aimless and half-hearted is a very arduous, very expensive and—most important—totally different process from education of the highly motivated.*

Transitional statement

12. As the number of apathetic students in a college increases, there is a fundamental change in the tone of the educational process. There occurs a gradual but inevitable shift in the entire educational approach—in teaching methods, and in the nature of assignments, in the curriculum and in the methods of handling students. As the institution re-orients itself toward educational practices suitable for youngsters of low motivation, it all too often forgets the art of dealing with youngsters of high motivation.

13. It applies to eager and alert youngsters the practices which it uses on less spirited individuals—assignments which do not stretch the mind, and procedures which assume a considerable degree of individual apathy. The attitude which comes to dominate a school is reflected in the forthright assertion of one progressive educator: "The school should *meet* the demands of the nature of childhood, not *make* demands."* In short, the classroom comes to reinforce the attitude which is cultivated by the rest of our prosperous society; namely, that the individual should never be faced with a severe challenge, that he should never be called upon for even minor sacrifices, that asking him to undertake arduous duties is a form of injustice.

14. One might say that this makes very little difference because eager and ambitious individuals will drive themselves to achieve, and the apathetic ones will not drive themselves in any case. In short, one might argue that our bland treatment of all young people does no harm and is at the very least humane. But the difficulty is that the degree of motivation which the individual possesses at any given time is very much affected by what is expected (or demanded) of him. Every emergency, every crisis reveals unsuspected resources of personal strength in some people and evokes heightened motivation in almost all. In speaking of the hero born of such a crisis, people say, "I didn't know he had it in

---

*Marietta Johnson, *Youth in a World of Men* (New York: John Day, 1929), p. 261.

him." But most of us, in fact, have a better, stouter-hearted, more vigorous self within—a self that's deliberately a little hard of hearing but by no means stone deaf.

15. We all know that some organizations, some families, some athletic teams, some political groups inspire their members to great heights of personal performance. In other words, high individual performance will depend to some extent on the capacity of the society or institution to evoke it. And woe to the society that loses the gift for such evocation! When an institution, organization or nation loses its capacity to evoke high individual performance, its great days are over.

Analysis of Paragraph Development

1.
2. } An anecdote used as an introduction to exemplify the theme of the essay.
3.
4. } Thesis of essay expressed alternately in the first and last sentences in the next two paragraphs.
5. Motivation problems introduced and exemplified.
6. Reasons why young people find it easier to attend college.
7. Transitional paragraph introducing effects of social trends.
8. Good and bad effects of social trends.
9.
10. } Qualities of eager and apathetic students.
11. Social benefits of present educational system and transitional statement indicating changes in educational process if system continues.
12.
13. } Discussion of important process changes in education resulting from lower standards of present system.
14. Further clarification of motivation difficulty in relation to expectation of others.
15. Concluding reaffirmation that society must evoke the individual's desire to excel if it is to remain healthy and viable.

Exercise 11.3 — Essay Assignment

Write an opinion essay on one of the topics below. Make sure you support your position with relevant facts and persuasive examples.

1. New immigrants in Canada need better educational opportunities.
2. I believe that the rapidly rising cost of long-term health care will seriously endanger our national health-care system.
3. We need more information about corporate welfare in Canada.

4. It makes economic sense for the Canadian Football League to merge with the National Football League in the United States.
5. Canada should tighten its pollution laws against greenhouse gases.

This excerpt from Michael Shifter and Peter Hakim's essay[3] is analytical. The writers discuss the recent changes that have been taking place in Latin American countries because of economic reforms. They break down and analyze the benefits accruing from these reforms—low inflation and increased foreign investment, among others—but suggest that the endemic problems of poverty, slow growth, high inflation, and poor distribution of income will not be solved without continued international assistance.

Latin America: a Broad Overview

Economic Reforms

1. Since the early 1990's, every Latin American country has—albeit to varying degrees and at different paces—extensively reformed and restructured its economy. Governments have sharply reduced barriers to international trade and investment, turning away from protectionism and inward-oriented development. They have curtailed their involvement in the production and distribution of goods and services and scaled back regulation of economic activity. Emphasis today is on competitive markets, private enterprise, foreign trade and macroeconomic discipline. In general, governments are working to control budget deficits, redirect expenditures, transform pension systems and revamp tax codes to generate greater revenue.

2. Economic reform has produced benefits in nearly every country of the region. The most impressive and important gains have come from controlling inflation, which has long plagued Latin America's economies. Over the past half dozen years, inflation rates have declined everywhere that they had been a problem. The yearly average for the region as a whole dropped to 11%, from roughly 1,200%, in just seven years. In 1997, no country had an inflation rate above 100%.

3. Other signs of progress include the revival of foreign investment and lending to the region. After nearly a decade of huge capital outflows in the 1980's, when Latin American nations were servicing huge debts and considered uncreditworthy, investments and loans have (until the recent economic crisis) been coming into the region—nearly $80 billion [U.S. Dollars] in 1997, mostly from private sources. Exports also, after stagnating for much of the 1980's, have doubled in the last six years. Latin America's per capita income has expanded every year but one since 1990, after declining by more than 10% over the previous 10 years.

4. Still, the region's macroeconomic performance has in large measure failed to meet expectations. Governments and many individuals had anticipated that reform programs would produce more rapid and consistent growth. Latin America's annual economic expansion has av-

eraged just over 3% in the 1990's. This, to be sure, is substantially better than the 1.6% average of the debt-ridden 1980's, and economic reform measures are seen as mainly responsible. Indeed, in 1997, the region registered its highest aggregate growth level—more than 5%—since the early 1980's. But the growth is only half the region's 6% average in the 1970's. Only a few countries—notable Chile, Argentina and El Salvador—have done much better than average.

5. The current global financial crisis is once again causing growth to slow in Latin America and postpones the prospects of sustained economic expansion. The crisis underscores the extent to which many Latin American countries remain volatile and vulnerable to international capital flows. Some of the larger economies, Brazil particularly, are threatened by full-scale collapse, which would set back economic prospects for years. Avoiding the worst-case scenario would require that the International Monetary Fund (IMF), the U.S. and other industrialized countries take an active role in shielding Brazil and other Latin American countries from the consequences of financial turmoil. In 1995, the economic contractions of Mexico and Argentina (two of the tree largest economies of the region) were especially hash, although both countries managed to recover in a relatively short period of time. Mexico required a massive international rescue package of loans totaling $50 billion—which it has since paid back. The current crisis is far worse.

6. Social conditions are dismal throughout most of Latin America—and are getting worse in many places. Pverty has declined slightly in the 1990's, largely because inflation—and the burden it imposes on the pooor—has been contained. Latin Amerca, however, still has the worst distribution of income and wealth of any region of the world, receive only 10% of the region's annual income, while nearly 60% of the income goes to the wealthiest 20%. Poverty is widespread in almost every nation, affecting most severely indigenous groups, racial minorities, women and children. Slow growth, high unemployment, low quality and inefficient social programs and the lack of social safety nets all contribute to the perpetuation of poverty in Latin America.

Analysis of Paragraph Development
1. Introduction describing how Latin American countries are working to restructure their economies.
2. Statistical examples demonstrating how economic reform has controlled inflation.
3. How increased foreign investment and lending have expanded the per capita income of Latin American workers.
4. Statistics proving that Latin America's macroeconomic performance has not met growth expectations.
5. Discussion, with examples, of the extent to which countries in Latin America still remain susceptible to international capital flows.

6. Conclusion demonstrating that despite low inflation, the unequal distribution of income will ensure that poverty in Latin America will continue to be a problem in the future.

Exercise 11.4 — Essay Assignment

Write an analytical essay on one of the topics below. Use as many statistics as possible to support your researched statements.

1. Canada's community-college system is a vital post-secondary resource for employment opportunities.
2. Drug-related crime in Canada is creating an underworld of youthful criminals.
3. Weapons of mass destruction are becoming more available to terrorist groups who seek to overthrow democratic countries throughout the world.
4. The North American Free Trade Agreement (NAFTA) has both positive and negative effects on Canada's economy.
5. The consequences of separation on the province of Quebec.

F. CITING YOUR SOURCES

For longer essays requiring library research, you need to acknowledge your sources within the text of the essay and collect them in a "Works Cited" section at the end. Therefore, you should be aware of the rules and conventions that govern these entries.

A handbook published by the Modern Language Association (MLA) recommends that you relate your citations in the body of the essay to the sources at the end. As a general rule, you include only the basic information the reader needs to find the source in the list of works cited. The author's last name and a page reference within parentheses is usually all you require to identify your source.

1. Examples of Citations within the Text
(a) *Direct Quote*

> This tongue-in-cheek cynicism is reflected in the following statement: "I never met anyone that I immediately liked" (Stone 26).

Note: No comma after author's last name; the period is placed after the parenthesis.

(b) *Page Reference Only*

> Harvey Stone responded to a request for an interview by saying, "I haven't had anything important to say since I was twelve and a half" (36).

Note: Author's name appears within the paragraph.

(c) *Information from Different Sections in the Same Source*

    (Stone 195, 206-207).

Note: no abbreviated "p." or "pp." before page numbers.

(d) *More than One Work by the Same Author*

    (Stone, *My Life as an Optimist* 129).

Note: A comma is placed after author's name.

2. Works Cited
In this final section you list all the sources used to write the essay or report. The list appears at the end of the essay on a new page, but continues the essay's pagination. Thus, if the conclusion is page 13, your "Works Cited" page will be 14. These listed sources may include books, journals, magazines, newspaper articles, tapes, films, and other published or unpublished material.

    Each reference item should include the author's name (surname first), title of the work, the location and name of the publisher, and the date of publication.

(a) *General Guidelines*
- The list of entries is alphabetized but not numbered.
- Titles of works without authors are placed in the alphabetical sequence, using the first letter of the title word.
- Entries are single spaced and separated from preceding entries by double spacing.
- The second and following lines of each entry are indented five spaces.
- The second reference to an author's name (and all succeeding references) is represented by a series of hyphens, indicating ditto marks.
- Only the first author's name is inverted when a work has two or more authors. If there are more than three authors, you may use *et al.* ("and others") after the first name.

(b) *Sample Entries*
BOOKS BY ONE AUTHOR
    Dryden, Ken. *The Game*. Toronto: Macmillan of Canada, 1983.

BOOKS BY MORE THAN ONE AUTHOR
    Norton, Sarah, and Nell Waldman. *Canadian Content*. Toronto: Holt, Rinehart and Winston of Canada, 1988.

BOOKS BY MORE THAN THREE AUTHORS
    Fierman, William, et al. *The New Republic of Central Asia: A Modern History*. Boston: Godwin, 1995.

ARTICLES IN PERIODICALS
Holland, Norman N. "Unity, Identity, Text, Self." PMLA 90 (1975): 813-22.

ARTICLES IN ENCYCLOPEDIAS
"Láser." *Encyclopedia Britannica*. 1977 ed.

ARTICLES IN MULTIMEDIA ENCYCLOPEDIAS
"Internet." *Grolier Multimedia Encyclopedia*. Vers. 5.01 CD-ROM. Grolier, 1992.

Note: Since all encyclopedia articles are alphabetized, no volume or page numbers are given, unless referring to a specific section in a multi-page article.

ARTICLES IN AN EDITED COLLECTION OR ANTHOLOGY
Cope, B., & Kalantzis, M. "Introduction: How a Genre Approach to Literacy Can Transform the Way Writing Is Taught." *The Powers of Literacy*. Eds. B. Cope & M. Kalantzis. London: Palmer Press, 1993, 1-21.

GOVERNMENT PUBLICATIONS
Canada. Department of Indian Affairs. *Mercury Pollution in Northern Ontario*. Ottawa: Queen's Printer, 1967.

Note: The name of the government is stated first. If the writer is unknown, substitute the government department or agency for the author's name.

(c) *Sample Page*

Atwood, Margaret. *Survival: A Thematic Guide to Canadian Stories in English*. Toronto: Anansi Press, 1972.

Baye, Betty Winston. "Giving Up Cigarettes Is Not Very Easy—But Neither Is Dying." *El Paso Times*. June 15, 1992.

Double Vision: An Anthology of Twentieth-Century Stories in English. Selected by Rudy Wiebe. Toronto: Macmillan of Canada, 1976.

Findley, Timothy. *Headhunter*. Toronto: Harper Collins, 1993.

Gibaldi, Joseph, & Walter S. Achtert. *MLA Handbook for Writers of Research Papers*. 4th ed. New York: Modern Language Association, 1995.

Gold, Joseph, ed. *In the Name of Language*. Toronto: Macmillan of Canada, 1975.

O'Connor, Flannery. "The Displaced Person." In *Flannery O'Connor: The Complete Stories*. New York: Farrar Straus and Giroux, 1979, 192-235.

Rowse, A.L. *The Elizabethan Renaissance: The Cultural Achievement*. London and Basingstoke: Macmillan London, 1972.

Shakespeare, William. *Shakespeare: The Complete Works*. Ed. Peter Alexander. London and Glasgow: Collins, 1951.

ABOUT THE AUTHOR

Joseph Lyons was born and raised in Pennsylvania, and his work experience was almost entirely in the academic area. He earned his B.A. degree from LaSalle University, his M.A. from Temple University, and his Ph.D from the University of Ottawa, Canada. His major field of study was English Literature and Applied Linguistics. He worked as both a teacher and an administrator. He taught and managed at a private educational institution—The Reading Laboratory in Philadelphia from 1966 to 1969, and he taught English Literature and Developmental Reading at the University of Ottawa from 1969 to 1972. He also held different academic positions at St. Lawrence College, Ontario, Canada: English Professor from 1972 to 1983; Chairman, Developmental Education from 1983 to 1987; Dean of Developmental and Continuing Education from 1987 to 1989. He was then recruited to serve as Head of Academic Studies at Dubai Women's College in the United Arab Emirates from 1989 to 1992 and as Head of English at the U.A.E. University from 1992 to 1996, where he earned a diploma in T.E.F.L (Teaching English as a Foreign Language) from Cambridge University.

Exercise Answers

Exercise 1.1 — Distinguishing Parts of Speech
1. Our old boat is docked *across* from the new *hotel*.   5   1
2. Please *take* your brother with you *when* you go to the store   7   4
3. *She* swears that she was not in school when the *fire* started.   2   1
4. Milos *and* Catherine *prevented* the fire from spreading.   6   7
5. *You* should wash the fruit *before* eating it.   2   4
6. *Keep* your *head* down!   7   1
7. *Where* is *Carlos* going?   4   1
8. *Montreal* has many *excellent* restaurants.   1   3
9. Monty *wants* to go on a ski holiday, *but* Claude prefers to go to the beach..   7   6
10. *My* aunt *works* as a nurse in the general hospital.   2   7
11. The final rock concert this year was held in the *stadium where* our football team plays.   1   4
12. *Which* word-processing software package do *you* use?   3   2
13. Rojas and *he* are not coming with *us* tonight.   2   2
14. Your *pretentious* demeanour will make you *unpopular*.   3   1
15. *Talk* to your parents before you accept *their* invitation.   7   2
16. They *are* not to blame for your *poor* grades.   7   3
17. Is *it* her mother who *refuses* to join the exercise group?   2   7
18. Bill McLeod *and* Helen Freidlander *were chosen* for the leads in the school play.   6   7
19. It was *she*, not *he*, who travelled to India last summer.   2   2
20. *When* will she *visit* us again?   4   7
21. She broke the *blue* lampshade while trying to remove it *from* the packing crate.   3   4
22. Franz Lorca is a *famous* opera singer from *Bolivia*.   3   1
23. The Montreal Canadiens *and* the Detroit Red Wings *will play* an exhibition game tomorrow.   6   7
24. *Their* privacy is *our* number one priority.   2   2
25. They *travelled* throughout Europe *with* their dog, Ralph.   7   5

Exercise Answers

26. *Where* will the plane land if the weather *is* unsuitable?   4   7
27. Deirdre is a very *private* person; so is *her* sister.   3   2
28. *How many* times has *Devon* struck out this year?   4   1
29. Do *you* know *where* the Harrisons are moving?   2   4
30. *Correct* the tests *with* the computer; the correction program is already loaded.   7   5

Exercise 2.1 — Locating the Subject and Verb

		S	V
1.	Into the water dove the competing swimmers.	swimmers	dove
2.	Several of the puzzle pieces are missing.	several	are
3.	Please inform Sarah that she is wanted on the phone.	(you)	inform
4.	When is our next anthropology class?	anthropology class	is
5.	Juan Martinez has a dental appointment today.	Juan Martinez	has
6.	Playing tennis is excellent exercise.	Playing tennis	is
7.	Some of the spectators are leaving early.	Some	are
8.	There were several choices that we had to make.	choices	were
9.	Our parents' anniversary is next Friday.	anniversary	is
10.	Many of our classes were cancelled yesterday.	Many	were cancelled
11.	Only one of us gave up smoking cigarettes.	one	gave up
12.	Who took the chalk off the blackboard shelf?	Who	took
13.	Grapes and peaches were on sale last Friday at the local supermarket.	Grapes, peaches	were
14.	Several of our hockey players are still injured.	Several	are
15.	Here is my favourite talk-show host.	talk-show host	is
16.	Douglas, after finally making the basketball team, had to cease all sports activities because of a heart murmur.	Douglas	had
17.	Some of the prizewinners were not eligible.	Some	were eligible
18.	Beyond the next hill lies the farmers' market.	market	lies

Writing Fundamentals

19. Please do not walk on the fresh cement.   (you)   do / walk
20. Planting a flower garden is hard work.   Planting a flower garden   is
21. Where did we meet last month?   we   did meet
22. Mr. Chang, after months of litigation, finally won his court case against his former employer.   Mr. Chang   won
23. How many hats does Greta own?   Greta   does own
24. More than seven laws were broken by the convicted felons.   laws   were broken
25. Outside the stadium there was a traffic jam.   traffic jam   was
26. All of our neighbours have paved driveways.   All   have
27. Swimming every day tones the leg muscles.   Swimming every day   tones
28. After the snowstorm we could not see our hedges.   we   could see
29. While vacationing in the South of France, Jessica met her future husband.   Jessica   met
30. Please try to be a little more patient with your baby brother.   (you)   try

Exercise 2.2 — Recognizing Phrases

1. Monica does not want to go *with the rest of us*.   Prep.
2. Kathy prefers *acting on stage*, not in films.   Ger.
3. *During the basketball game* the assistant coach became ill.   Prep.
4. The police officer *walking toward us* is my uncle.   Part.
5. *Swimming in salt water* is very refreshing.   Ger.
6. *Discovering the origin of the universe* will be a major scientific undertaking.   Ger.
7. Luke's favourite pastime is *playing chess*.   Ger.
8. One of our highest-paid rock stars, *a multiple award winner*, has just been diagnosed with HIV.   Prep.
9. *Competing in track and field* is my favourite sports activity.   Ger.
10. I am flying out of Montreal *at precisely 1:00 p.m.*   Prep.
11. *Shocked by the outcome of the trial*, the family members left the courtroom in embittered silence.   Part.

Exercise Answers

12. *Playing Scrabble with my sister and brother* is not my idea of a satisfying evening.   Ger.
13. The new car, *parked near the courthouse*, belongs to the prosecuting attorney.   Part.
14. *Once purchased by the Queen of Belgium*, the famous blue, pear-shaped diamond is now being auctioned in London.   Part.
15. Abdullah Shaban certainly enjoyed *playing soccer in our new stadium*.   Ger.
16. The old man *playing shuffleboard* was once a famous stage actor.   Part.
17. Our dog, Max, chased the squirrel *into the garage*.   Prep.
18. Mary-Lisa hates *being the centre of attention*.   Ger.
19. Farina and Talia decided to take computer programming courses on Tuesdays, *after their gym class*.   Prep.
20. *To be an airline pilot* is my chief ambition in life.   Inf.
21. *While acting in our school play*, Sheila slipped on a stage prop and broke her ankle.   Part.
22. *Famous for her role in <u>Anne of Green Gables</u>*, Catherine quickly became a member of a daytime soap opera cast.   Part.
23. *Working two jobs during the summer* enabled Kurt to pay his college tuition.   Ger.
24. *To qualify for the accounting job*, we had to take a three-hour test.   Inf.
25. *Enraged by her employer's lack of concern for the employees*, Danielle filed a grievance on their behalf.   Part.
26. The parking lot *next to the department store* is being repaved.   Prep.
27. *Hiking in British Columbia* is one of the activities we are planning for next summer.   Ger.
28. *To grow a perfect rose* is my wife's fondest dream.   Inf.
29. They drove carelessly *on the unpaved road*.   Prep.
30. The young outfielder *walking toward the bullpen* was my roommate in college.   Part.

Exercise 2.3 — Identifying Clauses

1. *After you finish watering the lawn*, please sweep the driveway.   Adv.
2. The English professor *who wrote the best-selling mystery novel* is now working on a screenplay for the CBC.   Adj.
3. Maurice's new truck, *which he uses to haul produce*, has a broken axle.   Adj.

Writing Fundamentals

4. When I first saw Melissa, she was a platinum blonde. Adv.
5. My new computer, which has a Pentium chip, is being repaired. Adj.
6. When my birthday arrives, I do not want a celebration party. Adv.
7. We believe that everyone is entitled to a fair trial. N
8. The card game will begin as soon as the other players arrive. Adv.
9. That Conrad Jellico will be elected the mayor of our city is a foregone conclusion. N
10. Who knows when our bus will leave the station? N
11. Our city council is concerned about the allegations that several construction firms overcharged the city for street repair. Adj.
12. How can we know what our school board's intentions are? N
13. When Celeste arrived on campus, the library committee had already concluded its business. Adv.
14. If you think that your vote will make a difference, we would be willing to reconvene the committee. Adv.
15. Garcia suggested that we wait for final instructions. N
16. Do not overreact when you hear your sister announce her candidacy for a city council position. Adv.
17. The mid-term test that was scheduled for next Friday has been rescheduled for the following Monday. Adj.
18. Kim Chung is the woman who won the applied science scholarship. Adj.
19. My uncle, who retired last month, is now a consultant for a government agency. Adj.
20. We were told that our airline fares were already paid. N
21. Our team responded to the fans' encouragement as soon as our coach told us that our playoff chances were in jeopardy. Adv.
22. The plane that flew us to South America is the same one that slid off the runway last week. Adj.
23. Who knows how television network officials think. N
24. When we heard about the brush fires near our property, we rushed right home. Adv.
25. What we know about past segregation practices cannot be revealed. N
26. Fred's old sawmill, which he almost sold last week, has just been declared a historical landmark. Adj.
27. Talk to whoever is in charge of the investigation. N

Exercise Answers

28. Our team could not score a touchdown *because our star quarterback was out of action.*   <u>Adv.</u>
29. Dr. Singh, *who was chief cardiac surgeon at University Hospital,* has just been awarded a lucrative research grant.   <u>Adj.</u>
30. It was my family's cottage *that was severely damaged by the last hurricane.*   <u>Adj.</u>

Exercise 2.4 — Developing the Subject-Verb Structure

(Students to complete independently.)

Exercise 2.5 — Detecting Sentence Fragments

1. Forest fires can be prevented.   <u>C</u>
2. Without having to pretend.   <u>F</u>
3. Telling them again and again.   <u>F</u>
4. Stop driving so fast.   <u>C</u>
5. While we were waiting for our airplane to arrive.   <u>F</u>
6. Nothing is ever certain.   <u>C</u>
7. Although we were not the last ones to leave the party.   <u>F</u>
8. Your homework must be done now.   <u>C</u>
9. Whatever anyone says about our inability to win without a strong offensive line.   <u>F</u>
10. Let's keep it simple.   <u>C</u>
11. Appreciating someone else's point of view.   <u>F</u>
12. Try keeping your room clean.   <u>C</u>
13. Remember to exit your document file before turning off your computer.   <u>C</u>
14. Saving your document before exiting.   <u>F</u>
15. Where are you going?   <u>C</u>
16. How will you get there?   <u>C</u>
17. Staying home every Sunday evening.   <u>F</u>
18. To determine your next major goal.   <u>F</u>
19. Deciding what college to attend.   <u>F</u>
20. Will you commute or live away from home?   <u>C</u>
21. Organizing your time and scheduling different activities.   <u>F</u>

Writing Fundamentals

22. What are the possibilities?   C
23. Exercising every day.   F
24. Stay out of trouble.   C
25. Not caring what other people think about breaking the rules of the institution.   F
26. Tell me your class schedule.   C
27. To be excluded from all sporting activities is unfair.   C
28. Can I be of any help?   C
29. Smoking is not permitted.   C
30. A troublesome period in the lives of the next door neighbours.   F

Exercise 2.6 — Correcting Run-on Sentences

(Since there is not always only one correct revision, answers may vary; the following corrections may serve as guidelines.)

1. I cannot think of the gentleman's name; maybe it was Frank.   R
2. Nothing can be done for the victim. **H**is family, however, should be comforted.   R
3. Please don't spread rumours; get the facts before you speak.   R
4. English is my most difficult course; I have to spend hours revising my essays.   R
5. Our local library has a good children's section, but not a very large literature selection.   C
6. Shopping for shoes is frustrating, **because** I can never find a size small enough for my tiny feet.   R
7. Even though our house is small, it is quite comfortable.   C
8. However difficult the journey, we must complete it on time.   C
9. We took the train to Toronto; we were just too tired to drive.   R
10. I'll order the food, **and** you get us a table.   R
11. Abdul Rahman was not born in Canada; however, he is now a Canadian citizen.   R
12. Trina hates the cold weather, **but** Janine loves to ski.   R
13. Did you bring your umbrella? I don't have mine.   R
14. We went to the game early, but we still could not find a parking place.   C

Exercise Answers

15. She can always be relied upon, however difficult the challenge.   C
16. Our school basketball team will be ready for the start of the season; in fact, we have already been picked to win our division.   R
17. The picnic table was set up, but the food had not yet arrived.   C
18. What will you do if your flight is delayed? Will you cancel your speaking engagement?   R
19. The virus on my hard drive was transferred from one of my floppy disks. It has already corrupted one of my files.   R
20. Who drove home last night? Was it Malcolm?   R
21. The golf tournament will have to be cancelled and the money refunded.   C
22. Making hotel reservations on the Internet is easy; you should try it.   R
23. I cannot learn how to set up a spreadsheet, however hard I try.   C
24. Don't forget to pay the phone bill. You can pay it at the bank.   R
25. Our city does not have a football team; however, it does have a highly regarded hockey team.   C
26. Wanting to please the efficient office staff, the general manager expanded their morning coffee break.   C
27. I'll collect our coats; you start the car.   R
28. Conchita has just bought a VCR, **and** now she can tape her favourite TV programs.   R
29. Whatever the cost and however long it takes, we must arrive at our destination by Friday morning.   C
30. Having met its sales quota for the month, the marketing department decided to organize an office party. We were all invited.   R

Exercise 2.7 — Revising Sentences in the Paragraph

(Revisions may vary.)

Food prices are increasing every year, which places an extreme hardship on people who must budget their money carefully each month. That is why many people have changed their eating and shopping habits. For example, shoppers no longer buy as much red meat, which is usually the most expensive item on the shopping list. Its price has risen at least fifteen percent over the last few years. Instead, fish and chicken are often substituted, because they are not only less expensive but more nutritious. Pasta is also increasingly replacing meat dishes. Indeed, meatless dinners and lunches are becoming quite common among people who are not only budget conscious but who also want good nutrition.

Also, consumers are not buying as much convenience food. Frozen dinners and prepared delicatessen foods are now beyond many people's food budgets. Fresh fruit and vegetables in season are more in demand. In addition, store coupons and supermarket specials are more common, for comparative shopping is now a necessity for many low- and middle-income families.

There are also fewer trips to fast-food restaurants and more reliance on healthful and inexpensive snacks made at home. Yes, our eating habits are certainly changing, not only because of rising costs but also because of our desire for good nutrition.

Exercise 2.8 — Recognizing Sentence Patterns

1. My brother lost the golf tournament, but he still won a prize.   Cd
2. Rudy Polanski and his brother, Stan, are my new teammates.   S
3. Neither the school board nor the teachers' association could suggest a compromise solution to end the stalemate.   S
4. The personal computer that I bought from a mail-order catalogue does not have enough memory.   Cx
5. Our garage is a new addition, but our patio came with the house.   Cd
6. My brother, who just graduated from a community college, already has a job out West, but my sister is still looking for employment.   Cd-Cx
7. The Thousand Islands International Bridge joins the state of New York and the province of Ontario.   S
8. Betty was flabbergasted when her number was drawn for the door prize.   Cx
9. I understand that your brother still smokes cigarettes but that your sister has just quit.   Cx
10. Don't go home yet; the party is just starting.   Cd
11. My printer, which is five years old, is working fine, but my home computer, which is new, has just crashed.   Cd-Cx
12. Retiring early is my main ambition, but I don't think that I will achieve it.   Cd-Cx
13. Johnny Chung rides a bike to school, but his sister walks.   Cd
14. After the movie, we all went to a fast-food restaurant.   S
15. Whenever our instructor gives us a test, she always tells us to manage our time properly.   Cx

Exercise Answers

16. Please reduce your intake of sugar and fried foods.   S
17. After planning our fishing trip for a month, we had to cancel it at the last minute.   S
18. Line up your putt; then stroke the ball gently.   Cd
19. Felix and Mai had to wait two hours for Kim and Michel.   S
20. What happens when our bus breaks down because the driver forgot to change the oil and check the tires?   Cx
21. Don't wait for us; we'll be late as usual.   Cd
22. We could not pay cash for our theatre tickets; instead, we used our credit cards.   Cd
23. For my parents' anniversary, which falls on the day after Christmas, we are sending them cruise tickets, but they may not use the tickets until the spring.   Cd-Cx
24. Bernhardt Saltzer, the tennis pro, will not play in the next tournament, but his brother will take his place.   Cd
25. Keeping secrets is difficult; telling them is easy.   Cd
26. My sister, who went to university on an athletic scholarship, is graduating next month.   Cx
27. Learning how to surf the Internet can be confusing.   S
28. Mary-Lisa drives too fast, and her brother, Steve, is worried about her.   Cd
29. Jackson Boulevard, which was recently repaved, is now closed because of median repairs, and the daily commuters are furious with the city works department.   Cd-Cx
30. However hard we try, we still cannot beat our high school rivals in football.   Cx

Exercise 2.9 — Coordination

(Since there is not always only one correct revision, answers may vary; the following corrections may serve as guidelines.)

1. Santino might be quiet, but he is certainly not shy.
2. Our small town has two theatres, four movie houses, and only one hockey rink, although we are building another one.
3. Danielle is a hair stylist, not a manicurist.
4. Our local golf resort has two eighteen-hole courses; each accepts daily green fees and offers annual memberships.
5. Denzil is either a travel agent or an airline steward.

Writing Fundamentals

6. Our community college is not only the largest in the province but also the most overcrowded.
7. Both of my brothers and my sister are basketball players.
8. Several students were caught cheating, so the instructor confiscated their test papers; however, they were not suspended from school.
9. Her ice skates were either misplaced or stolen from the locker room.
10. I bought expensive skis, comfortable boots, and even took a series of ski lessons from the local ski instructor; however, I still have trouble parallel skiing.
11. The football players were told to be on time for the bus departure and not to forget their food vouchers, but some arrived late and some forgot their vouchers.
12. Song Wu and Tai Ming are neither swimmers nor high-platform divers.
13. Her skin is both fair and unwrinkled.
14. Claudette was either in a car accident or delayed by inclement weather.
15. My uncle is a college instructor and a part-time musician.
16. Martina was warned not to jog without a warm scarf, but she did anyway, and caught a bad cold.
17. Jason hates writing essays but enjoys doing grammar exercises.
18. Our former beauty queen is now either an actress or a physical fitness instructor.
19. Deirdre wanted to join a ski club but is bothered by cold weather, so she decided to play indoor tennis instead.
20. His job is not only boring but also physically difficult.
21. Sky diving is both exciting and dangerous; it is not a sport for people who are physically unfit.
22. I am interested in politics, Canadian history, and environmental studies.
23. Pierre's new computer is not only fully equipped with a monitor and a printer but also loaded with the latest business software.
24. Mohammed plays tennis, golf, basketball, and racquetball.
25. Our physics professor is a basketball coach and a volunteer with the Red Cross.
26. Jennifer is our prime success story; her ideas have saved our company more than a million dollars during the last five years.

Exercise Answers

27. Our neighbourhood is located in a high-crime district and is therefore considered unsafe by both our city police force and fire department.
28. My winter suit may look new, but it is five years old.
29. The telephone company is not only raising its monthly rates but also charging more for collect calls.
30. Seamus McCann thought he wanted to be an airline pilot, but he suffers from claustrophobia; therefore, he is now a community-college professor.

Exercise 2.10 — Subordination

1. The runaway Zamboni injured more than ten people before it was finally brought under control.
2. Taylor's car, which is only two weeks old, was stolen yesterday.
3. I attended a professional football game for the first time in 1959.
4. Our new car, which was made in Germany, has a sunroof and anti-lock brakes.
5. The stock market crashed in October 1929.
6. We saw a spotted dog chasing a rabbit while we were walking by the new fire station.
7. The new television that my father bought has a twenty-seven-inch screen and stereophonic sound.
8. Our coach was carrying a canvas bag full of footballs when he entered the locker room.
9. Nidal Mahti visited relatives and friends in Pakistan last month.
10. Some of Doris' fingers became frostbitten while she was skiing without heavy woollen mittens
11. Hurricane Fran roared through our village and caused property damage in the millions.
12. While standing near the bus stop, Susan was almost run over by a swerving automobile that was trying to avoid a stray dog.
13. Our basketball team won its tenth game in September.
14. Last week Pietro nearly ran over his Siamese cat while mowing the lawn with his riding mower.
15. While skating on our back pond, Bernice fell and nearly went through the ice.

16. Tina developed severe muscle spasms in her lower back while driving in the pouring rain for nearly five hours.
17. I am not sunburned because I put on sunblock before we went to the beach.
18. We saw the moving van back into the parked car as we were leaving the movie theatre.
19. Our small neighbourhood food market, which was once a thriving business, is now losing customers to the large supermarket down the block.
20. Kristen tripped and tore the ligaments in her left knee while she was playing field hockey.
21. The Saginaw River severely damaged more than two hundred homes before its floodwaters receded.
22. The morning newspaper did not arrive because the delivery boy is sick.
23. Carlotta's first novel, which was a best-seller, is now being made into a movie.
24. Our young mayor was re-elected in 1996.
25. Maurice, while riding on the Toronto subway, saw a man snatch an old woman's purse and run through the concourse.
26. My sister just moved from Halifax, Nova Scotia, to Ottawa, Ontario, because she could not find a management job in Halifax.
27. Because the new movie has too much sex and violence for people under eighteen years of age, it has been rated "for adults only."
28. I saw a black bear catching fish with its paws in a mountain stream while I was vacationing in Banff last summer.
29. When Heidi finally arrived at the airport, her plane had already left the boarding gate.
30. Our examinations, which are now finally over, were the most difficult that I have ever taken.

Exercise 3.1 — Making Subject and Verb Agree

1. Neither of Danielle's parents (is/are) going to our picnic lunch on Saturday.   *is*
2. The computer salesperson, as well as the technician, (was/were) correct in analyzing the problem with my laptop computer.   *was*
3. Neither the faculty members nor the college president (is/are) aware of the morale problems among our student body.   *is*

Exercise Answers

4. Each coach, team member, and sports fan (agree/agrees) that our city needs a new track-and-field facility.   _agrees_

5. There (was/were) a safety inspector and two members of the Ministry of Health investigating the fire that started in our restaurant's kitchen last week.   _were_

6. In the middle of the town square (stand/stands) the statues of our city's founders, Myers and McGillicudy.   _stand_

7. There certainly (seem/seems) to be a solution for every problem.   _seems_

8. The new rose bushes, as well as the bag of topsoil, (is/are) in the back of my pickup truck.   _are_

9. (Was/Were) American as well as Canadian literature courses scheduled last semester?   _were_

10. The hospital administrator, as well as the physicians on staff, (think/thinks) that our hospital needs a new chemistry lab.   _thinks_

11. The number of high-school dropouts (have/has) decreased during the last five years.   _has_

12. None of the salespersons (was/were) on the lot when the new Volvo was stolen.   _was_

13. Everyone who saw the Broadway cast perform in *Phantom of the Opera* (was/were) amazed at their versatility in adapting the play to our small stage.   _was_

14. Philippe and I are among the few who (practises/practise) the broad jump and the hammer throw on Fridays after school.   _practise_

15. Anyone who thinks that he or she can function without the rest of the team members (is/are) very much mistaken.   _is_

16. Participating in the Red Cross blood drive (is/are) one of the members of our tennis team.   _is_

17. Neither the fresh peaches nor the skim milk (was/were) on sale this weekend.   _was_

18. *The Magnificent Ambersons* (was/were) included in the Orson Welles film festival at our local movie theatre.   _was_

19. Not one student in ten (knows/know) who wrote *The Ginger Man*.   _knows_

20. Kimberly, together with her brother Alex, (has/have) decided to attend our local community college next year.   _has_

21. Neither Renko nor I (are/am) attending the music recital tomorrow evening.   _am_

22. Our crafts guild members (was/were) discussing next week's quilt show when the earthquake tremor shook the house.   _were_

Writing Fundamentals

23. The selection of the jury (does/do) not mean that all ethnic groups will be represented. <u>does</u>
24. Mako's physics project, together with her excellent mathematics test scores, (makes/make) her the student most likely to win this year's science scholarship. <u>makes</u>
25. Every electrician, toolmaker, and welder in our union (have/has) a right to vote in our next election. <u>has</u>
26. We were informed that either Geoffrey or Liam (was/were) involved in the cheating scandal. <u>was</u>
27. Our farm, along with our house and barn, (has/have) already been selected for sale at the auction next week. <u>has</u>
28. Either the baseball players or the umpire (was/were) mistaken about the incorrect alignment of the left-field foul pole. <u>was</u>
29. Sayed's favourite meal (is/are) chicken and rice. <u>is</u>
30. One of the concert audience members (was/were) to blame for setting off the fire alarm. <u>was</u>

Exercise 3.2 — Making Pronouns Agree with Nouns

1. The computer users committee members are meeting this afternoon to discuss (its/their) financial report. <u>their</u>
2. Anyone who wishes to participate in the hockey tournament should submit (your/his/their) name by next Tuesday. <u>his</u>
3. Any person intending to vote in the city council election must first register (his or her/your/ their) name at the voting office by tomorrow afternoon. <u>his or her</u>
4. Everyone who intends to donate blood next week should give (their/his or her) name to the Red Cross representative on campus <u>his or her</u>
5. My neighbour was told that (you/he) had to make special arrangements for private trash collection. <u>he</u>
6. Having considered all of the alternatives, the entertainment committee still could not decide on (its/their) next venue for the Halloween Ball. <u>its</u>
7. Anybody who wants to babysit my little brother had better bring (his or her/their) Monopoly game; he loves playing board games. <u>his or her</u>
8. Tanaka, together with her two brothers, was asked if (she/they) wanted to join the swimming team. <u>she</u>

Exercise Answers

9. Everyone except Cleo passed (her/their) entrance exam.   __her__
10. Neither of the software writers could find (his/their) way to our new cafeteria.   __his__
11. Either the company president or the middle managers should have had (her/their) meeting last week with our union representatives.   __their__
12. The two new cars in the showroom window do not have (its/their) hood ornaments attached.   __their__
13. No team member will be permitted to arrange (their/his or her) own transportation to the tournament next Saturday.   __his or her__
14. Our investment club had (their/its) last meeting on Thursday.   __its__
15. Everyone in our Internet class should have (their/his or her) own home computer.   __his or her__
16. Both Francine and Hillary won (her/their) chess matches.   __their__
17. Neither the dancers nor the master of ceremonies wanted (his/their) performance to be videotaped.   __his__
18. Those of you who want to reserve orchestra seats had better send (their/your) money in by tomorrow.   __your__
19. Our Internet provider has increased (their/its) monthly fee by ten percent.   __its__
20. If anyone wants to have a thoroughly enjoyable time next weekend, (they/he or she) should attend our Riverfest celebration.   __he or she__
21. Every member of our union will have to turn in (his or her/their) strike vote ballot by tomorrow.   __his or her__
22. Both accident victims had (his/their) legs broken.   __their__
23. When Ricardo applied for a hockey scholarship, he was told that (you/he) first had to have a physical examination.   __he__
24. The local newspaper is printing all of (its/their) news photos in colour.   __its__
25. The student union committee argued for hours over the budget changes that (it/they) placed on the agenda last week.   __it__
26. Our board of education has informed us that (you/we) now have to build a childcare facility.   __we__
27. The coach, as well as the team members, thinks that (his/their) views are being ignored by the college officials.   __his__

Writing Fundamentals

28. No participant in the AIDS eradication drive will have to donate more than (their/his or her) time to Saturday's march.   <u>his or her</u>
29. Neither the lawyers nor the plaintiff could convince the jury that (her/their) arguments removed any reasonable doubt.   <u>her</u>
30. Each member of the curling association will be required to purchase (his or her/their) own team sweater.   <u>his or her</u>

Exercise 3.3 — Review of Agreement

	P	V

1. Somebody must be working late on the fourth floor; (he or she/they) (is/are) turning on all of the overhead lights in the front office.   <u>he or she</u>   <u>is</u>
2. Ranjit will enrol any student in his karate class, providing (they/he or she) (have/has) parental permission.   <u>he or she</u>   <u>has</u>
3. The college pep club (have/has) asked every student to lend (his or her/their) support in promoting next month's charity concert.   <u>his or her</u>   <u>has</u>
4. One of the young men in our class (believes/believe) that (his/their) grades were not properly recorded by the college registrar.   <u>his</u>   <u>believes</u>
5. Neither Hector nor Pierre (want/wants) to have (his/their) name submitted for class president.   <u>his</u>   <u>wants</u>
6. A pack of matches (was/were) left precariously near the fireplace; please remove (it/them) to a safer location.   <u>it</u>   <u>was</u>
7. Neither the police nor the fire fighters (was/were) aware that (their/its) salary scales were under review.   <u>their</u>   <u>were</u>
8. Every member of our neighbourhood watch committee (is/are) requested to collect (his or her/their) window sticker as soon as possible.   <u>his or her</u>   <u>is</u>
9. Sufficient RAM, as well as a fast modem, (are/is) necessary for anyone who wants (his or her/their) computer to properly surf the Internet.   <u>his or her</u>   <u>is</u>
10. If either the dentist or the dental technician (answer/answers) the phone, please tell (her/them) that I must cancel my appointment for next Tuesday.   <u>her</u>   <u>answers</u>

Exercise Answers

11. Among my favourite Canadian authors (is/are) Alice Munro and Margaret Atwood; I have read all of (her/their) novels and short stories.   __their__   __are__

12. Both my father and my uncle (feels/feel) that (he/they) should be the coach of our Little League baseball team.   __they__   __feel__

13. Claudia, as well as Beryl, (think/thinks) that the new Boeing 777 is the most comfortable airplane that (they/she) has ever flown on.   __she__   __thinks__

14. Victor Gonzales is one of those small-business owners who (believe/believes) that (they/he) should put the customer first.   __he__   __believes__

15. Every man and woman in this room (were/was) present when the conference-call message came from our home office; (he or she/you) should follow its instructions implicitly.   __he or she__   __was__

16. Chandra is one of the few travel agents who (provide/provides) the customer with (his or her/their) own computerized itinerary.   __his or her__   __provides__

17. The bridge club (are/is) meeting this Friday to decide on the venue for (their/its) next tournament.   __its__   __is__

18. No one can understand dire poverty until (they/he or she) (travel/travels) to Calcutta, India.   __he or she__   __travels__

19. Each of her sisters (are/is) working part-time to defray (their/her) tuition and travel expenses.   __her__   __is__

20. The building superintendent, along with the owners, (want/wants) each tenant to remove (his or her/their) clothesline from the balcony.   __his or her__   __wants__

21. There (weren't/wasn't) anyone in the audience who did not have tears in (his or her/their) eyes after the performance.   __his or her__   __wasn't__

22. Both our accountant and office assistant (has/have) already taken (his/their) summer vacations.   __their__   __have__

23. Neither the director of community relations nor the nursing-home volunteers (expect/expects) the city to reduce (their/her) monthly parking fees.   __their__   __expect__

24. Veronica, in addition to Mona, (keeps/keep) (her/their) valuables in our bank's safety deposit box.   __her__   __keeps__

25. Each of our sales associates (meets/meet) (his or her/their) weekly sales quota by Thursday afternoon.   __his__   __meets__

26. Every freshman, sophomore, and junior (are/is) required to collect (his or her/their) student identification card by Wednesday; seniors may collect theirs on Thursday.   his or her   is

27. Neither Fatima nor I (were/was) aware that the students, as well as the faculty, should pick up (his or her/their) graduation gowns on Saturday.   their   was

28. None of the grocery store clerks (were/was) allowed to remove (their/his or her) name tag during working hours.   his or her   was

29. Each of the two new employees (has/have) recently arrived from (his/their) respective country —Poland and South Korea.   his   has

30. The squash club (is/are) meeting tonight to announce (its/their) new bylaws and dues structure.   its   is

Exercise 3.4 — Revising the Paragraph for Agreement

(Since there is not always only one correct revision, answers may vary; the following corrections may serve as guidelines.)

At some point in our career we may be called upon to make a formal speech, and unfortunately we will probably not do a very good job. We will become nervous and hesitant, and forget what we want to say because we will try to memorize lines as if we were actors on stage. We will also stumble over words that we use effortlessly in social or informal occasions, and we will speak either too briefly or too long. In either case our ideas will not be properly developed, which will cause our audience to become either bored or restless. If you have ever been in this situation, I have some tips that may help you take the pain out of speech making.

    First, find out everything you can about the members of your audience. How much do they already know about your subject? For instance, do they know enough so that you can gloss over some of your points without going into detail? And do they have common interests and backgrounds? If your subject is aimed at a homogenous audience, such as community-college or university students, then you can use examples that appeal to their common experiences. Next, ask yourself why they are coming to hear you speak. What set of assumptions are they bringing that may cause your content to be either too narrow or too broad? If you assume, for instance, that you have knowledge to impart, then make sure that your thesis indicates the limited range of your subject.

    Second, do not try to memorize your speech beforehand. Instead, jot down notes on index cards that cover your main points. You may glance at them while giving your speech to keep yourself from wandering off the subject, but the language used should be natural and delivered in your normal voice, with the proper inflections and hesitations. Speaking from memory can be very artificial and mechanistic, which may cause members of your audience to feel that you are speaking down to them.

Third, use as many examples and visuals as you can to illustrate your ideas. Charts, graphs, and pictures on an overhead projector are extremely effective because they clarify your information and raise your audience's interest level. Concrete examples and visual information also eliminate vagueness and the excessive use of descriptive words.

Therefore, if you strive to know as much as you can about your audience by putting yourself in its place; if you avoid an artificial delivery by eliminating your dependence on memorization; and if you clarify and tighten your content by using significant visuals and concrete examples, you will find that your next speech will not only be easier to deliver but also more interesting to your audience.

Exercise 4.1 — Choosing Verb Forms

1. (Set/Sit) the salad bowl on the drainboard next to the sink.   Set
2. The rotted tree trunk has (lain/laid) in our backyard since last July.   lain
3. There is the worker who is (suppose/supposed) to help us erect the scaffolding.   supposed
4. Jasmine is the woman who (swum/swam) for our college swimming team..   swam
5. The Flannigans (use/used) to be our next door neighbours.   used
6. Caroline has already (began/begun) her quilting classes.   begun
7. The party guests had already (ate/eaten) when the dinner-music ensemble arrived twenty minutes late.   eaten
8. The Salvation Army workers had almost (frozen/froze) on the street corner during the cold spell a week before Christmas.   frozen
9. Only a few children (rang/rung) our doorbell on Halloween night.   rang
10. I do not believe that convicted murderers are (hung/hanged) anymore in North America.   hanged
11. My grandmother has (flew/flown) over 15,000 kilometres since my aunt moved to Vancouver.   flown
12. If Rachel and Tanya had (chose/chosen) another airline, they would not have been delayed five hours in Chicago.   chosen

13. The chorus had already (sang/sung) its opening number before most of the audience was seated.   __sung__
14. I did not know that Maurice already (seen/saw) our new play.   __saw__
15. How many paintings were (hanged/hung) yesterday at the art gallery opening?   __hung__
16. We tried to skate on the back pond, but the ice was (broke/broken) in several places.   __broken__
17. When I was dieting, I (drunk/drank) at least eight glasses of water every day.   __drank__
18. Toys were (laying/lying) all over the floor when I entered my son's bedroom.   __lying__
19. My younger brother has (grew/grown) two inches since last February.   __grown__
20. After Martina's term paper had been (wrote/written), her sister, who is a high-school English teacher, proofread it.   __written__
21. Our train had already (went/gone) by the time we arrived at the station.   __gone__
22. The football fans were just (rising/raising) the banner above their heads when a gust of wind blew it over the railing.   __raising__
23. How could the pitcher have (threw/thrown) the baseball over the catcher's head when the tying run was on third base?   __thrown__
24. Victor Chung may have (rode/ridden) on the snowmobile if he had worn warmer clothes.   __ridden__
25. Has anyone in the class (brung/brought) a copy of today's newspaper?   __brought__
26. Who (sung/sang) "O Canada" at the hockey game last night?   __sang__
27. Bernice's stamp collection was (stole/stolen) while she was visiting her uncle in Calgary.   __stolen__
28. The plate glass window was (broke/broken) when I arrived this morning to open the grocery store.   __broken__
29. If we had known that the movie was showing for only one week, we would have (saw/seen) it.   __seen__
30. The bedroom door slowly (swang/swung) open to reveal the bloodstained carpet.   __swung__

Exercise Answers

Exercise 4.2 — Correcting Verb Errors

Coins were first invented as a form of money by three separate

civilizations: the Chinese, the Greeks, and the Indians. Even

though these people *had* no contact with each other, they all   1   C

invented metal coins and *had chosen* them as the best form   2   chose

of money. The first coins *had been* very simple and heavy   3   were

and did not have an exact value. Silver coins *become* very   4   became

popular among the Greeks for several reasons. First, since

silver is so strong, people *have used* the coins over and   5   used

over without the money breaking. Second, the coins *were*   6   C

small, so they *are* easy to carry or to store at home. Third,   7   were

silver is a beautiful, soft metal, and coins that *have been made*   8   made

of silver *are* easy to imprint with designs, letters, and   9   were

numbers. Most importantly, however, the value or cost

of silver *will stay* the same longer than cheaper metals.   10   stayed

Writing Fundamentals

Exercise 4.3 — Using the Proper Pronoun Case

1. Fuad Shamaz and (I/me) bought the members of the soccer team pizzas for winning their final game of the season.   <u>I</u>
2. No one on the team is faster than (she/her).   <u>she</u>
3. Just between you and (I/me), the anniversary dinner will not be held at Sal's Restaurant.   <u>me</u>
4. We were not prepared for (his/him) complaining about the lack of team spirit.   <u>his</u>
5. It was not (he/him) who won the new car in the raffle yesterday.   <u>he</u>
6. (Whomever/Whoever) is ready may tee off first.   <u>Whoever</u>
7. Please inform Kerry and (I/me/myself) what time you will pick us up tomorrow evening.   <u>me</u>
8. My Web site was designed by (her/she) and Brian.   <u>her</u>
9. It must have been (they/them) who started the vicious rumour.   <u>they</u>
10. (Whom/Who) are the leading candidates for the job?   <u>Who</u>
11. (We/Us) club members had better vote in the next election.   <u>We</u>
12. None of us thought that (their/them) booing their own team was appropriate behaviour.   <u>their</u>
13. Everyone but (she/her) wanted to participate in the student-council election.   <u>she</u>
14. Please return the locker room keys to either Jasmine or (me/I/myself).   <u>me</u>
15. Our committee will present the most valuable player award to (whoever/whomever) has scored the most points during the hockey season.   <u>whoever</u>
16. No one but (he/him) could swim the length of the lap pool underwater.   <u>he</u>
17. Even the coach (hisself/himself) thought that our split end was out of bounds when he caught the ball.   <u>himself</u>
18. The second prize in the lottery was five hundred dollars, which was divided equally between Johnny Wu and (I/me/myself).   <u>me</u>
19. The church choir members (theirselves/themselves) thought that choir practice was rescheduled for Friday evening.   <u>themselves</u>
20. It was (they/them), I believe, who went white-water rafting on the Ottawa River.   <u>they</u>
21. Emma, the live-in house maid, and (he/him) are finally getting married.   <u>he</u>

Exercise Answers

22. I cannot understand (she/her) telling the cheerleaders that they are not sufficiently enthusiastic when leading the cheers.   her
23. My husband was not as excited as I about (my/me) taking flying lessons.   my
24. No one was more disappointed than (I/me) when our debating team lost last week.   I
25. Don't do anything rash until you hear from Rachel and (I/me).   me
26. Please give the donation to (whoever/whomever) qualifies as a worthy recipient.   whoever
27. Father did not know that both my sister and (I/me) are ski instructors in British Columbia.   I
28. Will you provide Michelle and (I/me/myself) the information that we require to reserve discount airline tickets?   me
29. I cannot understand (them/their) insisting that we report to work a half-hour early.   their
30. Is it (them/they) who will host the bazaar next Saturday?   they

Exercise 4.4 — Confusing Adjectives and Adverbs

1. Our Thanksgiving meal was (really/real) sumptuous.   really
2. The captain of our basketball team felt (bitter/bitterly) about not being selected for the all-star team.   bitter
3. Martha is an (awfully/awful) fine dressmaker.   awfully
4. The whole class felt (bad/badly) when our teacher, Mrs. Reagan, was transferred to another school.   bad
5. Our company's accounting office operates quite (efficient/efficiently) despite being understaffed.   efficiently
6. We did not eat any (different/differently) than the other tourists, but we still became ill.   differently
7. My husband always dresses (conservatively/conservative) when we have dinner with our friends.   conservatively
8. Both Carmen and Felicia did (good/well) on their mid-term examinations.   well
9. Kurt eats (sensibly/sensible) when we go out for buffet dinners.   sensibly
10. That small girl on the bench is (sure/surely) not a member of the school basketball team.   surely
11. I felt (strange/strangely) when I entered the room alone.   strange
12. All of us felt (good/well) about the size of our donation to the Children's Aid Society.   good

13. We advised Liam to drive (slowly/slow), but he ignored our admonition and received a speeding ticket on the highway. — slowly
14. Donata is the (most thinnest/thinnest) woman in our cooking class. — thinnest
15. I felt (sick/sickly) after I ate the chocolate fudge sundae. — sick
16. Clara told us that she played (poor/poorly) in our annual college golf tournament. — poorly
17. Timothy is much (more heavier/heavier) than his friend Sam. — heavier
18. My family is the (most/more) gregarious of any family in our neighbourhood. — most
19. Our hockey team is (most frequently/frequently) faster on the ice than our competitors. — frequently
20. Those lemons tasted very (sour/sourly) in our lemonade. — sour
21. Charles Chang is the (more qualified/most qualified) employee in our marketing department. — most qualified
22. Harold certainly looks (different/differently) since he had his hair coloured. — different
23. I believe that last month was the (most warmest/warmest) month on record. — warmest
24. Creative Solutions is the (more recent/most recent) software development company to move into our industrial park. — most recent
25. We cannot give you a (more accurate/more accurately) account of our department's monthly expenditures. — more accurate
26. This year our basketball team is the (most strongest/strongest) it has been since the 1993-94 season. — strongest
27. My rowing coach is (most knowledgeable/knowledgeable) about high-protein diets. — knowledgeable
28. Please don't play your saxophone too (loudly/loud). — loud
29. I think that Ottawa is the (most coldest/coldest) city in which I have ever lived. — coldest
30. Odette's is the (most elegant/more elegant) dress shop of the two in our small town. — more elegant

Exercise 4.5 — Revising the Paragraph to Solve Special Problems

Last winter my wife and I decided to take a summer golf vacation with two other young couples whom we have known for nearly ten years, before they were married. Since all of us were avid golfers, we thought that a two-week holiday focussing on golf would be a lot of fun.

We decided on the Carolinas. We thought that a week spent at Myrtle Beach, South Carolina, and a week in the mountains of North Carolina would be enjoyable and entertaining. We were right: my wife and I both agreed that it was one of the best holidays we have ever had.

We left Canada on June 15 in two cars, three people in each car. The trip to Myrtle Beach took us two full days, but we drove slower than the speed limits and made small side trips along the way, including a stop in Gettysburg, Pennsylvania, where the famous Civil War battle was fought.

In Myrtle Beach we stayed in a charming small hotel right on the beach; our rooms were adjoining, and each had cooking facilities. The couple who owned the hotel were the friendliest and most obliging people that my wife and I have ever met. They were also, themselves, really fine golfers, and gave us helpful tips on which courses to play. We decided, on their advice, to play four different courses, each with different degrees of difficulty, including extensive water hazards and large sand traps along the fairways. In the evening we ate in different ethnic restaurants, most of which served wonderfully fresh seafood. And the prices, we discovered, were quite reasonable for the quality of the food and the sophistication of the restaurants in which we and our companions ate.

We also took a day off from golf and spent some time on the beach. The water was awfully warm for that time of year, and the sand was white and clean, which we were not used to since we live in the Ottawa Valley, where beaches are few and far between. And, of course, what Canadian, including me, travels south and does not go shopping? So we shopped in factory outlet malls during the one rainy day we had that week. The women, for the most part, bought clothes and we all purchased golf accessories.

At the end of the week, on Sunday, we drove—more quickly this time—to the Blue Ridge Mountains of North Carolina, where we checked into a golf resort with lodging and restaurant facilities. The resort had twenty-seven holes of golf as well as finely manicured tennis courts and a large swimming pool. The mountain courses were quite interesting and challenging, with raised tees and greens, and fairways that followed the contours of rolling hills and wide valleys. The tall southern pine trees were really magnificent, and the view from several of the tee areas was breathtaking. We spent a great deal of time taking pictures of the beautiful vistas. Again, the food was first rate, and there was dancing and entertainment in the evening for whoever was energetic enough to stay awake after playing twenty-seven holes of golf. The weather, as in Myrtle Beach, was absolutely perfect: warm days and cool nights, especially in the mountains, where the air was fresh and dry.

At the end of our holiday, we all agreed that our choosing the Carolinas for a golfing holiday was a stroke of genius. We also agreed that we would recommend the holiday to anyone who loves golf, good food, and wonderful scenery.

Writing Fundamentals

Exercise 5.1 — Improving Pronoun Reference

(The revisions that replace or remove pronouns will vary; the following revisions may serve as guidelines.)

1. Carlotta spends a great deal of time collecting stamps because stamp collecting is her favourite hobby.   F
2. Eileen told Maureen that Eileen's hairdresser was seriously ill.   F
3. My uncle from Toronto bought my brother a new computer, a gift that took him completely by surprise.   F
4. My sister has never played tennis, but she is quite interested in learning the game.   F
5. The music on the radio is too sombre; it is not the kind of sound that I enjoy.   C
6. When I saw my first baseball game, I decided that I wanted to be a baseball player when I grew up.   F
7. When I went to the unemployment office, the clerks told me to return next Monday for an interview with an employment counsellor.   F
8. When the star baseball player hit a home run, everyone gave him a standing ovation.   C
9. Gregory asked Brian if he could meet Brian for lunch on Sunday.   F
10. Our gym instructor told us that the workout had been successful.   F
11. I attended my first cricket match, but I couldn't understand the game.   F
12. The menu outside the restaurant indicates that the soup of the day is cream of asparagus.   F
13. Everything I do seems to annoy you, which confuses me.   F
14. I never went to a bullfight, but I am fascinated by the sport of bullfighting.   F
15. Deirdre failed the final exam, which was the reason she had to attend summer school.   C
16. Because we left the football game early, we failed to see our team score the final touchdown.   F
17. The captain of the cruise ship asked the passengers if the cruise had been enjoyable.   F
18. The dentist told the doctor that the doctor's tooth had to be extracted.   F
19. Helen called the hospital and told the administrators that she had been overbilled.   F

20. Their exam scores were low, which disappointed them.   C
21. When the storm hit the coast of North Carolina, it achieved hurricane-force winds of one hundred and sixty kilometres per hour.   F
22. After living in France for the last ten years, I have come to enjoy living there.   F
23. Carl told Fred that Carl's tie was made of silk.   F
24. I spend a lot of money on stamps because stamp collecting is my favourite hobby.   F
25. William Frazier, in *Cold Mountain,* writes about a soldier returning to his home in the North Carolina mountains during the civil war between the northern and southern states.   F
26. When the airline pilots went on strike, their decision surprised us very much.   F
27. The members of our hockey team bought the coach a gold watch at the end of the season, which was a very nice gesture of appreciation.   C
28. The jury members were surprised when the judge informed them that they had to stay in the hotel overnight.   C
29. Beryl's volunteering to work overtime on Friday was appreciated.   F
30. In the Middle East the people speak mostly Arabic.   F

Exercise 5.2 — Revising the Paragraph for Clear Pronoun Reference

(Pronoun reference corrections may vary; therefore this revision may serve as only a guideline.)

1. When a foreign-language credit was a requirement for high-school graduation, this requirement greatly increased students' sensitivity to the structure of language, including English. The language requirement was important for students because there was a skills transfer, especially in the knowledge of verb tenses and of common prefixes and suffixes.

   Also, students developed a disciplined approach to learning grammar rules, which helped their knowledge of English syntax. This approach tended to make them more careful writers. It is too bad that students today do not have to study a foreign language, because this study would certainly make them better users of their native tongue.

2. When I first travelled overseas I was worried that the people would not understand me, for I could not speak a foreign language. But I was mistaken, because I found that in every European country I visited the people could understand what I said. The reason for their understanding, of course, was that most of them had to study English in both grade school and high school.

Their knowledge of English made me feel inadequate, because the people were at least bilingual—some even trilingual—and everyone I met was eager to talk to me to increase his or her knowledge of English, especially our slang expressions. This experience made me suspect that my lack of knowledge about other people and other cultures stemmed from my unwillingness to learn a foreign language.

Therefore, since my first trip overseas five years ago, I have learned two foreign languages fluently and am conversant in two more. This knowledge also increased my appreciation of other cultures, because I soon realized that language is the key to understanding how people think and feel. This is a lesson that I will not soon forget.

Exercise 5.3 — Misplaced Modifiers

(Corrections may vary.)

1. Without a tool kit, no one could fix the bicycle.   M
2. On Monday, Raymond asked Leslie for a date.   M
3. On Sunday morning we started the automobile race without qualified mechanics in the pits.   M
4. Frequently, people who overeat have high cholesterol.   M
5. By 7:00 p.m. most of the dinner guests had already arrived.   C
6. Frequent singing relieves tension.   M
7. If the coach is agreeable, the team intends to have a pizza party on Saturday night in the locker room.   M
8. Please inform us on the enclosed postcard if you received your free box of chocolates.   M
9. By the end of the meal I had consumed almost all of the lemon meringue pie.   M
10. We attended the annual fundraising party for AIDS research at our high-school gymnasium.   C
11. Do not buy a used car without a maintenance record from a friend.   M
12. Please believe me, my father did not intend to offend you by offering to pay for your wife's dinner.   M
13. Our volunteer recycling team collected almost three hundred discarded aluminum cans.   M
14. Everyone in my class completed his or her assignment before the due date.   C

Exercise Answers

15. I finally found my wristwatch without the gold band under the car seat.   M
16. My son's pen pal from New Orleans visited us on Saturday.   M
17. The mechanic told me to have my car's oil changed on Friday.   M
18. Greg and Sally finished their homework only ten minutes before class.   M
19. We will not agree, under any circumstances, to accompany you to the class reunion this Saturday.   M
20. We often go to the movies on Friday night.   C
21. With trepidation, our hockey team played last year's championship team.   M
22. She telephones her sister almost every night at 8:00 p.m.   M
23. Mai Ling's gold ring, with a two-carat diamond, was lost in the airport.   M
24. I am certain that Denise did not intend to insult the cocktail waitress last night.   M
25. Often, drinking Gatorade prevents dehydration.   M
26. Never drive at night without fog lights on country roads.   M
27. Only Gerta ran in the five-kilometre race.   M
28. Frank swam nearly ten kilometres across Lake Tuckahoo.   M
29. Ranjit sold a necklace with a broken clasp to Chandra.   M
30. Our Little League team played without proper uniforms last Saturday.   M

Exercise 5.4 — Revising the Paragraph to Correct Misplaced Modifiers

Last summer, in Grove Park, we held our annual company barbecue, which included only chicken, hot dogs, and hamburgers. By eliminating steak, we saved nearly two hundred dollars. Also, if the park authorities had agreed, we wanted to have soccer games and Frisbee-throwing contests, but they refused to give us permission because of lack of space and potential danger to other picnickers.

    Despite this restriction, though, we still managed to have fun. We organized potato-sack races for the children and horseshoe-throwing contests, with real horseshoes, for the adults. There were also watermelon-eating contests in which nearly everyone participated. It was a perfect afternoon, without oppressive heat or humidity, for the families of our employees. And we had only one minor injury: our vice-president of marketing cut his finger with a knife while slicing a watermelon on a slippery plate.

Writing Fundamentals

Exercise 5.5 — Dangling Modifiers

(Revisions may vary.)

1. Concerned by the threat of lightning, the head official delayed the golf match.   DM
2. During the drive between Edmonton and Calgary, one could see many serious accidents on the icy roads.   DM
3. While I was cross-country skiing without sunblock, my face became painfully sunburned.   DM
4. To play golf in the low eighties, you need to practise for many hours.   DM
5. Before buying my new car, I did a lot of comparison shopping.   C
6. After I waited two hours for the plane to arrive, the airline announced that the flight had been diverted to another airport because of inclement weather.   DM
7. Concerned by the spreading brush fires, the firefighters ordered the homes evacuated.   DM
8. While waiting for the bus to arrive, Serena used her mobile phone to make a dinner reservation.   C
9. Once I was on the open road, my worries seemed to disappear.   DM
10. As an expert in tax law, I think that this business deduction is completely unwarranted.   DM
11. After I listened to him speak, my opinion of his management skills did not change.   DM
12. When sailing on the St. Lawrence River, I saw the Thousand Islands International Bridge appear suddenly through the morning mist.   DM
13. When I first met Beverly, I thought that she was a fashion model.   C
14. Like many of today's TV programs, this show's violence and sex are what makes it so popular with today's youth.   DM
15. When the wall was thoroughly plastered, the painter decided to let it dry overnight.   DM
16. For you to become a successful actor, voice training is essential.   DM
17. Seeing the snow fall in late afternoon, I felt like a child again in the province of Quebec.   DM
18. During our lunch hour the fire alarm went off inadvertently, and the building had to be temporarily evacuated.   C
19. When jogging in the hot sun, you should wear a sweatband.   DM
20. After a large dinner, a heavy dessert is not a good idea.   C

Exercise Answers

21. To remain thin, you must exercise and eat a low-fat diet.   DM
22. As a long-time resident of Montreal, I think this city needs better, and more modern, public transportation.   DM
23. When you are sunbathing on the beach, watch out for the Frisbee players.   DM
24. While word-processing on my computer, I always save my work during—not after—the writing process.   C
25. After Zelda became pregnant, the doctor put her on a strict diet.   DM
26. Regretting her refusal to participate in the bake sale, Kathy decided to volunteer as a ticket seller for the charity bazaar.   C
27. To enjoy the winter months, families can cross-country ski, which is a great family sport.   DM
28. After I read Stephen King novels in bed, the light must always be on..   DM
29. Because he knows when to stop drinking alcohol, Harvey is always elected the designated driver.   DM
30. While Donna was attending the Calgary Stampede, her purse was stolen from her hotel room.   DM

Exercise 5.6 — Revising the Paragraph to Remove Dangling Modifiers

(Revisions may vary.)

The motor trip that my wife and I took along the Rhine and Moselle river valleys was a once-in-a-lifetime experience, for it was both delightful and educational. Flying from Montreal to Frankfurt, we encountered rough weather that caused our flight to arrive late. But after we spent a quiet and restful night in a Frankfurt hotel, the next morning we rented a small German car and drove to Mainz, where we began our Rhine River trip.

Taking the two-lane road that ran alongside the river, we saw small towns and villages. We visited vineyards and wineries where different grades of white wines were made and bottled. We also took a cable-car ride to a lookout point above the river, where the small ships looked like toy boats in a bathtub. And in the old town of Boppard we saw the ruins of an old Roman fortress. One morning, while taking a boat cruise along the Rhine, we heard a guide point out the history of that waterway, especially as a daunting means of transportation during the time of the Robber Barons, who levied heavy tolls and exorbitant custom duties on people travelling along the river's stretch from Mainz to Cologne. After sightseeing, shopping in the small villages, and visiting ancient churches and cathedrals, we stayed overnight in *gasthauses*—which can be compared to bed and breakfast inns throughout North America—as a welcome respite.

When we reached the town of Koblenz, we joined the Moselle river valley. The wine vineyards there were on the sides of steep hills that guarded the river, and the workers had to be tied around the waist with a rope to tend the grapes. While we were driving along the Moselle, several small towns were having wine festivals, in which we actively participated. We also ate our lunches—wursts, schnitzels, and red cabbage—in quaint *biergartens*, toured several castles, and visited Roman ruins in the old town of Trier.

During the trip we encountered many friendly German villagers, who extended us their hospitality and good will. We even learned to say "bottoms up" in German. At the end of the trip, we realized that we had just travelled through one of the most beautiful parts of southern Germany, and that our knowledge and appreciation of the German people and their history had increased tenfold. We also learned an important lesson: one should never try to lose weight while touring through the German wine country.

Exercise 5.7 — Correcting Faulty Parallelism

(Revisions may vary.)

1. I moved to Vancouver because of its milder winters, the close access to the University of British Columbia, and because I wanted to be near my youngest daughter. P
2. My uncle George was a bricklayer, a construction worker, and finally a professional wrestler. P
3. Our high-school gym teacher, who is a strict disciplinarian and who is the treasurer of the local teachers' union, has just been indicted for embezzlement and bribery. P
4. Calvin not only wants to learn how to play tennis, but also wants to learn golf and curling, too. P
5. My new car is comfortable, economical, and easy to drive. C
6. The golf pro's putting is much more accurate than Paul's putting. P
7. She is either an actress or a fashion model. P
8. The Muslim faith, which is one of the world's fastest growing religions and which is attracting new worshippers in Canada every year, requires strict fasting during the holy month of Ramadan. P
9. Tam Sung's apartment is not only small, but also unfurnished. P
10. I was asked to pick up the laundry, put gas in the car, buy headache pills at the pharmacy, and then rent a movie at our local video store. P
11. He is either going to the local community college or the University of Western Ontario. P
12. Fenimore always has supported and always will support the Calgary Stampeders football team. P

Exercise Answers

13. My tennis game is not as well developed as Luke's game. P
14. The airline that I am using offers neither frequent flyer miles nor non-stop service from Vancouver to Montreal. C
15. I cannot decide which kind of fruit I want: a pear, an orange, or an apple. P
16. She jogs every day for at least an hour. P
17. Our city's pollution bylaws are not as strict as your city's bylaws. P
18. Françoise is participating in, as well as benefiting from, the new community campaign to modernize garbage collection. P
19. Donn is both an officer and a gentleman. P
20. My parents always have voted in the national election and always will. C
21. We were told that our evening flight would be delayed indefinitely and that we should be prepared to wait until the early morning flight. P
22. My daughter babysits for our neighbour's little girl quite willingly. P
23. Cross-country skiing is good for the heart and lungs and is highly recommended for muscle tone. P
24. I can play poker, pinochle, gin rummy, and canasta. P
25. Manuel's credit-card debt is not as large as Paco's. P
26. He is not only a navigator but also a pilot. C
27. Mandy and Mickie are cousins and best friends. P
28. My cat, Max, catches neither mice nor any other rodent that could possibly injure him. P
29. The hockey game that we saw last night was rough, exciting, and full of penalties. P
30. If I had my choice of owning either a Mercedes or an Oldsmobile car, I would choose the Mercedes. P

Exercise 5.8 — Revising the Paragraph to Improve Parallelisms

(Revisions may vary.)

It is not easy to lose weight permanently and safely, for there is no magical diet pill that will guarantee substantial weight loss without risk. Furthermore, fad diets not only do not work but may even be harmful to your health. The most important facts to remember are that permanent weight loss takes time, involves a change in lifestyle, and requires exercise. Through the correct combination of the right foods and exercise, you need to establish a daily deficit of approximately five hundred calories to lose that pound a week.

Writing Fundamentals

You need to control your eating not only for the duration of the diet but also for long after you have lost the desired pounds. Food rich in fat calories is more readily converted to body fat than food high in carbohydrates and proteins. A high-fat diet is a risk factor for heart disease, for diabetes, and for some kinds of cancers. Diet experts advocate a fat intake of 25 percent of total calories, which is substantially lower than the 38 to 40 percent most North Americans consume and which is ideal for maintaining a long-term weight loss.

After a certain amount of time, your fat deficit, along with exercise, can slim your body to a point where it functions so efficiently that you stop losing weight. At this point, having become used to both the dietary changes you have made and to your daily exercise regimen, you can then go ahead and cut your fat intake far enough to reach the target weight you have set for yourself. But you must remember that losing weight always has required and always will require a combination of diet and exercise—one without the other will not, in the long term, be effective.

Exercise 5.9 — Review Exercise: Sentence Clarity

(Revisions may vary.)

1. I moved to North Carolina for the milder weather, for the golfing opportunities, and for the lower cost of living. **P**
2. Once we were out on the open sea, our worries seemed to disappear. **DM**
3. As the representative for the clean air committee, I do not think that this proposal will help our cause. **DM**
4. Tanya informed Paula that Paula's lost dog was finally found by Tanya's brother. **PR**
5. Always purchase a computer with a fast modem and sufficient memory from a reputable store. **M**
6. Whenever I go to the post office, the clerks find something wrong with the way I wrap my parcels. **PR**
7. She always has voted and always will vote for the political party that supports affirmative action. **P**
8. When you type a letter, you should use your word processor's spell-check capability. **DM**
9. To safely and efficiently lose weight, you must ensure that your exercise routine includes at least a half-hour of either walking or jogging. **DM**
10. Mendez ran almost fifteen kilometres in the marathon race. **M**

Exercise Answers

11. The flight attendant forgot to tell us to buckle our seat belts during the turbulent weather, and this lack of information was noticed by all of the passengers in my section.   PR

12. Sergio not only finished first in the marathon race, but also broke the speed record.   P

13. After we arrived at our lakefront cottage, we carried in our belongings, stowed our fishing gear, slid our boat into the water, and then decided to go swimming.   P

14. The football players who are often late for practice are placed on probation and suspended for one game.   M

15. All of us wanted to cancel the volleyball game and have our picnic lunch inside the school cafeteria if the rain had continued.   M

16. Caroline's English test score was much lower than Phil's and Kurt's.   PR

17. I have never seen an African bee, but I am terrified of African bees.   PR

18. While attending the estate auction, we saw the grand piano slide off the mobile stage and smash into a dining-room table.   DM

19. Kylie is interested in, and excited by, the new Canadian rock star.   P

20. Emory is either a ballet dancer or a soccer player.   P

21. The gym instructor told us to meet the school bus at 9:00 a.m. on Friday.   M

22. The coach asked her players if the game had been easy.   PR

23. With sadness and regret, the hockey team played its last game.   M

24. If the rain stops, please allow me to attend the outdoor rock concert.   M

25. Our college tennis team is far better than your college's team.   P

26. After I spent a gruelling six weeks of spring training at football camp, my family was glad to have me back home in Canada.   DM

27. The rain in the mountains melted the snow and caused some flooding.   PR

28. Out of a field of fifty-four teams in the golf tournament, only the team of Durer and Sullivan broke par on the first day.   M

29. We finally decided to purchase the car that had a sliding moon roof and an ABS package from the used-car dealer.   M

30. When the flounder was completely fried, Sally removed it from the Teflon pan.   DM

31. Garth plays tennis because he enjoys the competition and the exercise, and because his girlfriend is a tennis pro.   P

Writing Fundamentals

32. Once we were on top of the CN Tower, the cars looked like small toys racing along the thin parkway.   DM
33. Stacy always has exercised and always will exercise strenuously at least three times a week.   P
34. Claude's new detective novel was favourably reviewed and is now on the best-seller list.   P
35. For you to swim competitively, your legs and shoulders must be very strong.   DM
36. My husband forgot our wedding anniversary, which disturbed me very much.   PR
37. He is either lazy or not interested in success.   P
38. I have never seen a great white shark, but I am deathly afraid of great white sharks.   PR
39. Johnny Chung won only ten dollars playing blackjack.   M
40. My father is irritated by, and disappointed in, his employees' tardiness and lack of ambition.   P

Exercise 6.1 — Spelling

1. We cannot **except** any more donations at this time.   accept
2. I think **your** in that new play we saw last night.   you're
3. Would you please **advice** my daughter about the available opportunities for post-secondary education?   advise
4. She does not know **weather** to major in dentistry or medicine.   whether
5. We cannot **alter** our rules on attendance and lateness.   C
6. There are **to** many cooks in the kitchen.   too
7. Josef was **borne** on July 1, Canada's birthday.   born
8. **They're** peace proposal was unacceptable to the Security Council.   Their
9. Whomever they **chose** as a candidate must be acceptable to the election committee.   choose
10. I'd rather sail through the **Straight** of Gibraltar than through the **Straight** of Hormuz in the Arabian Gulf.   Strait
10. He is thinking of **dyeing** these plain cloths a bright orange.   C
12. The holy **rights** of the Anglican Church are similar to those of the Catholic Church.   rites
13. The formal recognition of his past accomplishments was the best **complement** he could have received.   compliment
14. Darlene is **quiet** strong for her size and weight.   quite

15. Our city council is **liable** to overturn the school board's decision on further funding for school construction.   C
16. Smoking on campus is **prescribed** by our school's clean-air policy.   proscribed
17. These immigrants come from one of the **dessert** countries along the Arabian Gulf.   desert
18. Who's in charge of our **personal** department?   personnel
19. I do not know whether **its** Thursday or Friday.   it's
20. May I have a **peace** of pie for dessert?   piece
21. He looks too young and inexperienced to have **lead** soldiers into battle.   led
22. Please do not **loose** your temper when addressing city council tonight.   lose
23. When did your legal counsel file the **liable** suit?   libel
24. Can you **exceed** to her wishes with good conscience?   accede
25. Who's in charge of the **stationery** department?   C
26. I don't know how the personnel department will **adopt** to his aggressive management style.   adapt
27. Do you know **were** the principal is right now?   where
28. Do you think that this **coarse** of study will help you obtain a decent job?   course
29. He has too many **vises** to be a prefect of discipline at our school.   vices
30. We just passed the building **cite** for our new gymnasium.   site

Exercise 7.1 — Commas That Separate Independent Clauses and Elements in a Series

1. Monica has taken up the game of tennis, but she still plays golf regularly.   W
2. I cannot decide whether to have tea or coffee with my meal.   C
3. My favourite fruits are oranges and grapes.   C
4. Our team won the game, but we also lost our star fullback.   W
5. My college is not large, but it does have high academic standards.   W
6. Milo Gomez, Bill Granger, and Gino Tezza all graduated with high honours.   W
7. Her plane arrived late, but she was still in time for the graduation party.   W
8. The rock concert was sold out, but we managed to get standing-room tickets.   W
9. Quincy mowed the lawn and then ate his lunch.   C

Writing Fundamentals

10. Jamal is both intellectually astute and emotionally stable.   C
11. The pharmacist recommended Aspirin and cough syrup for my head cold, but he did not tell me to use an antibiotic.   W
12. No one knew who turned out the lights and slammed the door during the poker game.   C
13. Yesterday I painted the bathroom, cleaned out the shed, fixed the toaster, and bottled the homemade wine.   W
14. Liam was selected as a candidate for student government, but his brother was passed over.   W
15. Consuela does not own a motocycle or drive a car.   C
16. Did your brother ever have chicken pox or whooping cough as a child?   C
17. Helene is either a business owner or a physician or a trial lawyer.   C
18. My house is almost twenty years old, but my car is only one year old.   W
19. Calgary is not only where I work but also where I was born.   C
20. My father is a carpenter, and my uncle is an electrician.   W
21. Our English teacher told us to read good literature, to keep a daily journal, and to try to add new words to our vocabulary by looking up word meanings in a dictionary.   W
22. Macy visited Edmonton and Calgary and Vancouver last summer during her school vacation.   C
23. Mario and Jack were partners in our annual golf tournament, but they do not often play together during the week.   W
24. She is neither a cheerleader nor a member of the school band.   C
25. Zelda, Nora, Marisa, and Melinda all play soccer for our college team.   W
26. Please eat sensibly and exercise every day.   C
27. She is, I am certain, an honours student, and her brother is the captain of the football team.   W
28. Don't forget to feed the cat, turn out the lights, and lock the front door before you leave.   W
29. Neither wind nor rain nor sleet will keep us from attending the championship hockey game.   C
30. Carrie, my cat, and Edgar, my dog, are not good friends, but they are not mortal enemies, either.   W

Exercise Answers

Exercise 7.2 — Commas That Separate Coordinate Adjectives and Confusing Sentence Elements

1. Without Gloria, Tess would not have gone on a European vacation. __W__
2. Dimitri has a small European car, not a large American car. __C__
3. The rainy, dreary, depressing Monday afternoon seemed to last forever. __W__
4. Down below, the men were working on the sewer line. __W__
5. Our new home is large, airy, bright, and cheerful. __W__
6. Outside, the rain poured down in heavy sheets. __W__
7. My father bought a used electric hedge trimmer and a new fifteen-inch chainsaw. __C__
8. Before ten, nineteen shoppers were outside, waiting for the department store to open. __W__
9. The sleek jungle cat pounced on the small antelope. __C__
10. Our black and white Dalmatian swam after the brown and white ducks in our village pond. __C__
11. The frigid, snowy, gloomy winter afternoon was a good time to read by the fire. __W__
12. After jogging, the team had to do forty push-ups on the stadium grass. __W__
13. Up above, the swiftly moving clouds were threatening rain. __W__
14. While Sarah was sewing, her orange and white cat jumped on her lap. __W__
15. The hot, humid, sultry summer day was not what we expected when we planned our class picnic. __W__
16. Conchita purchased a pink and white golf shirt and two dozen long-distance golf balls. __C__
17. Our powerful, rugged, expensive four-wheel-drive utility vehicle was just what we needed for our camping trips. __W__
18. While Millie was dressing, her pet parrot flew onto her shoulder. __W__
19. The flat desert landing strip was large enough to land a 747. __C__
20. The loud, raucous, smoke-filled rock concert was a financial failure. __W__
21. Inside, the crowd cheered wildly for Mark McGwire. __W__
22. Our large, furry, docile tabby cat sleeps in front of our fireplace. __W__
23. After nine, fifty people rushed into the stadium to claim their free baseball caps. __W__

24. Mai Ling made a green silk dress and light blue slacks for her sister.   C
25. With her German shepherd, Drake, Wilma feels safe and secure.   W
26. Your large, expensive, gas-guzzling car will cost you more than you think to run and maintain.   W
27. Before bathing, Vincent always trims his beard.   W
28. Sheila's black and white terrier puppy is still not housebroken.   C
29. His parents are young, tall, handsome, and rich.   W
30. However hard it is to maintain, Herman refuses to sell his twenty-foot yacht.   W

Exercise 7.3 — Commas That Set Off Non-restrictive Modifiers, Appositives, and Introductory Phrases and Clauses

1. My sister, who is a long-distance runner, has just won the annual marathon race.   W
2. The chainsaw that I bought yesterday was stolen from my car trunk this morning.   C
3. When my brother arrived in Ottawa from Halifax, our entire family met him at the airport.   W
4. Stan Myers, who is my accountant, just won a new car in the hospital lottery.   W
5. Before you jump to conclusions, we must discuss our new investment plan.   W
6. Friday evening's seminar, Technical Report Writing, was rescheduled for Tuesday evening.   W
7. Teachers who fail to take attendance before each class will be placed on report for disciplinary action.   C
8. My brother Tom has just left for Vancouver.   C
9. Our local butcher, who just recently won the Father of the Year award, is being investigated for failing to pay his back taxes.   W
10. When I first saw my future husband, he was playing Frisbee with my best friend.   W
11. Without a second thought, Paula spent her last thirty dollars on a new pair of shoes.   W
12. Nathan Kepler, the famous bowling champion, will visit our college next week.   W
13. The new camper that my father just bought has defective brake lights.   C
14. Brian, my best friend, is a trial lawyer.   W

Exercise Answers

15. Her cousin Rachel is a fashion model in Montreal.   C
16. During yesterday's baseball practice, our star pitcher hurt her left elbow.   W
17. Sales personnel who ignore customers' requests will be immediately terminated.   C
18. Our mayor, Sheila Berg, will not hold a press conference until next week.   W
19. Students who want to try out for the lacrosse team must report to the gymnasium at 3:00 p.m. tomorrow afternoon.   C
20. After due deliberation, we find that we cannot accept your proposal.   W
21. Our city's new curling rink, which cost the taxpayers over half a million dollars, had to be rewired for new lighting fixtures.   W
22. Attila the Hun was both respected and feared by his numerous enemies.   C
23. Without our lead actor, the show cannot go on.   W
24. The man who fixed our water heater has just been arrested for grand theft.   C
25. My favourite singer, Céline Dion, is appearing in Toronto next month.   W
26. After Kathy Chung survived the airplane crash, she vowed never to fly again.   W
27. Our parish priest, who used to be an all-star baseball player, has agreed to coach our Little League baseball team.   W
28. While searching for her sister's wallet, Clare found her old coin purse.   W
29. My aunt Helen, the family legal expert, has just changed her last will and testament.   W
30. The printer that I ordered through the mail last month has not yet arrived.   C

Exercise 7.4 — Commas That Set Off Sentence Modifiers, Absolute Constructions, and Contrasting Elements

1. Our health clinic is, in fact, associated with our general hospital.   W
2. I am certain that we will be on time, weather permitting.   W
3. She will surely repeat her victory of last year.   C
4. The new city arena is, without a doubt, the most modern in our county.   W
5. The machinists' union, unable to muster a strike vote, returned to the bargaining table.   W

Writing Fundamentals

6. The high-school football coach was disappointed, not devastated, by his team's loss last week. W
7. Our school counsellor is absolutely terrific. C
8. All things considered, we were lucky to have survived the sixteen-kilometre march. W
9. She should change her diet, not her dress size. C
10. However hard we tried, we still could not score the winning goal. W
11. Harriet's flight was delayed, not cancelled. W
12. The camping trip was, I am certain, scheduled for a week from Thursday. W
13. I cannot be certain that her first name is Zelda. C
14. We absolutely will not, under any circumstances, tolerate your uncooperative behaviour. W
15. Leniency, not revenge, is a far more humane solution. W
16. Ottawa is, I am almost certain, the capital city of Canada. W
17. Nellie is a seamstress, not a quilter. W
18. Enid Gooch is certainly the brightest student in our class. C
19. However long it takes, we will find the missing evidence. W
20. The building was finished on time, notwithstanding the carpenters' strike and the late delivery of roofing material. W
21. Without a moment's notice, the tornado hit the trailer camp. W
22. However much you want to succeed, you cannot continue to ignore self-sacrifice and hard work.. W
23. The basketball player was 6'9", not 7'1". W
24. We are indeed fortunate to have such an understanding mathematics teacher. C
25. Without realizing his mistake, Pierre continued to wax his skis with car polish. W
26. The correct spelling of the word is "advice," not "advise." W
27. I am certain that Marc took the wrong personnel folder to work. C
28. Our new fire engine is blue, not red. W
29. *Forever Young* is the title of the new movie that opened last night at the Rialto Theatre. C
30. I cannot, in principle, agree to your outlandish proposal. W

Exercise Answers

Exercise 7.5 — Commas That Set Off Names, Speakers, Echo Questions, and Mild Interjections

1. Tell me, Donn, what time did you get home last night?   W
2. "Please don't worry about your father," said my mother pleadingly.   W
3. "We will not lose our next game," said the coach forcefully, "because we will all focus on not making any dumb mistakes."   W
4. Yes, Lisa, I have already purchased our theatre tickets.   W
5. The English teacher did not say that she was going to give us an in-class essay tomorrow.   C
6. Oh my, what a mess you have gotten us into.   W
7. They are certainly a fine dance troupe, aren't they?   W
8. "Stop right there," shouted the police officer, "and place your hands on top of your heads."   W
9. My aunt Flora and her partner won the bridge tournament this year.   C
10. Wow, what an impressive air show our city has organized.   W
11. "Your jeans are filthy," complained my mother.   W
12. Our plane is leaving at 10:00 a.m., isn't it?   W
13. Please wax the car, Fred, before you go to the concert.   W
14. "Many people in the world do not have enough to eat," said our guest speaker, "and many more do not have access to clean drinking water."   W
15. We did not say that you could smoke in the restaurant.   C
16. Well now, aren't you ashamed of yourself for overeating?   W
17. I think you know by now, don't you, that lying to the school counsellor doesn't make any sense.   W
18. Stop shouting, Kim; we can all hear you.   W
19. The conductor announced that our train would not arrive in Winnipeg for another hour.   C
20. "I cannot help it," announced Lorna, "the pollen in the air is making me sneeze."   W
21. Well, well, you finally passed your physics course.   W
22. "Leave your books and personal belongings behind," said the vice-principal, "when the fire drill begins."   W
23. No, sir, the men will not be late for roll call tomorrow.   W
24. "Wait your turn," said the woman, "I was in the queue before you arrived."   W

Writing Fundamentals

25. You returned before 1:00 p.m., didn't you?   __W__
26. Please return your library book, Phyllis, before you are fined by the librarian.   __W__
27. "Don't drive too fast," ordered the park ranger.   __W__
28. Uncle Bill didn't leave yet, did he?   __W__
29. I think everyone realizes, don't they, that we have a school holiday tomorrow?   __W__
30. Oh well, nothing ventured, nothing gained.   __W__

Exercise 7.6 — Comma Review Exercise

1. My mother is a stockbroker, and my father is a physics professor.   __W__
2. If you want to play football you must lift weights, jog eight kilometres every day, and eat a high-protein diet.   __W__
3. The calm, cool, collected poker player won steadily all evening.   __W__
4. We did not see the new Broadway musical, but we did manage to attend the opening of the art museum.   __W__
5. Like clockwork, the mail carrier comes every day at 8:00 a.m.   __W__
6. Before ten, forty shoppers were waiting for the shoe store to open.   __W__
7. Our community college, which is located near the St. Lawrence River, is having a Founder's Day celebration.   __W__
8. Cynthia DeFalco, my hairdresser, is visiting Rome next fall.   __W__
9. The bus that was in an accident just last week is now back on the road.   __C__
10. Before we leave for our annual vacation, we must notify the post office to hold our mail.   __W__
11. The lead actor, I am certain, is related to a famous concert pianist.   __W__
12. "Yes, Virginia, there is a Santa Claus."   __W__
13. My brother Phil works in a law office.   __C__
14. Now, now, don't cry over spilled milk.   __W__
15. Our bus leaves for Banff tomorrow, not next Tuesday.   __W__
16. The house that has green shutters is the one that was burglarized last month.   __C__
17. "I cannot understand," announced the teacher, "how any of you passed the chemistry test."   __W__
18. Curtis enjoys playing the trumpet and singing off-key.   __C__
19. Please don't touch the railing, Mike, it has just been painted.   __W__

Exercise Answers

20. We are community-college students, not university students.   W
21. No one told us that we had to attend Professor Davis' lecture on African history.   C
22. "Stand still," commanded the drill instructor, "or you will be on extra duty for the rest of the week."   W
23. My uncle Francis arrived late, stayed for dinner, watched television until midnight, and then asked to be driven home.   W
24. I am certain that she is the one who bought the computer.   C
25. My family's cottage, which is located near Georgian Bay, is now up for sale.   W
26. Before eating, Danny always takes an antacid pill.   W
27. You're playing tennis this afternoon, aren't you?   W
28. Because of the minor earthquake last week, the covered bridge is undergoing structural repair.   W
29. Oh dear, another busload of tourists is arriving.   W
30. Fix the water leak, Ted, before our water bill grows any larger this month.   W
31. "Do me a favour," said Clemenza with irony, "don't do me any more favours."   W
32. With friends like that, who needs enemies?   W
33. We should be arriving in Edmonton in another twenty minutes, shouldn't we?   W
34. He graduated from the University of Ottawa, not the University of New Brunswick.   W
35. The team members entered the stadium without their coach.   C
36. Sophie, the night bartender, went back to school to finish her computer-science courses.   W
37. Up above, the clouds looked threatening.   W
38. If we do not win our next game, the coach will have a heart attack.   W
39. The Lotus Garden, which is our new Chinese restaurant, won the "restaurant of the year" award from our Chamber of Commerce.   W
40. Terry O'Sullivan is, without a doubt, the best baseball player I have ever coached.   W

Exercise 7.7 — The Semicolon

1. Some of us are playing tennis; others, though, want to go swimming.   W

Writing Fundamentals

2. I can work on my computer for hours; time seems to fly when I am on the Internet.   W
3. Yolanda is an excellent chess player; she wins nearly all of her matches.   W
4. We missed the last train to Toronto; fortunately there was a late bus that we managed to take.   W
5. Jack Daniels, our vice-president; William Frankel, our treasurer; Clara Stuben, our personnel director; and Son Ming Chu, our systems analyst, all attended the management meeting yesterday.   W
6. Drive carefully; I don't want to have an accident on this lonely road.   W
7. Our college does not have a faculty lounge; we have to use the same lounge as the students.   W
8. Doris, Janet, Chris, and Maureen, the hairstylist, are all going to the fashion show this afternoon.   C
9. The workers were not being paid the minimum wage; therefore they decided to sue the company.   W
10. The ship could not stay afloat, however fast the crew pumped water from the hold.   C
11. Carrie is a vegetarian, and so is her older brother.   C
12. "Don't touch the paintings," warned the museum guide, "or we will have to end our tour."   C
13. Try studying more efficiently; for example, turn off the stereo when you are preparing for a test.   W
14. "How many kilometres is it from Kingston to Toronto?" asked the tourist.   C
15. Count your blessings; the tornado did very little structural damage.   W
16. We are almost out of firewood; perhaps it is time for you to cut some.   W
17. Because she has chosen to ignore our warnings on missing practice, we are therefore considering banning her from the school basketball team.   C
18. Slim, Kurt, Chubby, and Sandy all failed the final examination.   C
19. Please tell everyone that I will be late; I have to take my car to the garage.   W
20. The snowstorm was extremely severe for this time of year; for instance, we were without power for thirty-six hours.   W
21. "I cannot wait any longer," said the bus driver, "because the storm is getting worse."   C

Exercise Answers

22. I know how difficult it is to quit smoking; nevertheless, you must try.   W
23. Stay on your diet, however much you enjoy chocolate.   C
24. After we returned home, we found a message on our answering machine that said we had won money; but, of course, it was just another misleading scheme, like others we have received in the past, to get us to take a magazine subscription.   W
25. I think you are wrong, Scott; Melanie Snyder is not a Canadian citizen.   W
26. The fruit market is out of avocados, but you can buy some at the corner grocery store.   C
27. We could not understand Professor Clark's lecture; it was too obscure and irrelevant to our present course of study.   W
28. Some people love to exercise; others enjoy a sedentary lifestyle.   W
29. Notwithstanding your considerable influence with the school board, you will not be re-elected as treasurer.   C
30. Warn the others; I'll close the shutters and get out the candles.   W

Exercise 7.8 — The Colon and the Dash

1. Tracy bought the following items at the department store (:) stockings, lipstick, note pads, towels, shampoo, and toothpaste.   CN
2. Our mayor made the following statement before he left office (:) " My opponent rigged the election."   CN
3. Trout fishing, long hikes in the woods, horseback riding along picturesque mountain trails, and daily tennis games (—) these are the things we did on our holiday.   DS
4. In *Time* magazine (—) or was it *Maclean's* (—) I read that a civil war is likely to break out in Bangladesh.   DS
5. I won't tell you again (:) put away your toys and make your bed.   CN
6. She wants only two things in life (—) power and security.   DS
7. Last Friday (—) or maybe it was Thursday (—) our history teacher resigned his position.   DS
8. The ski trip was a total success (:) the weather was perfect; the snow pack was free of ice; the group lessons were fun; and the food at the ski lodge was delicious.   CN
9. I think you know who made this statement (:) "There's a sucker born every minute."   CN
10. Their scoutmaster (—) I think his name is Andrew (—) slipped and broke his ankle last week.   DS

Writing Fundamentals

11. My uncle (—) he is a high-school principal (—) won the Father of the Year award. DS
12. My brother, who is a coach, made the following statement to his Little League baseball team ( ) "Winning is a state of mind; it takes desire, sacrifice, and hustle." CN
13. Her sister lives and works in Halifax, Nova Scotia (—) or is it Moncton, New Brunswick? CN
14. Sports and girls (—) they are all my brother thinks about. DS
15. The food that we need for the picnic (—) bread, meat, pickles, mustard, catsup, cookies, and fruit (—) is being purchased by Dave and Michelle. DS
16. The hockey announcer made this ludicrous statement on the air (:) "Fighting is a part of the game." CN
17. Greed and selfishness (—) these two vices are ruining our country. DS
18. I don't know which computer to buy (:) the lap top or the desk top. CN
19. I was told how to get ahead in the company (:) arrive early and leave late. CN
20. The Internet (—) that's all she talks about. DS
21. Maury's two dogs (—) Coco and Max (—) won honourable mentions at our annual dog show. DS
22. The following statement was made by a famous author (:) "I write because I am not qualified to do anything else." CN
23. The latest hurricane (—) I think its name was George (—) devastated the southeastern coast of the United States. DS
24. We have only two choices (:) put up or shut up. CN
25. My Aunt Maude's antique store has everything (:) old furniture, clocks, canes, jewellery, glassware, silver, and pottery. CN
26. We drove through three provinces on our trip to the East Coast (:) Ontario, Quebec, and New Brunswick. CN
27. Carter's golf bag is made of cowhide (—) or is it horsehide? DS
28. The discount store is having a huge sale on computers (:) IBM, Macintosh, Hitachi, and Compaq. CN
29. Yesterday Mr. Yablonski made this surprising statement (:) "Do as I say, not as I do." CN
30. Running three kilometres every day (—) nothing is better for your heart and lungs. DS

Exercise Answers

Exercise 7.9 — Quotation Marks and Italics

1. The autobiography that Carol just published is entitled *Just Me Again*.   W
2. "Relax," she said, "no one knows where we are."   W
3. The computer teacher asked us if we wanted to download the prime minister's speech from the Internet.   C
4. The musical *Chicago* is now playing in Vancouver.   W
5. "Who Wants to Know?" is the title of the scathing editorial in our local newspaper.   W
6. Who wrote the book of short stories entitled *The Moons of Jupiter*?   W
7. My brother refers to Sharon Stone, the movie actress, as a "babe."   W
8. *The Heritage* is the name of our apartment building.   W
9. *60 Minutes* is my favourite television news program.   W
10. Kay's expression for the latest fad in fashion is *au courant*.   W
11. "How do you install word-processing software on your computer?" asked Jefferson.   W
12. I finally told Paul what he needed to do in order to upgrade his computer memory.   C
13. *Macaroni's* is the name of our new Italian restaurant.   W
14. Are there one or two *t*'s in your sister's name?   W
15. The play *As You Like It* is my favourite Shakespearean comedy.   W
16. "Keep trying for the athletic scholarship," advised Abdul Jabbar, "because you certainly have the talent to play on the university team."   W
17. "Swish" is our nickname for Clifford, our star halfback.   W
18. Who starred in the movie, *The Way We Were*?   W
19. What was the name of the television show that had Spock as one of its main characters?   C
20. Does the word *altar* refer to a part of a church?   W
21. What does the Italian phrase *buena sera* mean in English?   W
22. "The violin is a very difficult instrument to learn how to play," said my piano teacher, Mrs. Califano.   W
23. *The Holiday Centre* is the name of our newest shopping mall.   W
24. Madeline told Jiminez that her father does not approve of their relationship.   C
25. "Sailing to Byzantium" is one of William Butler Yeats' most famous poems.   W

Writing Fundamentals

26. The term *birdie* in golf means a score of one under par on any given hole.   W
27. The magazine article entitled "Our Canadian Wilderness" was both entertaining and informative.   W
28. Our committee spokesperson announced to the gathering of faculty members that we do not have enough money to build a new cafeteria.   C
29. My German girlfriend calls herself my *frauline*.   W
30. My father's speedboat is named *Sandy's Dream*.   W

Exercise 7.10 — Capitalizing Correctly

1. The best seafood restaurant in our town is called squids.   Squids
2. My wife's birthday is next monday, February 17.   Monday
3. Donald's Cousin is arriving by train this evening.   cousin
4. Katy has just been hired as a waitress at Carl's Home-Style restaurant.   Restaurant
5. Last Sunday my mother reminded us that we should not forget our Father's birthday.   father's
6. Our computer-science instructor made the following statement to the entire class: "your computer is an intellectual tool, not a physical plaything."   Your
7. Next semester I will study math, history, English, and french.   French
8. The community college in our city has two more campuses in other Ontario cities.   C
9. The Grand Canyon in the state of arizona is awe-inspiring.   Arizona
10. There are at least two hundred african students attending our university.   African
11. Reedy creek is the name of our local golf course.   Creek
12. The town council has decided to postpone building the new ice arena until next year.   C
13. Sayed Nawri has just been awarded his canadian citizenship.   Canadian
14. "Yes, Yasmin," she said, "The carpet is handwoven."   the
15. Our vice-principal used to teach a computer-science course at the University of New Brunswick.   C

Exercise Answers

16. Last semester I took a course in american history.   <u>American</u>
17. We played golf last Summer on one of the Thousand Islands.   <u>summer</u>
18. Milovik was born in croatia, which is a part of Yugoslavia.   <u>Croatia</u>
19. My best friend, Marvin Shore, works for an electronics firm on the outskirts of our town.   <u>C</u>
20. We are building our manufacturing plant just west of the central post office.   <u>C</u>
21. Our imported carpet was made in afghanistan.   <u>Afghanistan</u>
22. Sharon's little girl still believes in the Easter bunny.   <u>Bunny</u>
23. My wife's best friend was born down east.   <u>East</u>
24. The health clinic is located on Thirty-First Street, near Cary Road.   <u>first</u>
25. One of our parish priests is named father Ryan.   <u>Father</u>
26. The new pastry chef is Australian, not spanish.   <u>Spanish</u>
27. We were told that Mr. Moray, our gym instructor, is a christian Scientist.   <u>Christian</u>
28. where is Saudi Arabia located?   <u>Where</u>
29. The heart patient was released by Dr. Sidlowski yesterday afternoon at three o'clock.   <u>C</u>
30. Midlothian secondary school won the track and field competition last Saturday.   <u>Secondary School</u>

Exercise 7.11 — The Apostrophe

1. Its the same magazine article that you read last night, isn't it?   <u>It's</u>
2. Can you tell me whose supposed to present the basketball trophy?   <u>who's</u>
3. I am not sure if the ballpoint pen is her's or yours.   <u>hers</u>
4. Were we invited to the Harris luncheon this Tuesday?   <u>Harris'</u>
5. James brothers are all Ontario scholars.   <u>James'</u>
6. The next time you turn in an essay, Bruce, please make sure that you dot your *i*'s and cross you're *t*'s.   <u>your</u>
7. Who's your seventh-grade teacher this semester?   <u>C</u>
8. Is that used car you bought a 97 Plymouth or Buick?   <u>'97</u>
9. I think its about time that your sister returns her library book.   <u>it's</u>
10. Her dogs bone is under the kitchen table again.   <u>dog's</u>

Writing Fundamentals

11. The summer of 98 was the hottest on record.	'98
12. I cannot understand they're position on abortion.	their
13. Let's surprise my brothers friends before they leave.	brother's
14. I hope your satisfied with your impressive performance onstage last night.	you're
15. There was something I've wanted to ask you're father, but it has slipped my mind.	your
16. My truck looks new, but it's engine is almost worn out.	its
17. The United States foreign policy is confusing to us Canadians.	States'
18. I think that he'd already gone to the mens room by the time their dinner companions arrived.	men's
19. There not supposed to cross the yellow line outside the employees' locker room.	They're
20. I hope we're not scheduled to go to the soccer game this afternoon.	C
21. Rachel insists that her mother's recipe isn't lost, just mislaid.	C
22. The new computer is either her's or his—not theirs.	hers
23. My business partners are developing next year's budget.	C
24. Our swim teams loss was a complete surprise.	team's
25. My 94 Lincoln has been driven only thirty thousand kilometres; it's still like new.	'94
26. Her children's toys are spread all over the tables surface.	table's
27. Did someone's car keys' fall down the subway grate?	keys
28. Is this book yours or mine?	C
29. Mr. and Mrs. Broderick's son owns three drugstores in our city.	C
30. The motorcycle is our's, not hers.	ours

Exercise 7.12 — Parentheses and Brackets

1. Mario Ben Venisti *(the famous Italian hairstylist)* was on the airplane that crashed into the sea last week.	PR
2. Jack Weston *(1942-1998)* was our town's mayor for twenty years.	PR
3. Vanessa Massimini *(she was a famous Italian movie star in the 1930s)* was a member of the Italian resistance during the Second World War.	PR
4. The Mafia don *(also known as The Godfather)* died yesterday of natural causes.	PR

Exercise Answers

5. "The Sears Tower, just outside of Chicago, has been sold to a consortium of Japanese businesses." *[The writer needs a geography lesson; the Sears Tower is in the heart of Chicago.]*   BR

6. "The Calgary Stampeders hockey team *[sic]* won its fifth game in a row last night."   BR

7. Our company had a substantial increase in profits last year *(40 percent)*.   PR

8. The text of one of Ernest Hemingway's most popular novels *(The Sun Also Rises)* is being read in its entirety on one of our local FM stations.   PR

9. Don't forget that you have a series of errands to run before you leave for the cottage: *(1)* pick up the laundry, *(2)* buy grass seed and lawn fertilizer, *(3)* drop off the house keys to Aunt Rachel, and *(4)* fill up the car with gasoline.   PR

10. "One should not go to the top of the CM Tower *[sic]* in Toronto on a foggy day."   BR

11. My grandmother *(1925-1990)* worked as a nurse until she died.   PR

12. "The Persian Gulf is where the American aircraft carrier is on patrol." *[The more acceptable name for that body of water is the Arabian Gulf.]*   BR

13. Last Canada Day *(July 1)* we went on a picnic in St. Lawrence Park.   PR

14. "The home-run race between Mark McGwire and Sammy Sossa *[sic]* was the most exciting sports competition of 1998."   BR

15. "Our inflation rate last year was negligible." *[It was actually 1.6 percent.]*   BR

16. Her instructions were explicit: *(a)* assemble in the college parking lot, *(b)* check to see that we have the necessary provisions for our hiking trip, *(c)* collect our lunches in the school cafeteria, *(d)* wait for the bus at the southeast corner of the lot.   PR

17. Zeke Polonski *(the famous hockey player)* is now a sports announcer on the radio.   PR

18. "Our unemployment rate is the lowest it has been for twenty years." *[The speaker is mistaken; the actual number is twelve years.]*   BR

19. "Margaret Lawrence *[sic]* is one of my favourite Canadian novelists."   BR

20. Our Riverfest celebration *(July 8 and 9)* this year was the most successful one we have ever had—more than twenty thousand people attended.   PR

Exercise 7.13 — The Hyphen

1. The plumber told us that he had to realign our water pipes before he could install our new water heater.   C
2. We just discovered that the money in our pension fund had been misappropriated.   C
3. I think twenty-six people out of forty voted to increase next year's budget.   W
4. Most gasoline stations today have self-service pumps.   W
5. My twelve-year-old nephew has just joined a chess club.   W
6. Our first snowstorm this year occurred in mid-October.   W
7. Her month-old baby is already trying to crawl.   W
8. Farida's car is at least nine years old.   C
9. Yuri Ganikov has always been anti-Fascist.   W
10. Charlene is an above-average law student.   W
11. We are scheduled for the twelve-thirty lunch period.   W
12. The annual trade show is scheduled for June 10-12 at the municipal auditorium.   W
13. Last year's Christmas decorations will have to be reused, since our budget for decorations has been cut again.   C
14. The food and clothing that we collected for the poor are more plentiful this year.   C
15. The hotel that we stayed in last night had in-house movies.   W
16. Let's re-establish our position as the number one basketball team in our league.   W
17. The pollution control department did a better-than-average job this year.   W
18. Both my grandmother and grandfather are in their eighties.   C
19. The Toronto-Vancouver flight was two hours late.   W
20. My stepbrother no longer lives at home.   C

Exercise 7.14 — Periods, Question Marks, and Exclamation Points

1. Please stop repeating yourself; it is an annoying habit.   W
2. Would you please find the janitor? I forgot the key to my office door.   C
3. 8:30 p.m. is too late to have dinner.   W
4. Will you pick up the guest speaker this afternoon?   W
5. I get all the world news from our national CBC station.   C

Exercise Answers

6. Mrs. Parker thinks that her new IBM computer is wonderful.   W
7. Will you please be quiet while I am talking.   W
8. Well, our team finally won its first game.   W
9. What time is she expected to arrive? At nine o'clock?   W
10. Clarence is enrolled in a Ph.D. program at the University of British Columbia.   W
11. Watch out! The scaffolding is falling!   W
12. Fitch Mfg. and Bryson Inc. are discussing a merger.   W
13. Please watch your step as you enter the elevator.   W
14. Is CTV broadcasting the hockey game at 8:00 p.m.?   W
15. Marsha apologized to Evelyn, didn't she?   C
16. Watch out! The building is collapsing!   W
17. You should ask her if she is married, divorced, or single.   W
18. Mrs. Tonka, Mr. Bradley, and Dr. Towndrow are meeting at 12:30 p.m. to discuss the new zoning laws for the medical centre.   W
19. Please be careful; you'll spill your coffee if you walk too fast.   W
20. Did the plumber ask if you had flood insurance?   W

Exercise 7.15 — Punctuation Review Exercise

1. Please find out when we should leave for the airport; then call me at home with the answer.   W
2. Carlos and his partner—her name is Jennifer—came in second in the doubles competition at our annual tennis tournament.   W
3. Who was the person who said the following: "You can't fight city hall"?   W
4. Tim was not fatigued, although the rest of us were exhausted.   C
5. The party organizers—Ben, Connie, Eddie, and Karim—did a wonderful job.   W
6. Hockey—that's all my two sons think about.   W
7. "Don't forget your dictionaries," said the English teacher, "you will be able to use them for your test tomorrow."   W
8. The term for using cocaine in a cigarette, I think, is "smoking crack."   W
9. The *Toronto Star* had a very interesting editorial page yesterday.   W
10. What prompted Fred to change his major from English literature to chemical engineering?   W

Writing Fundamentals

11. Tanya failed the geography test; however, she will be given an opportunity to rewrite it next Tuesday.   W
12. Behave yourselves at the rock concert tonight.   W
13. The name of our new domed stadium is the *Queen Dome*.   C
14. I think NASDAQ is the name of a major stock exchange.   C
15. Danielle earned her **M.Sc.** in computer science.   W
16. So, you finally bought a luxury car.   W
17. Simon Granz, vice-president; Graden O'Leary, treasurer; Paula Carmichael, financial planner; and Greta Schuman, personnel manager, are now meeting with the company president, Doris Neil.   W
18. Do you think that **it's** too late to make amends?   W
19. Jack Hunt asked the golf pro if he could have a putting lesson.   C
20. Ida's mother named her new compact car Martina   C
21. The Taj Mahal is India's most famous tourist attraction.   C
22. "When Summer Comes" is the name of a short story in Martha's book, entitled *Summer Tales*.   W
23. "I will never leave my office because of a personal financial problem." [The next day the mayor was charged with embezzlement and resigned.]   W
24. Did Margaret Atwood write *The Handmaid's Tale*?   W
25. We have not been paid for our work to date, and therefore will not complete the job until we are paid in full.   C
26. Juan refers to large cigars as "stogies."   W
27. Do you believe that **they're** going to fulfill their part of the bargain?   W
28. Sam is strong and honest; Reese is slim and sly.   W
29. My brother will study history, mathematics, sociology, and Spanish next year.   W
30. The New York musical *Rent* is coming to the National Theatre in Ottawa next month.   W
31. "Keats is my favourite Irish poet." [The writer has confused Keats with Yeats.]   W
32. Sadler Inc. and Tamarack Mfg. both make aluminum products.   W
33. Why can't Cloris maintain a higher grade point average?   W
34. My three cats—Mina, Claude, and Silvia—have to be placed in a kennel for a week because my cat sitter is ill.   W
35. Did Dr. Chang perform the heart surgery on your father?   W

Exercise Answers

36. "Last summer my family camped along the Cabbott Trail [sic] in Nova Scotia." __W__
37. Keep away! Gas is leaking! __W__
38. *Two Gentlemen of Verona* is my favourite Shakespearean comedy. __W__
39. I think Morris asked Ellen if she would marry him. __W__
40. The real estate agent recommended a pre-inspection on the house. __W__

Exercise 8.1 — Detecting Clichés

(Answers will vary.)

1. We must make quick decisions and get down to business.
2. It is obvious that she is planning to buy our entire company.
3. Our crew narrowly escaped the fire because the crew captain remained calm.
4. Just remember that our time is valuable, so we should start our business trip as early as possible.
5. I don't want to disclose secrets, but Charles became quite upset when he was confronted by the police.
6. Magda made a hasty decision when she decided to give us a general estimate of the value of her beachfront property.
7. The business partners did not agree, so they decided to cancel their partnership agreement.
8. We curtailed his proposal because it would have cost our company too much money.
9. Katya was warmly welcomed when she stepped off the plane.
10. Let's keep him away from the company while we consider his job application.
11. The news that our business venture was going to fail was sudden and unexpected.
12. Jenkins received money secretly during the election campaign.
13. Erin's mother lost her temper when she was told that Erin was going to have a baby.
14. Our accountant knows his business, so let's leave him alone to do his job.
15. Penelope's mother lived a long life because she always remained quite busy.
16. Donald is emulating his successful father, who always worked very hard.
17. If we curtail our spending, we can survive this financial crisis.

Writing Fundamentals

18. My father died when he was eighty-six.
19. Donna told us a sad tale when she was asked to pay her debts.
20. His reluctance to be decisive was to be expected.

Exercise 8.2 — Changing Clichés to Fresh Expressions
(Students to complete independently.)

Exercise 8.3 — Replacing Jargon
(Answers will vary.)
1. We must solve the problem by conferring with their legal representatives.
2. If our cost-cutting program is to be effective, we must formulate a quality control management plan.
3. I must talk with your plant manager and get his advice on our production figures.
4. Our political position should prepare our constituents for our stand on environmental issues.
5. Let's stay on the topic, so that we can meet the deadline set by our union negotiators.
6. The figures that I presented to you were just estimates.
7. Can you understand her position on our absentee policy?
8. We should all agree before implementing the proposed changes in our management structure.
9. Elvira did not lie; she merely stretched the truth.
10. We couldn't have had better autumn weather (or "a better autumn").
11. I think that she is prepared to accept our business proposition.
12. Our marketing team met with the software specialists and created a perfect strategy for selling our new product.
13. Mr. Yates was discharged (or "fired") when his team's product line was not ready for our winter sales promotion.
14. The history professor could not understand the point of Andreas' argument on why the Second World War should not have been won by the Allies.

15. Please do not discuss business when we meet with our union stewards about the Christmas party arrangements.

16. Moses Mobley manages a used car lot in Toronto.

17. The bombs that were dropped by our bombers killed many enemy troops.

18. Are you aware of your increased responsibilities as a supervisor?

19. Our new, more expensive department store will include a fashion coordinator and a beauty salon.

20. The mayor must be kept informed if we expect him to meet with representatives of our business community.

Exercise 8.4 — Alternatives to Jargon
(Students to complete independently.)

Exercise 8.5 — Making Sentences Concise
(Answers may vary.)

1. I think that she has finally realized that her brother will not give up smoking.

2. In conclusion, I think (or "believe") that our company cannot comply with your financial demands.

3. Did you have the opportunity to join our hiking group?

4. Our baseball team is not yet ready to compete for the league title.

5. Because Gertrude will deliver her baby in September, we will not oblige her to work on the weekends.

6. My geography teacher told me that he would consider my request to delay submitting my term paper.

7. Willard's new sofa is similar to the sofa that my mother bought for our family room.

8. I cannot agree, in principle, to your stand on taxation.

9. I promised our student president that I would discuss his proposal with the principal next Monday.

10. We will be leaving by train for Vancouver soon.

11. All of us, without doubt, identified the perpetrator.

Writing Fundamentals

12. Our committee meetings will be closed to the public until the information leaks to the news media are stopped.
13. Emory often saw Felicity act onstage.
14. I cannot think of any reason why our students would have been near the closed hockey rink last Wednesday evening.
15. Sheila decided to attend Martin's Halloween party last Tuesday.
16. Our hockey team members could have scored many goals if its passing game had been more precise and timely.
17. After the intense snowstorm, the city council decided to purchase two new snowplows.
18. Recently, our school received three new computers from our school board.
19. Pauline has cancelled her subscription to the drama society because it will not consider showcasing young Canadian playwrights.
20. We will consider your job application later.

Exercise 8.6 — Removing Redundancies

(Answers may vary.)

1. Her (old) antique vase is a (exact) replica of the one in our museum.
2. The (end) result of his experiment was barely adequate (enough) to be included in our chemistry paper.
3. A (cold) shiver went down my spine when Raoul opened (up) the coffin lid.
4. Our tour guide gave us the (true) facts about the history of the Battle of Quebec.
5. Her car seemed to disappear (from view) when it entered the fog bank on Carpenter Road.
6. Most students seldom (ever) concern themselves about the (strict) accuracy of their spelling on homework assignments.
7. The destruction of the village was complete (and total) after the terrifying hurricane hit the island.
8. Our town experienced an (serious) economic crisis last year, but our new mayor is (bound and) determined to turn things around this year.
9. Nora's black cocktail dress was very expensive (and costly), but she swears that the money was well spent because the design is (very) unique.
10. As our plane soared (up) above the cloud bank, the clouds appeared red (in colour) as they reflected the setting sun.

Exercise Answers

11. The acid rain, throughout the years, has eroded (away) our city monuments.

12. Please ask our instructor to repeat (again) the instructions for writing the mid-term examination.

13. You cannot expect the (inexperienced) rookies to play like our (experienced) veterans.

14. The (computer) software company promised us a (free) gift if we would order its accounting package.

15. We tried to negotiate the sale, but the sales person told us that the prices were (firm and) fixed.

16. There wasn't a single (solitary) sales item left one hour after the store opened, and that's the (honest) truth.

17. The deplorable condition of our lake is (plain and) obvious.

18. We had to surrounded the enemy (on all sides) before they finally surrendered their armaments.

19. The printer and the computer have to be connected (together) with a special cable that we sell in our computer supplies store.

20. When Willard asked for my (personal) opinion of his new motor home, I told him that I thought it was too small (in size).

Exercise 8.7 — Revising for Effective Diction

(Revisions may vary.)

The strategies for teaching the fundamentals of writing on the post-secondary level should be used in a variety of contexts, and emphasis should be placed on both the process and the end product of student writing. Students should be given the requirements to write expository essays, creative pieces, reports, and research papers; they should also be able to interpret diagrams, tables, and graphs. And, if possible, their writing should be done on computers and stored in electronic portfolios.

It is important that students develop an awareness of the various stages of writing, regardless of their proficiency or grade level. In the initial planning stage, for instance, the students should focus on generating and organizing ideas. They should also consider the importance of determining readership when selecting the content of their essays and reports. During the drafting and evaluation stages, they should concentrate on critiquing their writing so that they can produce further drafts to improve accuracy and syntactical quality.

Teachers should also make students aware of the coherence in written texts. Sample reading texts can provide useful models for analysis, and the planning strategies of outlining, which focusses on main and supporting ideas, can also help students develop a coherent framework for their writing.

Writing Fundamentals

Teachers also need to provide substantial support for students to help them develop the high-level skills embodied in research and report writing. For example, students will need a great deal of practice in paraphrasing, summarizing, and avoiding plagiarism; they will also need instruction in converting the visual information contained in diagrams, tables and graphs into readable prose. Furthermore, they need to be taught how to supply in-text or bibliographic references in an acceptable format.

Finally, the students must be provided with appropriate and realistic contexts for their writing. These should include many topics that are relevant, meaningful, and motivating—ones that the students can easily identify with and access through library or Internet research.

Exercise 9.1 — Preparing an Outline

(Answers will vary.)

#1
(a) **Types of Food**
    I. Meat
        A. Steak
        B. Veal
    II. Vegetables
        A. Potatoes
        B. Broccoli
        C. Beans
            1. Wax beans
            2. Lima beans
    III. Fruit
        A. Apples
        B. Grapes
        C. Peaches
        D. Bananas
        E. Citrus fruit
            1. Grapefruit
            2. Oranges
    IV. Poultry
        A. Turkey
        B. Chicken

(b) **Professions**
    I. Doctor
        A. Surgeon
            1. Heart
            2. Brain

B. Ears, nose, and throat
C. Urologist
D. Pathologist
E. Psychiatrist
II. Teacher
A. Elementary
B. Secondary
1. High school
C. Post-secondary
1. University
2. Community college
III. Engineer
A. Electrical
B. Civil
C. Aeronautical
IV. Lawyer
A. Corporate
B. Labour
C. Tax

(c) **Rivers of the World**
I. North America
A. Mississippi
B. Colorado
C. St. Lawrence
II. Europe
A. Germany
1. Rhine
2. Moselle
B. Italy
1. Tiber
C. France
1. Seine
2. Loire
D. Russia
1. Volga
III. South America
A. Amazon
B. Orinoco
IV. Asia
A. Yangtze
V. Africa
A. Nile

#2
(a) **Famous World Cities**
    I. Central America
        A. Panama
            1. Panama City
    II. North America
        A. United States
            1. East Coast
                a. New York
                b. Boston
                c. Philadelphia
            2. West Coast
                a. Los Angeles
                b. San Francisco
                    i. Golden Gate Bridge
                    ii. Chinatown
        B. Canada
            1. Ontario
                a. Toronto
                b. Ottawa
            2. Alberta
                a. Calgary
                    i. Calgary Stampede
            3. British Columbia
                a. Vancouver
    III. Europe
        A. Western Europe
            1. Germany
                a. Berlin
                b. Munich
            2. France
                a. Paris
                    i. The Eiffel Tower
                    ii. The Louvre
            3. Italy
                a. Rome
                    i. The Colosseum
                    ii. Venice
        B. Eastern Europe
            1. Russia
                a. Moscow
                b. St. Petersburg
                    i. The Hermitage Museum
            2. Poland
                a. Cracow
                b. Warsaw

Exercise Answers

(b) Shakespearean Plays I Have Seen throughout North America
  I. United States
    A. New York
        1. New York City
            a. Comedies
                i. *As You Like It*
                ii. *All's Well that Ends Well*
            b. Tragedies
                i. *King Lear*
                ii. *Othello*
    A. Illinois
        1. Chicago
            a. Comedies
                i. *Twelfth Night*
            b. Histories
                i. *Richard II*
                ii. *King John*
  II. Canada
    A. British Columbia
        1. Vancouver
            a. *Hamlet*
            b. *Macbeth*
    B. Alberta
        1. Edmonton
            a. Histories
                i. *Richard III*
                ii. *Henry IV, Parts 1 & 2*
    C. Ontario
        1. Ottawa
            a. *Julius Caesar*

(c) My Favourite Ethnic Restaurants in Our City
  I. North Side
    A. German
        1. Stengel's
        2. Town Haus
    B. Italian
        1. Faragetti's
        2. Milano's
    C. Greek
        1. Athena

  II. West Side
    A. Eastern European
        1. Russian
            a. Tatiana's
        2. Polish
            a. Pulaski's

III. South Side
    A. Middle Eastern
        1. Lebanese
            a. Kalba's Bistro
            b. Hassan's Pearl
        2. Egyptian
            a. The Nile Café

#3

(a) *I visited several famous museums while I was an exchange student in Europe.*

I. Western Europe
    A. Paris in the spring of 1976
        1. The Louvre
            a. I saw a great collection of Impressionist painters.
                i. Monet
                ii. Manet
                iii. Cezanne
            b. The Italian Renaissance paintings were also quite impressive.
                i. Titian
                ii. da Vinci's *Mona Lisa*
                iii. Tintoretto
    B. Madrid in October, 1976
        1. The Prado Museum
            a. I saw a magnificent collection of religious art.
                i. Rafael
                ii. Fra Angelico
                iii. Rubens
                iv. Velàzquez

II. Eastern Europe
    A. Russia in December, 1976
        1. St. Petersburg
            a. I visited the Hermitage Museum.
                i. French painters from the nineteenth and twentieth centuries
                ii. Byzantine art from fifth to twelfth centuries
                iii. Carved stones and Assyrian reliefs from ninth century BC

(b) *Global warming will be one of the most serious problems of the twenty-first century.*

   I. The Causes

   A. Emissions of carbon monoxide from gasoline-burning vehicles

   1. Very little effort by advanced Western countries to reduce pollutants from vehicle exhaust systems

   a. The major automobile manufacturers build more vans and utility vehicles that burn more fuel per kilometre
   b. The three major North American automobile companies make little effort to build and sell compact and subcompact cars that burn less fuel
   c. There is little or no interest by automobile companies in manufacturing electric cars that would eliminate exhaust emissions

   B. Emissions of carbon and sulphur dioxide from industrial smokestacks

   1. Little effort by industry to seek alternative fuels

   a. Many large manufacturing companies still rely heavily on fossil fuels such as coal and oil
   b. Utility companies do very little research on alternative sources of energy such as wind and wave power

   C. The burning of major rain forests

   1. Brazil and Indonesia continue to destroy rain forests

   a. Trees and foliage are burned to open more land for farming
   b. Governments do not provide leadership or financial incentives to stop the devastation
   c. The United Nations does not consider the burning of rain forests a high priority

   II. The Results

   A. Ice caps melt, causing oceans and rivers to rise

   1. Seaside cities, villages, estuaries, and resorts flood

   a. Low-lying countries like Bangladesh and Sri Lanka will lose living space and farmland
   b. Millions of hectares of farmland and estuaries throughout the world will disappear
   c. Hundreds of billions of dollars will be lost due to the worldwide floods

B. World climates radically change
      1. Temperate climates become tropical
         a. Crops will die and billions of people will suffer famine and disease
         b. Rainfall will increase dramatically
      2. Cold climates become temperate
         a. Ice and snow will melt
         b. Arctic tundra will disappear
      3. Tropical countries become arid
         a. Deserts will expand and increase
         b. Tropical grasslands will disappear
         c. Animals and plants will die

#4
(a) Topic: *My experience as a tourist during the last ten years*
   I. Europe
      A. France
         1. Paris
            a. Nightclub tour
            b. Seine River cruise
            c. Notre Dame Cathedral visit
            d. Eiffel Tower visit
      B. Germany
         1. Berlin
         2. Munich
            a. Attended Oktoberfest
               i. The Hofbrauhaus
               ii. Festival Biergarten
      C. Denmark
         1. Copenhagen
            a. Little Mermaid
            b. Tivoli Gardens
      D. British Isles
         1. London
            a. Changing of the Guard at Buckingham Palace
            b. Shopping at Harrods department store
            c. Cruising on the Thames River
   II. Middle East
      A. Egypt
         1. Cairo museum visit
         2. Nile cruise
         3. Tour of the pyramids

    B. Persian Gulf
        1. United Arab Emirates
            a. Dubai City tour
            b. Camel rides in the desert
III. Indonesia
    A. Jakarta
        1. City tour
    B. Bali
        1. Shopping
        2. Golfing
        3. Scuba diving

(b) Topic: *Checklist for developing a collaborative learning environment*

I. Classroom

A. The physical organization
    1. Does the classroom organization allow for cooperation, sharing, and group work?
        a. Are traffic patterns to storage areas, large tables, printers, doorways, and black- or whiteboards clear and unfettered?
        b. Is the lighting flexible enough to allow for overhead projections and computer displays?

II. Teacher

A. Teaching strategies
    1. Do I use multiple techniques, and are they consistent with the desired goals of my lesson plan?
    2. Do my evaluation techniques reflect the interactive learning process?
    3. Do I use a variety of group activities that encourage new and diversified group formations?
    4. Do I implement interactive skills that generate a learning environment conducive to self-directed learning?

III. Students

A. Are students involved in decision-making, planning, organizing, and evaluating classroom activities?
    1. Can they seek resources to assist their own learning?
    2. Do they practise assessing their own strengths and weaknesses?
    3. Do they use peer evaluation techniques?
    4. Do they learn through a variety of class, group, and individual activities?

Writing Fundamentals

(c) Topic: *The personal essay revision process*

    I. Content
        A. Do you have all the information you need to make your argument?
        B. Are the general statements supported by evidence?
        C. Is your thesis statement logical and complete?
        D. Does your introduction inform the reader what the essay is about?

    II. Organization
        A. Have you used a consistent pattern of development?
        B. Are your arguments properly sequenced?
        C. Are your paragraphs unified and connected with transitional words and phrases?
        D. Do you have a conclusion that summarizes the development and that restates the topic idea?

    III. Diction and Grammar
        A. Have you avoided jargon and clichés?
        B. Have you used precise words to convey your meaning?
        C. Are the main ideas stated clearly?
        D. Have you avoided sentence structure errors?

    IV. Mechanics
        A. Are all words spelled correctly?
        B. Is your essay properly punctutated?
        C. Have you enclosed all direct quotes in quotation marks?
        D. Did you use the correct bibliography and citation format?
        E. Are all typographical errors neatly corrected?

#5

(a) Topic: *Members of my family who are currently attending, and who have attended, universities and colleges across Canada*

    I. Alberta
        A. University of Edmonton
            1. My brother Phil studies history
            2. My nephew Edgar just received his B.A. in English literature
            3. My sister Francine is studying mathematics
            4. My cousin Dennis studied geography and played football
    II. British Columbia
        A. Simon Fraser University
            1. My niece Phyllis is majoring in physics
            2. My brother Cliff studied chemistry
        B. British Columbia Institute of Technology
            1. My nephew Morris studied computer science

Exercise Answers

III. Ontario
    A. Universities attended
        1. University of Toronto
            a. My mother earned her law degree
            b. My uncle played hockey and studied electrical engineering
        2. Queen's University
            a. My sister Claudia studied mechanical engineering
            b. My aunt Betty earned her B.A. in history and her M.A. in English literature
    B. Colleges attended
        1. St. Lawrence College
            a. Kingston
                i. My cousin Flora studied to be a child-care worker
        2. Algonquin College
            a. Ottawa
                i. My niece Jeannette is studying nursing
                ii. My nephew Roland studied early childhood education and played baseball

#6

Topic: *The dramatic increase in fast-food restaurants in our city*

Thesis Statement: The fast food restaurants in our city serve a variety of foods and offer a number of services.

I. The pizza restaurants offer two different services.
    A. Pizza Hut and Domino's Pizza offer drive-through service.
    B. Tombstone Pizza, Pizza, Pizza, and Don Corleone's Pizza offer free delivery.

II. The hamburger restaurants cook hamburgers in different ways.
    A. Charbroiled hamburgers are cooked by Burger King and Hardee's
    B. Fried hamburgers are cooked by McDonald's, Wendy's, and Wimpey's.

III. We now have four chicken restaurants: two are takeout restaurants and two are new.
    A. The takeout restaurants are KFC and Swiss Chalet.
    B. The restaurants that opened last year are Chicken Lickin' and Southern Delight.

IV. We also have four seafood restaurants: two are new and two have free delivery.
    A. The restaurants that opened last year are the Dockside Restaurant and Squidd's.
    B. The free-delivery restaurants are Trident Seafood and The Chowder House.

Writing Fundamentals

    V. Our steak houses are both family-style and takeout.
       A. The family-style restaurants are the Outback Steakhouse and Sid's Steakhouse.
       B. The takeout restaurants are Ponderosa and Steak Express.

    VI. We have three Chinese restaurants that opened last year.
       A. Their names are Golden Leaf, Lotus Blossom, and China Moon.

#7 (Students to complete independently.)

Exercise 10.1 — Paragraph Unity

1. My dog and cat have become fast friends. When I purchased a tabby kitten to provide company for my dog, Max, I did not expect them to be so dependent upon each other. Now they do everything together. Max and Barney—my cat—sleep and play together: they take turns chasing each other throughout the house, and then, when they become exhausted, take naps with their paws on each other's body. They even, occasionally, eat each other's food, which doesn't seem to annoy either of them. And when one of my pets is ill, the other broods and mopes around the house until the illness passes. I have never seen anything as strange or affecting as their close relationship. I hate to think of what would happen if one of them should pass away.

2. Our city has many recreational opportunities for both young and old. There are, of course, baseball diamonds, soccer fields, and hockey rinks for our youth, and tennis and squash courts, curling rinks, cross-country ski trails, and jogging paths for the physically active of all ages. But we also have several fine golf courses that cater to an older group who cannot participate in physically demanding sports. Our senior citizens also enjoy walking and bicycling. Furthermore, in our parks we have hiking trails, bicycle paths, and ice-skating ponds that can be enjoyed by the whole family. In addition, picnic areas abound throughout our city. We are indeed fortunate to have a city council that cares so much for recreation and sports opportunities for all of our citizens.

3. My sister is the busiest person I know. Besides working part-time in our college library, she also does volunteer work in our psychiatric hospital. In addition, she is an active athlete: she golfs at least twice a week, belongs to a local tennis club, and curls for a team in our women's league. She is also taking a quilting course in the evening at our community college and is serving on a parent-teacher committee at the school her daughter attends. Her energy, it seems, is inexhaustible

4. My college is not keeping up with the information age and the computer revolution. We have only four computer labs to service over two thousand students, and most of these computers do not even have Pentium processors. Also, our printers are old ink-jet types, not laser printers, and they are al-

Exercise Answers

ways breaking down. Furthermore, the only computers with Internet access are in the library, and they are always in use. Nor do we have an internal network that enables us to use e-mail to converse with our teachers. Because of this lack of computers in our school, very few students know how to use the latest word-processing and spreadsheet programs. I think that the administrators at our college all need to take professional development courses in managing a computer-based learning environment.

5. The Christmas season has become too commercial. The department stores start advertising "Christmas specials" in the middle of November, and gift giving has become an unfortunate substitute for the Christmas spirit. Santa Claus has become nothing more than a conduit between a child and a department store. There is no longer any religious significance in Christmas trees or Christmas music. "Rudolph the Red-Nosed Reindeer," cheap tinsel, and coloured bulbs are now the order of the day. Everyone goes on a buying frenzy, and liquor stores always do a booming business because of all the office parties where prodigious amounts of liquor are consumed. I think that Christ has permanently gone out of Christmas and has been replaced by the gift catalogue.

Exercise 10.2 — Selecting the Topic Sentence

- (a) 2. Since I bought my car, it has never run properly.
- (b) 1. Basketball is my favourite sport.
- (c) 2. Our school picnic was a great success.
- (d) 3. All members of my family are physically active.
- (e) 1. Many American companies have manufacturing plants in Canada.
- (f) 3. Why aren't handguns outlawed in the United States?
- (g) 1. Why do people still smoke?
- (h) 1. Toronto is an attractive city for tourists.
- (i) 2. Reading good literature is both enjoyable and intellectually rewarding.
- (j) 1. I enjoy Shakespearean drama.
- (k) 2. The diet I am following is very difficult.
- (l) 3. My English teacher expects too much from her students.
- (m) 1. Our bus system is a mess.
- (n) 3. Telephone sales are both annoying and misleading.
- (o) 3. I will never again buy a luxury car.

Exercise 10.3 — Position of the Topic Sentence

- (a) 5
- (b) 1 and 6
- (c) 5
- (d) 6
- (e) 5

Writing Fundamentals

Exercise 10.4 — Paragraph Types

(Answers will vary.)

A. INTRODUCTORY STATEMENT
1. Salvatore, my brother, was voted the most valuable player on our baseball team.
2. I use my computer for both schoolwork and pleasure.
3. I read extensively for various reasons.
4. Our Christmas parade this year was a complete disaster.
5. Members of my family have varied and interesting hobbies.

B. TRANSITIONAL STATEMENT
1. Unlike our strong hockey team, our baseball team looks as though it will be weak this year.
2. On the other hand, the cottage that my uncle purchased is not suitable for family vacations.
3. Once we left France, though, our travel experiences became quite unpleasant, to say the least.
4. Red meat, though, should be assiduously avoided.
5. But on the way home we encountered major difficulties that ruined our relaxed holiday mood.

C. CONCLUDING STATEMENT
1. Obviously our university needs an infusion of cash in order to operate successfully as a post-secondary institution.
2. The government may force our company to close if it does not soon stop harming the environment.
3. Given these extraordinary costs, our city will have a hard time convincing the taxpayers to support these lavish sports facilities.
4. It is obvious that our local government cares very little about the economic future of our city.
5. Our graduation ceremony was certainly very poorly planned and administered.

www.ingramcontent.com/pod-product-compliance
Lightning Source LLC
Chambersburg PA
CBHW080542230426
43663CB00015B/2681